Guide to Planning the Perfect Family Vacation

From the Team at RealFamilyTrips.com

Copyright © 2015 by Inspire Conversation LLC. All rights reserved.

Contact Information at www.RealFamilyTrips.com

This book or any portion thereof may not be reproduced or used in any manner whatsoever without the express written permission of the publisher except for the use of brief quotations in a book review.

Dedicated to our dear children, Noah, Julia, Anna, Sophia, Avery, and Vera. Your presence brings a constant joy to our lives; your thoughts help us to grow together as individuals and as a family, and your love makes each and every day better. Sharing our many journeys with you is one of the greatest gifts of all.

Table of Contents

Introduction: The Joy is in the Journey 1
Part I: What Makes a Great Family Vacation? 5
    The Value of Planning 9
    Enriching, Hands-On Experiences 16
    Inspire the Next Generation 21
    Discover Extraordinary, and Ordinary Places Together 26
    FUN 31
    Quality Family Time 38
    Active, Engaged, Curious 42
    Free Time and Options 48
    Balance the Activities 53
    Watch the Pace 58
    Experience Different Cultures 65
    If Things Go Wrong (They Often Do) 70
    Vacation IS a Vacation 75
    Great Experiences to Treasure for a Lifetime 79
Part II: Location, Location, Location 81
    Expand Your Vision on Where You Can Go 83
    Our Family's Vacation Wish List 87
    Our Family's Favorite Vacations and Destinations ... 128
Part III: Travel Tips And Hacks 155
    Getting or Renewing a US Passport 159
    A Guide to Online Resources for Travel Advice 168
    Shots, Inoculations, Safety, and Insurance 171
    There's an App for That 185

Seasonal Travel Concerns 203

Money and Travel 209

Make the System Work For You 219

Having the Right Gear 226

What the Experts Say About Family Travel 234

Packing Lists and Checklists for You to Use 251

Part IV: Guide to Online Resources and Booking 263

The Websites We Use (And You Should Too) 266

How to Book Better and Smarter 285

An Overview of Basic Good Booking Practices 293

Part V: Making a Trip Work for You 303

Cruising: The Good, The Bad, and the Exciting 306

Flying Solo, or Joining Another Family? 320

How Active Are You? 327

Planes, Trains, and Automobiles 330

Making Each Stop Work 339

Rest Days 344

Preserving Memories 347

Other Types of Vacations 353

Closing Thoughts and Additional Information 358

Our Goals and Hope for You 358

Other Books by Us 360

The Team at RealFamilyTrips.com 363

The "Fine Print" 368

Image Credits 369

Introduction

The Joy is in the Journey

There is an old adage that says "the joy is in the journey…not just the destination." This is a great way to view the creation of an amazing family vacation. One needs to appreciate the process, and find happiness in the planning of a trip, not just the trip itself.

There is certainly much joy to be had at your vacation destination, whether it is one of the world's great cities, an idyllic island retreat, or a fantastic locale just down the road from your own home. At the same time, it is important to savor the entire process, and see travel as a series of great opportunities as opposed to a few exciting days.

Great travel is about more than just the time spent between leaving and reentering your front door. The experience of a vacation takes place before, during, and after your time spent away. A family vacation should be a journey of personal discovery, family growth, exploration, and adventure.

Moreover, family travel is a lifelong pursuit. Over the 18 or so years each of your children is under your care, you have time to show them the world in amazing ways. Your collected travel experiences can set them up for a life of not only engaging with the world at large, but being more worldly in their daily interactions.

Family travel offers opportunities not available at home, nor through exploring the world by ourselves. When we share the journey with those closest to us, we have a chance to make each other better, and experience a closeness few other activities can impart.

This work constitutes our shared experience, vision, hopes, and dreams. This is a book about making family travel great, and great family travel possible. Through five parts, we will explore the biggest questions and address the major concerns. We will consider thoughts related to what great travel means, as well as challenge you to find your own meaning.

The joy truly is in the journey. We hope that like us, you will be able to enjoy planning your next trip as much as taking it. When you look at the world as an amazing landscape of possibilities, there is never a dull moment and another adventure always awaits you. You may choose to read this book straight through, jump around to parts most relevant to an upcoming trip, or enjoy it in pieces over the course of your continuing journeys. We hope that you will see the value in all of it.

Some of the ideas and stories contained in these pages reflect our own real experiences. These are meant to share our own journey, and provide relatable bits of our own travels. Even if you have different style, goals, or notions about what travel means to you - we hope you can find something that will aid you on your path. Tailor the advice and the experiences shared - to your own family's needs, personalities, likes, dislikes, and dreams - and find how our experience may benefit you.

Real Family Trips was founded on the idea that better travel is possible for any family equipped with the right information. Today's world certainly offers content in spades, but it is flung across the far corners of the Internet and spread throughout too many books to count.

We know that families are busy - you want to, and should - be focusing your energy and time on your children at home. According to a recent article by Travel + Leisure, planning a vacation is a great deal of work. This prestigious magazine cites a 2013 study conducted by Millward Brown Digital which determined that people made an average of 38 visits to different travel sites in the 45 days leading up to their vacation. We believe this number can be even higher for families, as the complex nature of traveling with children can lead to even more information you need to gather. Our site and this book are about helping you to cut back on this time spent researching, by directing your efforts on things that matter and helping you find places to focus your searches.

Savor the moments you share together and make the most of the time while they are still kids. We hope that by condensing and curating the important information, and combining it with real family experiences, we can simplify and enhance the process of travel. We want to share our joy and allow any family to enjoy a great vacation, without having to sacrifice precious time at home.

The creation of this book has been a journey, and to share it with you is a great joy. We hope that this book inspires and moves you to experience great voyages of your own. We hope that you too can find fun and excitement not just in where you go, but in how you get there, and what you do along the way.

Part I

What Makes a Great Family Vacation?

Great family vacations are within your reach. Right now, today, you and your family hold the capacity for a wonderful set of experiences that will help you each to grow as individuals, and for your family relationships to deepen and grow.

While it may seem like a mystifying experience, the act of taking great trips together is really more art than science. It is a practice born out of a mix of planning, experience, knowledge, and the energy of your own family. Combine these elements - mix in a great destination and a desire for fun, excitement, and learning - and you have the recipe for a vacation that will provide memories to last a lifetime.

The good news is that we have experience and knowledge to share, as well as advice on how to make a great plan. All you need to add is your family.

Contained in this section are a collection of thoughts about travel that were amassed over years of real trips with children ranging in age from infants to teens. These trips have been filled with highs and lows (though fortunately very few of the latter), and through them we have gathered some great thoughts and tips about how best to travel, as well as the many things that can be gained from the experience.

Later sections of the book will focus more on the *how* of everything, from booking to other logistics; the *where* of choosing a destination, and the *when* and *what* of vacation types and great activities. The *who* is your family. Thus, in this first part of our book, we talk about the *why*.

Family travel is about getting away, relaxing, and sharing time together. It is also about so much more. It is about growth and exploration, fun and excitement; it is about dropped jaws and the picture on your mantel that you can't help but smile at whenever you pass it. A great vacation is about creating moments in which there is no place you would rather be, and no one you would rather be with than each other.

Anyone can take a vacation. We like to think that we have taken some great ones, and that travel of this sort is both transformative and life affirming. Travel opens doors and changes lives. A great trip isn't about the couple days, or weeks, that you are there. Great family travel is timeless and stays with you forever.

But just what is great travel, and how does one go about traveling better?

The Value of Planning

Great family vacations don't just happen. You could have tickets to the best destination on Earth, a stellar hotel lined up, and the whole family excited about the possibilities - but once you get there, things do not meet your expectations. Do you ever feel like your friends keep coming back from vacations with stories for days and memories that leave you feeling like you missed out? Why is your time away falling flat?

It can be tempting to think that some families are just *better* at taking trips than others. On the other hand, you know your family. You love your children. You invest a lot of money in getting the best of everything that you can afford, yet can't seem to achieve the sort of vacation bliss you are looking for. The issue isn't your family. Every family is capable of taking great vacations; it just takes a bit of work. Sometimes, depending on the destination, it may take a lot of work.

All too often we have encountered families who return from the far corners of the globe, or remarkable getaways at fancy resorts, only to have very little to show for it. Too often have we seen a family that spared no expense and set their family up for the best of the best; yet their report on the time they spent in paradise is all too often, "Eh, just another beach" from parents and children alike.

To think that simply selecting and arriving at a great destination is going to provide an exceptional vacation isn't seeing the full picture. Additionally, spending money is not directly proportional to the levels of fun and satisfaction had while away. In fact, money can have very little to do with it. While having top accommodations and a first class experience can be great, they don't promise fun or satisfaction. Some of the best trips can be accomplished on a relatively small budget if money is spent wisely. Don't think that lavish expenses guarantee you a great trip, and don't think you need to spend big to have an amazing vacation.

So just what *does* make for an amazing vacation?

Many things go into it, all of which we will explore in the coming pages. The goal is to captivate children, and to provide experiences that engage and amaze. A great vacation has you living completely in the present moment, fixated on the here and now. A captivating experience can be as simple as a beautiful sunrise, or as extreme as a zip line through a rainforest. These moments can be different for every family and more importantly, you will find them in a variety of places throughout a given vacation. The unifying factor is that they be compelling and engaging and fit so perfectly to your family and the given moment that you can't even imagine thinking about what happened yesterday or what may come tomorrow. You and your children are simply right there, enjoying it all together.

These moments *may* come spontaneously, and hopefully will (more on that to come), but for the most part they come from solid planning and being flexible enough to divert from your plan when needed, or if the mood strikes you.

In other words, to have a great vacation, you are going to have to plan much further than "eat breakfast, then, maybe head to the pool?"

Don't get us wrong, there is a lot to be said for relaxing while away, and any good vacation should have its share of "off" times. It should also have opportunities for fun, education, family bonding, and a host of other experiences. Great vacations have balance and a certain pace to them. They are also born out of careful planning and knowledge of the opportunities available to you.

A game plan for your trip should offer a solid promise of fun and excitement. When you can leave with a list of locations within your destination, a few bookings for terrific activities or excursions, and a general idea of what your family might want to do with each day, you are way ahead of the game. A well planned vacation helps keep you from getting bored, and will see your children waking up each day eager to see what you have planned. The same way a child will talk about and look forward to their birthday for weeks in advance; knowing that their parents have picked out fun and engaging things to do will make vacation like a weeklong celebration of life.

Your plan can be as simple or as complicated as you like. Cater to your own family. You may be like us, and enjoy packing each day with as much as you can possibly fit in, from morning until late at night. This sees you getting the most out of your destination. Many destinations will end up being truly "once in a lifetime" experiences for you or your children, or at the very least, for you *and* your children. Knowing what you have available to you once you arrive means that you don't return home feeling remorse for "the one that got away." For those who feel that sleep is something better left for when you are home, an action-packed vacation can help you really capitalize on the unique opportunities of a far-flung locale.

You may be the type that wants to take it slower. You may have a very young child or children, or may prefer a higher degree of spontaneity. This is great, but the importance of *some* level of planning still holds true. Maybe you only plan one "big" thing each day of your trip, and leave lots of time open.

Think of your plan as your baseline for a great vacation. By researching what is available to you and having a least a handful of exciting things ready for you each day, you guarantee a certain level of enjoyment. Ensure that you never have a boring day by having something captivating on each leg of your trip. You can still leave plenty of time for relaxing, or for spontaneous excursions and seeing where the feeling takes you, but you'll never have a "lost day." Vacations, like most things in life, require a certain amount of momentum. This is especially true of traveling with children. It can take only one boring day to turn kids off to a destination. Teenagers can be especially vulnerable to this feeling. Once a place has lost its "cool," you'll be battling to pick up strength again and have a harder time getting going in the morning. Have great things lined up so that you and your children greet each day with a sense of excitement for what is to come. In this day and age, there is a wealth of resources for travelers that it is easier than ever to do a good amount of research beforehand.

Guidebooks can be a great resource. A good guidebook can give you background information on a destination, an overview of what you need to know to get a lay of the land, as well as a variety of activities, accommodations, food, and more. We will admit to a little bias in this department, but we are proud of the guidebooks we at RealFamilyTrips have put together. As of the printing of this volume, we have guides for Israel and New York City, with more planned for the future.

The Internet has a wealth of information regarding travel. There are official sites like ministries of tourism for a variety of locations, as well as the official sites of hotels, airlines, cruise lines, restaurants, activities, and museums, to name a few. There are also review sites that aggregate a variety of information in one place, booking sites that amass widespread offerings, and travel blogs that detail personal accounts and favorite choices.

We discuss a variety of specific web resources in Part IV of this book, and share our own contributions on RealFamilyTrips.com. The point is, that there are many great resources available to you. It is up to you to make use of them, for as much or as little as you like. We recommend doing more research as opposed to less, as planning is never lost. The more you know before you arrive, the better equipped you are to make the most of your time.

Keep in mind that resources change and evolve over time. At some point, the ones discussed in this book (or at least some of them) will give way to new, perhaps better, resources and ways to plan a vacation. Once you are in the habit of planning, and once you are tapped into available sources of information, each future trip will get easier. Even when one site closes and gives way to another, you will know what to look for when you start to plan. Once careful planning is a part of your vacationing, you have already won.

Besides selecting the "big three" of your vacation (where to go, how to get there, and where to stay) you will also want to plan activities and things to do. This gives you that aforementioned baseline for your trip, and guarantees a level of fun and satisfaction before your trip even begins. However, the value of planning doesn't begin or end there.

Careful research will also provide a few fringe benefits:

Background on your destination will provide important context for what you experience. It is one thing to see a great piece of history, or go on a fun hike. Those very same experiences will mean much more to you and your family when you understand why they helped shape the evolution of a country, or the people who made the trek before you.

Details about a destination like how far your money goes, or whether local shops will accept credit cards or your home currency so you don't have to convert your money, are just two examples of how a little research beforehand can save you valuable time "on the ground" once you have arrived at your destination. Knowing where there are dress codes, what the options for food are, and how to get around - are just a few more instances where time, money, and sanity can be saved by knowing about where you are going before you get there.

The Best options may be subjective and vary from family to family, but should become clear to you when you put in a little legwork before you leave. Knowing what is out there, and selecting the options that work for you and your children, can prevent that feeling of "missing out." When there are a ton of different activities, and especially if many of them are similar to one another, a great game plan can allay that feeling of "this is great, but is there a *better* boat ride" that can create a nagging feeling that pulls you out of the moment. Similarly, when you can plan and present options to your children, and let them choose what they like, they can take a feeling of ownership over a vacation. Suddenly, they are doing exactly what they want to be doing, and not simply something you picked for them, or whatever was on a pamphlet in the hotel lobby.

Transportation for a family can be a hassle, even under the best of circumstances. You might have trouble moving multiple children of varying ages around with you on your home turf. The concerns of a strange new place can only compound this. Do you rent a car, take cabs, or use public transportation? How long will it take to get from point A to point B? How to transport your family around is one of the most important steps of planning ahead, and can save you time, money, and stress that will otherwise get in the way of having a great time. Again, this is an instance in which you typically will have several options. It could simply be using a reputable "maps" website (or app) to give you an idea of travel times. You may want to make reservations for cars (rented or driven by others) in advance, or you may want to print out directions to pack in a carry-on so that you can be totally independent once you arrive. The best solution will be dictated by your destination and your activity choices, but having at least a strong idea before you arrive will help you tour (and sleep!) better.

Budget is a concern that varies from family to family, but the fact is that most of us have to think about it. Many only go so far as to account for the transportation to, and accommodations for, the trip itself. If you really need to watch your spending, the Internet has opened up a wealth of information that can help you nail down *all* the details you like beforehand. You can find out admission costs for each activity, costs for transportation and meals, as well as where you can go once you arrive to get the best prices on the things you plan on buying, doing, and eating. Develop a financial plan beforehand and ensure that your trip is about having fun, not crunching numbers in paradise.

Hours of Operation are just another one of those things that you can very easily obtain in advance in this day and age. It may be knowing what time a museum opens on a given day (or if it opens at all) or what time the breakfast at your hotel ends so you don't miss it. Knowing what time places open and close helps avoid disappointment when you arrive, and this detail of planning can save time and money. Also keep in mind that if you are traveling internationally, the holidays of other cultures, countries, and religions will come into play. Did you know that Thai New Year, or Songkran, basically shuts down businesses in the country for three days from April 13th to 15th? Well, if you are going to Thailand you should know this, and staying on top of the local calendar will help you know what to expect.

These are just some of the important things to plan for and their benefits. Many will be expanded on in later pages, with other concepts added to the list. Not only does careful planning help make for a better vacation, it helps save time, money, and keeps you in a better frame of mind.

If all this weren't enough, good planning is also a part of responsible parenting. Knowing about which areas are safe and which should be avoided, as well as the age appropriateness of shows or exhibits, will keep your family out of harm's way. You want the best for your children and when it comes to protecting both their safety and their modesty, knowledge is power.

Great vacations are born out of solid plans. While you don't need to make vacation planning your second job, you will reap what you sow as far as putting effort into making your vacation great. There is a fine line between overthinking it (at the cost of your life at home) and under-doing it (expecting the fun to find you) but we encourage you to lean in the direction of heavier planning. Even the places you don't end up going to will help you feel better about the ones you do. Your plan is your ticket to guaranteed fun, and that enjoyment will breed more happy feelings that will permeate your family and the time spent on your trip.

Focus on developing a basic outline of your trip, complete with enough fun ideas to constitute a good starting point. You can still allow time for things to "happen" and you need to understand that some things will change, but your plan will provide the spark from which a great vacation will emerge. Allow your plan set a pace for your trip, give it momentum from the beginning, and be something you can all enjoy getting excited about. Let your children *know* how much fun can be had before you ever leave your front door. This is how captivating experiences and amazing adventures begin. Put in the work beforehand, so you can all enjoy all your time once you arrive.

Enriching, Hands-On Experiences

Seeing, hearing, and reading are simply not the same as *doing*. Vacation provides the most incredible opportunities for hands-on learning and real world experiences that one can enjoy. This is especially true for children. Because children are still in their formative years, they more easily dive into the world around them. Typically, they are eager to engage with new and different surroundings in a way that will help to shape them, and lend real world knowledge to their lives as they grow.

School is fantastic, and we would never knock the importance of a formal education. We would argue, however, that there are few better supplements to formal education than travel.

Being in a new location affords children the opportunity to apply the things they learn in the classroom or in books to the real world. It is one thing to read about ancient Egypt, quite another to see the pyramids in all their splendor. It is wonderful to practice a foreign language in the classroom, and something wholly different to try it out with a native speaker in their own country.

Knowledge gained while away can also translate back into the classroom upon return. Not only is a project based on something seen and experienced while away more fun to work on, it is that much more rewarding for your child to share their newfound knowledge of something that is now a part of their lives.

Travel as a means of, and an addition to, education is one of the easiest ways to see long term value in vacationing. See your time away as an investment in your child's future, as well as an opportunity to enjoy time away together. Facts learned and sights seen while away will mean that much more to children. By incorporating education into the fun of family vacation, a zeal for knowledge will be planted in your children that will follow them throughout their lives.

Many parents are concerned that a vacation based around (or even containing) educational stops will seem boring to kids. This simply doesn't have to be the case. By choosing stops that make learning more engaging, and by mixing them up with fun and relaxation, vacation can teach children just how much fun learning can be. It can instill in them that education is about piquing their curiosity and expanding their world, more than just trying to get good grades.

There can also be a tendency to "dumb down" activities for children out of a fear of things going over their head. Children, however, will surprise you, especially when they start traveling at a young age. Learning on vacation is different than learning in school or in day to day life. It tends to be more hands-on, situational, and inherently engaging in a variety of other ways. The simple joy and excitement of being in a new place gets blood pumping, resulting in brains and bodies that perk up with an ability and desire to handle more than usual. A subject that may otherwise be over a child's head may penetrate when a family is touring on vacation, more so than if the same topic were being taught in school. The strong visuals and other stimuli of a museum, historical site, or other unique location make greater impressions than simply reading about them or seeing images in a book.

At the very least, an educational encounter experienced at a very young age may plant a seed. Even if a child is too young to fully grasp a concept or understand an exhibit - images, thoughts, and emotions are imprinted. A child is more likely to want to learn about a subject later in life when they have a positive memory associated with it from a young age. They may choose to come back when they are older, or otherwise seek out and fill in the knowledge they were unable to grasp on that first visit. Don't look at it as a lost experience, but an initiating experience with a place or subject.

At the same time, keep in mind that to be educational, a stop on a trip doesn't have to be a museum or an exhibit. Part of the beauty of traveling is the opportunity to make learning hands-on and *real*. Get dirty, go off the beaten path, and *experience* something firsthand.

There are too many possibilities to list, with so many opportunities for practical education while traveling.

You might seek out a workshop that allows you to engage in a traditional craft or art. Berlin, Germany has a rich history of street art, and local graffiti artists conduct hands-on workshops that allow children to create their own street art on canvas. This unique type of activity teaches kids about something local, engages them with the people who know it best, *and* creates a unique souvenir for them to take home and remember the experience by.

Seek out the locations that are more interactive and lend themselves to taking you *inside* the subject matter. A colonial village will engage children with activities and historical reenactments in a way that looking at a statue or reading a plaque simply cannot. Put yourselves in your children's shoes and think about what would be most exciting to them. Don't think of this as "dumbing down" your trip, but rather see it as an opportunity to kindle the flames of knowledge. Every parent knows that kids can see right through it when you try too hard. Stop trying to make your vacation educational and start trying to make it fun. The learning will happen when any of you least expect it.

Active excursions can become learning experiences when you do a little preparation beforehand. Hiking around a dormant volcano in Hawaii would surely be a stunning and exciting venture in its own right. Many families would be content to simply take in the view, stretch their legs, and enjoy the walk. While there is nothing wrong with that, if you learn even a little about the particular site, and the science of how volcanoes work, you have information you can share with your children that will help science and nature come alive as you hike. If you visit a national park, this can be as simple as making sure you stop in the visitor's center before setting out on your journey. Read some panels, grab a pamphlet, or ask questions in order to gain some context about the area before hiking it. Make your afternoon in the sun one that engages children's minds and bodies equally.

Even mealtime can be an opportunity to learn and experience. Seek out a really traditional and authentic restaurant that serves local cuisine. Try ordering in another language, or taste a traditional dish you otherwise wouldn't have a chance to try. Participate in a tea ceremony, visit a specialty bakery, or a coffeehouse. Seek out something that doesn't exist where you live and let your children see something new, then allow them to participate.

Don't just leave the educational aspects of your trip to museums. Almost any place you visit can teach you something if you ask questions. You will of course want to exercise some discretion in approaching random people, but the attendant at a bike rental shop, the barista at a cafe, or the concierge at your hotel might have a thing or two to share with you if you are polite and inquisitive. Ask about places to go and things to see, as well as what things mean. Ask about facts and activities equally, and don't assume that someone won't know something. While you help to stoke an inquisitive streak in your children, exercise your own. You might just all come out learning something you never expected.

Setting examples for your children while you travel can provide a lot of benefits to all of you. By setting the tone and being inquisitive, you encourage them to do the same. By rolling up your sleeves and engaging in an activity that requires some effort, or gets you a little dirty, you show them just how fun mom and dad can be. We aren't promising that after vacation your teenagers will think that you're cool, but they may just learn a thing or two from (or about) you that will engender respect and help them in their own lives.

This is also a good place to mention the value of a solid tour guide. A reliable and reputable tour guide can help enhance your vacation greatly. Not only do they have a better handle on the logistics of getting around and an idea of the best things to do, they have a wealth of knowledge about the area that you likely don't.

A truly great tour guide knows the history of the area, and can offer insight into important things that happened there. They should also have a feel for local culture and tradition, and be able to help your family get a taste for them. Perhaps the greatest benefit to having a guide is the one on one time, and the opportunity to have exclusive access to someone who can help you go deeper. Group tours can also be a good option, but you have to share your question time and follow the plan of the other people in the group. Even time spent in transit with a knowledgeable tour guide and/or driver is not lost. If you can spend a half hour in the car asking questions about the place you are about to go, you can be better prepared (and more excited) for when you arrive.

Whether you work with a tour guide or plan everything on your own, search out the opportunities for practical education and hands-on experiences. If you have the option between watching something and doing it, choose to do. If vacation is about finding captivating moments that grab your family and keep you in the present moment, never is that more possible than when you are sharing in an activity together. Seek out the opportunities to learn that place you in the thick of things, and you will find yourselves smarter and happier for the effort.

Inspire the Next Generation

Many parents fear that taking a "big trip" - such as an expensive cruise, an expansive European tour, or an exotic getaway to Asia - will be "lost" on their children. This kind of thinking delays these sorts of trips. As children grow, their schedules fill up. There are only so many precious years before they strike out on their own. The time is now, and children can absorb a lot more than we give them credit for.

We have already touched on the notion of travel as education; however it is important to note that it goes beyond the scope of what we traditionally perceive as "education." Travel opens doors for children, both while away and upon their return home.

There are few better means to teach your children than through travel, and no better classroom than the world around us. Exposure to other cultures and ways of life will equip them to be more open-minded people, and to appreciate others around them. Traveling to far flung locations will inspire them to set large goals and widen their view of life. Spending time together traveling will cement deep bonds, and provide memories to last a lifetime.

In short, travel is an amazing way to help make your children smarter, and to inspire them to do and to be better.

Vacations can be a time to nurture a child's imagination and curiosity. This can begin at the onset of vacation planning and carry-on throughout the length of the trip, as well as following your return home. Ask your children about places that interest them, things they have studied in school, or books they have read. You might also consider their favorite activities when planning your vacation. Take your children to the birthplace of their favorite food, the site of their last history unit in school, or the place their favorite animal calls home. Engage them in the process of planning your trip, look at a map together, and think about the possibilities.

The same comes to the planning of details for your trip. When it comes to picking activities or selecting places to stay, showing your children what the options are can be a lot of fun. If you have your own ideas, a budget to stick to, or other concerns, simply limit the options you show them in order to avoid disappointment. Who knows, an innocent question from one of your kids about whether or not you can climb this, or swim there, or touch that, may inspire an activity you didn't even know existed until you looked into answering it for them.

Allowing your children to participate in planning is a bonding experience, and one that encourages them to be creative and imaginative about the process. It also helps build excitement for the coming vacation. When you have their minds swimming in the fun and excitement that awaits, you've sown the seeds for an amazing vacation before stepping out the front door.

At the same time that you look to engage your children's interests in selecting a destination and activities, it is also important to push them a little. One of the benefits of great travel is that it can take children out of their comfort zone in a wonderful way. By pushing the boundaries of what feels "safe" and "usual" to your kids, you help to expand these boundaries.

We all know that if kids were allowed to do nothing but what they wanted to at a given moment, the world might be filled with children who ate nothing but pizza and who spent all day on their devices. Think of travel as a way to "get kids to eat their vegetables" (perhaps quite literally) by dressing them up in a new and exciting skin. If your kids are always on the go, try to slow things down with a museum or a tour that forces them to stop and listen for more than just a minute. If your kids are more on the couch potato end of the spectrum, challenge them to run, climb, swim, or otherwise get up and out of themselves.

Vacation makes pushing these boundaries easier by presenting things in a new and exciting light. The thrill of a different place and setting can help push children to jump on something they normally wouldn't try. It can help combat the classic attitude of "I've never tried it, but I *know* I don't like it" by presenting children with a new angle on things. To return to the food analogy for a second, that steamed green bean they refuse to even touch on their plate at home might get devoured while on vacation as part of an authentic yasai itame (Japanese vegetable stir fry) without them even thinking twice about it.

This isn't about tricking children, but taking advantage of new places and happy attitudes to expand their view of what is fun, as well as what is possible. When children engage in great travel they let go and allow the experience to broaden their horizons. With careful reinforcement, parents can use this opportunity to teach valuable lessons about life. The result of this process will be kids who develop a true zeal for learning and experiencing new things.

Kids grow and move so fast that it can sometimes be hard, both for parents and for children, to really step back and notice what is going on. Vacation presents a slice of life, perhaps a week at a time, to really absorb and reflect on. For example, ending the summer with a well-balanced vacation, featuring a mixture of activities, education, and downtime, will allow you to have conversations about balance with your kids before returning to another busy school year.

We have encouraged you not to delay "big trips" until children are older because even when young, kids can absorb a lot from these experiences. Rather than seeing only what exists in the town, city, or area where you live - travel presents an opportunity to open children's eyes to new things and hold their hands as your family walks the great stage that is our world.

There is a lot to be gained from travel. Children are more likely to think critically and empathetically about the world around them when they have some conception of it. Even if they will not remember the specific person they met at age 5 while in another country, they will know that they met *a* person; they will remember that it felt good, and they will seek out other new experiences in life as they begin to make their own choices.

Travel can also be a chance to give back and to give of yourselves while away. Don't think of charity work as something that is limited to while you are home, as volunteering while away can provide incredible opportunities without parallel. While away on a recent trip our family was able to volunteer at an organization that delivers meals and care packages to the underprivileged. Packing up boxes of donations was a rewarding experience and a lot of fun in its own right, especially when done together as a family.

This experience taught our children that the place we were visiting was not *just* a vacation destination, but a real place with real people, some of whom had real problems. It didn't darken the fun and levity of the vacation or even that morning, but it did lend a dose of reality and perspective that helped our children to be grateful, and to develop a sense of what is right and wrong.

There are many such opportunities, to either build an entire vacation around volunteering (such as a trip to build homes for Habitat for Humanity) or simply build in a couple hours of giving back on a trip that is otherwise all about fun and excitement. Visit a foreign soup kitchen, stop in at an animal shelter, or see if another local organization needs help. It is also a great way to mingle with locals and meet other travelers who share your values and passion. Giving back while being away is a great opportunity to make vacation about more than just being someplace else, but *experiencing* someplace else.

Show your children how exciting life can be, and give them gifts that will last through their entire lives. There are just so many benefits to family travel.

These benefits exist on two levels. The first is the literal. The new people, places, and things they experience will open them up to possibilities and provide them with a practical education on life. This can and will happen before, during, and after the trip. As you research, experience, and reflect back on what you saw and learned, each vacation will provide a wealth of new knowledge for your children to carry with them.

The second level exists as part of a much bigger picture. The concepts introduced through travel: open mindedness, worldliness, curiosity, charity, balance, preparedness, a sense of fun, and many, many more - will be easiest to reflect on after getting back from your trip. These will develop not just from a single vacation, but instead, over the accumulated course of travels. By becoming the family that travels well together, each vacation will cement important principles in your children that will help shape their lives. The entire body of family travels will become a unique course of studies carried out over their entire childhood, and expanded upon in their adult lives.

So should you wait to take a big trip until later? The decision is yours, but each big trip has many benefits both in the immediate future, and the long run for your children. You never know until you go, and you'll only delay the benefits if you wait for "later" to come.

Discover Extraordinary, and Ordinary Places Together

One of the main points we will try to stress over the course of this book is that travel doesn't *have* to be anything. Many people get hung up on preconceived notions of what a vacation should be. These can be rooted in one's own childhood experiences, inherited from film or literature, or based on impressions of what the people around us do when they go away. The simple fact is that your family vacation should be what *you* want it to be. Nothing more, and nothing less.

That being said, the single undeniable and unifying factor about a trip is that it involves going *somewhere* other than where you live. We would like to emphasize, however, that simple definition as one meant to open doors and expand minds. You could choose to traverse a few miles or a few time zones. Neither is inherently better or worse. Some of it has to do with personal taste, some with budget. Ideally, over the course of your children's lives, it should probably include a bit of both.

We've talked about "big trips" already. These can be wonderful experiences that create lasting memories and deserve a special place in your considerations, as well as your actual plans. Travel most certainly can be, but also doesn't need to be, about a series of weeklong international ventures, expensive five star resorts, or luxurious retreats.

There is a lot to be said for taking your children abroad, and letting them experience places where they don't speak the language, recognize the culture, or know what to expect. This chance to expose them to new and different ideas will help shape them as they grow.

At the same time, even when expensive travel is within your means, it is a good idea to make your vacations a mixture of the grand and the down-home. You may be fortunate enough to be able to take your kids away several times a year. You may only have time and budget for one "big trip" each year, or every few years. Whatever your schedule and lives allow, the best you can do is create a variety of experiences that run the gamut and showcase for your children the variety of experiences that constitute travel.

First of all, you should dispel the notion that any type of trip, any variety of destinations, or any means of travel or accommodations are inherently "better" or "worse" than any other. Granted, when it comes to *your* family, there may be things that work and things that don't (due to budget, family makeup, personal tastes, etc.). The fact is that you don't know until you go. Except for a few major concerns that can't be ignored (like medical issues, cultural adherences, and the like) you shouldn't cross anything off your list until you have tested the waters. Who knows, the camping trip you though might be miserable could be the best experience of your summer. Similarly, the European odyssey that you just *knew* would bore your kids may end up being the thing they talk about for the rest of their lives. Step out of your comfort zone and try something new.

View cruises, resorts, and far flung locales as equal options to road trips and camping. Don't rule out Monaco *or* Montana. Take in the masterpieces of the Louvre with the same zeal as the 12 painting gallery next to the laundromat. Be excited about both the feather bed and the open field under the stars. Challenge yourselves to try and experience new things. You will learn about your children and yourselves. Even the "bad" experiences aren't lost when you share them together. Travel is about living another life for a short period of time. Sometimes it will look a lot like your life at home but with a different backdrop. At other times it should look and feel completely different. If you don't approach travel with this view, you may have no idea what you are missing.

Children learn to identify and adapt to patterns very early. If you take the same type of vacation, they begin to get used to the idea. You might spend a significant amount of money, pick the best resort, and visit a different country every year. You may soon realize, that after a few years of this, Jamaica will begin to look like Hawaii which will become indistinguishable from Bermuda. If you simply do the same thing, kids will begin to see vacation as "that time where we go to the fancy place" and for better or for worse, expect it.

Extraordinary excursions can be broken up by more "ordinary" places to keep things fresh. If you want to take a big international trip each winter, then find a fun, not-too-far away locale to road trip to during the summer. Cruise the islands or get an Italian villa one year, then spend the next staying in a rented apartment in the heart of a city. Take your children to places that look like their home but have different people and traditions, then expose them to something they have never seen before.

By mixing up the sorts of places you go, not only will you eventually zero in on what you like best, you help keep children on their toes. Kids are kids, and they crave what is new and exciting. Even butler service on a private island will become old hat to children after a couple of repetitions. By varying experiences, you keep kids on the edge of their seat. Suddenly vacation time is no longer "time for another beach" or "time to see another city" but rather, "I can't wait to see what mom and dad picked next!"

There can be a temptation to try and match what your friends and those around you are doing. It seems like everyone goes to the same beach, maybe even at the same time. You may also want to enjoy the same sorts of vacations you did as a child, or even visit the same places. By all means, do this. At the same time, it is important to mix these up with your own ideas and try out new suggestions. Travel is one area of life where it doesn't pay to "go with the crowd" but rather, it is important to forge your own path. Explore your options, and mix up your far-flung ideas or practical notions with the things your and/or the kid's friends enjoy.

Travel also doesn't have to become an "only once a year" affair when you free yourself from the idea that travel is only worth it when it is expensive. You may well spend a lot of time, and a lot of money, planning your major annual getaway. It may leave you, as parents, feeling drained. It may also create the impression that you only have the energy to do *that* the one time each year.

Instead, consider that while you may only have the time and energy for that one *big* trip, there is no reason you cannot supplement it with several smaller ones. Take long weekends and school breaks to do day trips, or quick getaways for a few days or so. Maybe you barely cross state lines. If you live in a city, get out of it. If you live in the suburbs or a rural area, get to a city.

There are a lot of options for small trips that are more affordable and require less planning. National and state parks are generally free or inexpensive to enter, require minimal fees for things like camping or equipment rentals, and depending on the park, may offer wonderful experiences. You don't need to put a lot of time or money into a trip that will both inspire and educate your children.

The advent of rental apps and websites, and day-of hotel booking software means that you can find affordable lodging when you are willing to be a little flexible. The best ways to save on flights and cruises are to book them either very early or at the 11th hour when companies try to fill their seats and cabins. Take these ideas (and more that we will share in Part IV) like parts that you can mix and match. Turn the ideas of luxury and economy on their head. Make the extraordinary vacation more affordable by finding ways to stretch a budget. Make the "ordinary" destination an entirely different experience by selecting the best of the best for it. Add trips you couldn't have conceived of before by thinking outside the box and getting creative.

If part of travel is about making children more worldly, it makes sense that this is best accomplished by seeing not only more parts of the world, but more types of locations and varieties of experiences. Since one important component of family vacation is building memories, keep in mind that these memories will be more distinct and meaningful when they don't all run together as a series of similar experiences.

We would encourage you once again to look at your family's vacations as a series of experiences, all working towards a common goal. Think of the 18 or so years you have with each of your children under your roof as a canvas on which to paint a rich picture of the world. Mix up the ordinarily wonderful, extravagant trips, with the wonderfully ordinary local trips. Show children the highs and the lows, the simple and the serene. This will provide them with a more rounded image of the planet, as well as a more balanced conception of vacation. Don't spoil or deprive them. Shatter your expectations over and over again, not by simply going bigger, but by traveling smarter and more unexpectedly.

Where there is a will, there is a way - and there is value in almost every destination. The most important thing, your family, will be constant. In the meantime, mix up and vary the locations and the style of your travel. Free yourself of the notions that either "big" vacations are beyond you, or "small" vacations are beneath you - whether directly or not, your children will thank you for it.

FUN

With all this talk of serious benefits, intellectual gains, and making important decisions - it can be easy to forget perhaps the most important part of a vacation - fun!

Travel offers an incredibly valuable and enriching experience for families. Think of educational gains, family unity, great memories, and the countless other benefits of great travel as dividends. They pay themselves out, in their own time. You need to invest the time and the effort (and yes, the money) to get yourselves out there. However, in addition to spending your time actively seeking out "ways to grow" while away, it is extremely important to focus on enjoying yourselves.

There is a reason this book begins with a chapter about the value of planning. From a solid plan, the stage is set for all the benefits and incredible opportunities afforded by a great vacation. We will speak more later about the ways in which reflecting on a great trip after the fact can reinforce the experiences and cement the gains. With careful planning and the fun of reliving the experience you can set yourself up for great opportunities and savor them for a lifetime.

The feeling of being right where you want to be and doing what you want to be doing, is both one of the great rewards of travel, as well as the means by which to reap further rewards. If ever you are going to overthink things (you don't *need* to, but let's be honest, some of us do) this should be done before you leave. Put your home time into planning so you can put your vacation time into enjoying. Once you arrive, live with both feet on the ground and enjoy being in the moment.

Having fun while away is incredibly important. By definition, fun means you are enjoying yourselves and we would all rather be having fun than doing something we feel we need to. Fun is also the magical ingredient in establishing great memories and life changing experiences. It is a simple fact of human nature that we tend to remember the best and the worst of things, with the middle ground being more elusive.

Since you certainly don't want the latter option to be a part of your vacation experience, maximizing fun will lead to more memorable trips, stronger family bonding, and greater opportunities.

Even a remarkably intricate plan, perfectly executed, is really just a case of getting what you wanted. If you were to plan a day with six stops, allow for travel time and factor in enough leeway to make it all work - surely you would have accomplished something fantastic. At the same time, if you went through this day and did all the things you had planned on, but without ever really enjoying them, wouldn't that feel a lot more like work than vacation? It isn't enough to simply do everything you wanted. Without plenty of enjoyment, vacation is less valuable and meaningful. It becomes more about the parents who did the planning, and not about the family sharing in a great time.

Another way to think of it is that fun will enhance every aspect of your trip. Having a fun morning with some activity you all love, or something exciting you have never tried, will generate adrenaline and endorphins that carry you through the rest of the day. Suddenly a family still brimming with excitement from their early excursions is that much more apt to enjoy their afternoon at the museum. When you are enjoying yourselves, that once in a lifetime photo opportunity on top of a mountain, or in front of a masterpiece, will be filled with warm, genuine smiles that make it mean so much more. When you try to get the kids moving at 6 in the morning, the experience will be remarkably different after a day of fun than a day spent doing "important things."

Children need time and space to be themselves. While it is important to push their limits and boundaries, especially while traveling, they also need to feel comfortable. You will have a much harder time getting them to try something new, much less appreciate it, if they aren't having fun along the way. You can plan all the opportunities for growth in the world, but without many pleasurable moments, they are all too likely to be lost in the shuffle. Kids have a tendency when young to shut down if not doing what they like to do. Without building enough fun and exciting things into your plan, amazing opportunities can be squandered. If you don't keep the fun levels up, you risk losing your kids and your vacation.

Seek out things that your family members enjoy, both as individuals and as a unit. Cater to the kid who loves science with a technology museum, or a hands-on wildlife experience. Look into tickets to a local sporting event for the child who can't get enough of their athletic pursuits. If your family loves to go to the movies together, find one while you are away, or visit the theatre for a live performance that feels like a "vacation version" of your favorite pursuit.

For families with multiple children, and multiple ages, it is important to vary activities to meet everyone on their level. Space out activities and mix them up so that every so often, there is something to meet each member of the family and keep them engaged. Visit a "kiddie" location early, followed by something to challenge your teen later in the day. Mix in things that everyone can enjoy. Find a balance and pace that keeps anyone from getting bored and gives you each something to look forward to. When vacation becomes less about being fun for everyone, you all suffer. After all, as a family, you sense each other's happiness and sadness more profoundly. If anyone isn't being taken care of, you will all feel it.

While you may choose to make vacation more about your children, and/or things shared as a family, do not forget the parents. This may be a parent's once in a lifetime experience as well. Ideally most of your stops will be about things that everyone can enjoy, and enjoy together. There is certainly nothing wrong with putting *most* of the focus on your kids. At the same time, remember that if you feel like you are sacrificing the things you enjoy, your kids will sense it and it will affect their time. It may be as simple as building in ten minutes between stops to grab a coffee that you really like, or building in a little time for shopping if that is what you enjoy. Find compromises. Get them each a treat at the coffee shop, and pick a shopping location that has things for them to browse while you get what you need. As much as it is important to build in stops that are *more* important for particular family members, there is no reason anything should be entirely about them. There are ways to find fun for everyone, while catering to a specific need.

While talking about the kids meeting their parents halfway, it is also important to note that the reverse needs to be true as well. Parents need to push their comfort zone and get their hands "dirty." You can't expect your kids to do this if you aren't willing to yourself. This also sets a good example not only for while you are away, but for them to emulate throughout their lives. Besides, how often do you get to show your children that you yourself are a kid at heart?

Try to do as many activities with your kids as possible. Within reason, and subject to health concerns, let yourself loose and don't just leave the play to them. Engaging with children in the fun activities that are important to them is, itself, very important to them. Jump into the activities with both feet. We aren't just referring to the "usual" ones like skiing, snorkeling, or riding a roller coaster. Seek out and share in the truly outrageous activities your kids are dying to try. Jump off that ledge into the water below. Swing from the Tarzan rope at the obstacle course. Hold your nose and wade through the muddy, smelly water on that hike. Let your kids see you be fun and vulnerable. Open up and enjoy yourself. These types of moments make for incredible bonding experiences and treasured memories. Show your kids how much fun you can have, and it will surely add to their own.

It is also important to free yourself of the notion that there are things you *need* to do at a given destination. Surely you couldn't visit New York City for the first time and not see the Statue of Liberty, right? Won't people look at you funny if you tell them you went to Paris and never went near the Eiffel Tower? Not that we would ever knock either of those locations, but if you know that they simply hold no interest for you or your family, don't force yourself to dedicate valuable time to seeing or doing something you don't want to.

It is important to push boundaries and step outside your collective comfort zone a little bit, but not at the expense of enjoying yourselves. You know your own family better than anyone. Just because another family thought something was great, don't push yourselves to do it just to keep up, or because you think you should. If you are unsure about how your children feel about a particular activity, ask them! There is no sense in making unilateral decisions and trying to make things happen the way they are "supposed to" - in life or in travel.

There is simply never going to be enough time to "do it all" when you go away. People live their entire lives in the places you will visit and don't enjoy every activity that they have to offer. Even two weeks in another city or country will see you returning home saying "I wish we had gotten to *that* place." Vacation time is precious and not to be squandered. Don't waste time doing things that don't appeal to you. Your children aren't going to grow up to say that they were glad they saw the things they were "supposed to" on vacation, but they will never stop talking about the fun you all had together.

A good rule of thumb is to push boundaries by trying things that are new or that you are unsure of. Never been to a luau? Unsure of what it would be like, or if any of you would enjoy it? By all means, *try* one while you are in Hawaii. At the same time, if you know that the food there consists of things your kids have tried and hate, or if the last time you took them to dinner and a show they simply shut down, don't force the issue. Try new things, but don't re-try things no one likes simply because you are away and feel you should. Exercise judgement, and keep your family in the loop.

This concept of "increasing levels of fun" may seem vague and elusive, but in practice it comes down to a few simple principles.

The first is in the planning. Part of the reason it makes sense to do extensive research beforehand is to make sure you know the full scope of options for your family. Whether you do your own research online, invest in a solid guidebook, borrow ideas from other families - or ideally combine some level of all of these things - get the lay of the land. When you can sit down and feel you are well versed in the options available to you, you are equipped to make the best possible choices for your family.

Many people seem to do this in reverse, selecting a location and starting with the things they "should" do. After including major museums, monuments and attractions in a city, they then look to fill in the rest of the time with fun activities that grab their eye. While this approach may work in some locations and for some families, for others it may result in a hodgepodge of disconnected stops. Our suggestion is instead, for you to look at the full array of activities and begin planning your trip. Start from the beginning, with a blank slate and the intention to choose the ideas that fit your family. You may end up forgoing some major landmarks when you realize how many unique stops there are that would appeal to your family's passions and interests. You might end up with a very different trip than you imagined when you first set out to plan, but this can be a good thing. When you can say that you chose the activities most appealing to your family, it doesn't matter what you skipped over. You are setting yourselves up for the vacation you will enjoy.

When we started creating guidebooks at RealFamilyTrips, our goal was to provide out-of-the-box vacations for families who don't have time to plan. At the same time, we recognized that there is no "one size fits all" solution. Families are different and complex. For each of our pre-planned trips, we include a robust selection of "alternate activities" that can be swapped in for stops on the main itinerary. For our book about New York City, the main trip and the alternates were about equal in length. This is because when there are so many possibilities, and with so many families, tastes will vary and it is important to have options. There is no sense in being told what to do. Vacation is about getting away - do what you *want* to do. Nothing sets you up for fun quite like an exciting itinerary.

The second way to increase your fun while away is to have your plan, but not be married to it. We will talk more about the value of spontaneity later, but for now suffice to say that you couldn't possibly foresee or account for every fun possibility on a given trip. If visiting another country you have never been to, no matter how extensive your research, you simply won't know what it feels like until you get there. There will be stops not mentioned in any book or website. There will be things that just happen. Your family, your mood, and your day will dictate what fun is. You just need to have your eyes open to it.

Fun is subjective. What is fun for one person may not be to another. What is boring on a given day may be loads of fun the next. You simply can't anticipate all the variables. If careful planning sets the stage for guaranteed fun, the ad libbing you do while away is what brings the play to life. Your attitude will have a lot to do with how much fun you will have. If you are looking for a good time, you are that much more likely to find one.

Fun will be what makes your good vacation great. Sharing in amazing times will bring you closer and create personal moments you can share for a lifetime. Letting loose and enjoying yourselves will make your vacation so much better. Fun comes from a healthy mix of the planned and the unplanned. If you make having a great time the theme of your vacationing, you will find that each trip you take becomes more and more valuable.

Quality Family Time

Vacation allows for some of the most unique and special opportunities for family bonding you will ever get to experience with your children. As important as the day to day of your lives together are, the chance to be removed from it all and enjoy each other's company will be invaluable in cementing your relationships and helping you grow.

Home life is full of distractions. The bustle of daily living, interference from work, social obligations, and so many other things pull us in different directions from our families. If it isn't your schedule getting in the way, it is that of your children. Modern kids can often be just as, if not busier, than their parents. Between school, sports, activities, friends, and the much needed time to be kids - the current age leads to families that have to fight for time together.

While it is incredibly important to build in shared family time at home, vacation does most of the work for you. Freedom from distractions while away creates a natural and euphoric release from hectic schedules, which sets you up for more family unity. At the same time, each trip you take can aid in creating and enhancing the quality of your shared time upon return. Vacation can bring you closer and keep you closer. It is a simple matter of appreciating the time and making the most of the experience.

Travel affords opportunities for each member of the family to grow as an individual, and for the family unit to grow as a whole. The special circumstances afforded by exploring a strange and exciting place together help facilitate this growth. In time, this growth can become a natural part of each trip.

Growing as individuals is about challenging each of you to try new things, learn from locations and experiences, and push yourselves a little. This can be easiest to see in the youngest members of your family. To see a toddler work to keep up with older siblings is a chance to see them grow right before your eyes. Younger children get to be a part of the same activities as their older siblings and parents in a way that is less often seen at home. Part of this comes from the fact that everyone is out of their element. For a child to explore a new place with siblings and parents who are similarly in the dark, is a disarming proposition; it levels the playing field and helps younger children enjoy the fact that they are tackling the same obstacles as their older family members.

When parents and siblings of varying ages experience something new and exciting side by side, they share in the victory as well as the fun.

Seek out particularly new and exciting options for this very reason. Take your children to a restaurant and introduce them to a really authentic, local dish that you love. Then be sure to order something none of you have ever tried and enjoy sharing in the uncertainty and excitement together. This allows you to all be equals, members of a family, trying something new together.

Look for new experiences so that you can all share in them, and aspire to unique experiences that create special memories. Go spelunking in that cave, climb that hill, or go snorkeling at that reef. Try the things that are rare and different to create memories that are special to you. A great and unique experience is like a little secret that you share as a family. While also doing the "popular stops" and the things your friends have enjoyed have their place, it is that very different and exciting stop that may end up being the memory that remains important to you for years to come.

It is important to carry these memories and feelings with you upon returning home. Preserve the experience and return to it as a family so that you can continue the happy feelings and the growth opportunities you all experienced while away.

Take lots of photographs and videos. It may seem like a no-brainer, but it will continue to be important to you into the future. Take pictures and record videos of the things you do and see, as well as of each other. Rather than have a designated family photographer, allow everyone to take turns behind the camera. This ensures that one person doesn't end up sitting out the fun while they focus on documenting the trip.

It also helps kids feel involved. They will feel ownership over pictures they took, and look back on them with fond memories.

When you get home, assemble the pictures before you get too far away from the experience to appreciate their significance. Create an album, either physically or digitally, that puts them in order and allows you to really relive the experience as viscerally as possible. Many companies will make high quality photo books for you. These hard bound volumes are an investment, but they allow you to incorporate text and pictures, create a really aesthetically pleasing presentation, and preserve your memories. They can serve as great coffee table books, becoming part of your home and a reminder of shared joy. They can also serve as great gifts for kids. For a birthday or holiday following a trip, a personalized photo book of the vacation (or featuring pictures taken of or by one of your children) can create a delightful present that they will treasure.

We have also found photo collections, whether they be an album, a book, a slideshow, or another form - to be a great way to share the memories with others. Friends and extended family will want to hear about your trip, and it is easier (and better) to show than to tell. The photographs provide an opportunity to empower your children to be storytellers, recounting the family trip while prompted by photographs. Sit down with people who weren't there, and allow your children to explain what each photo means, how they felt about it, and what they learned. This cements the experience in their mind, and helps them to really demonstrate what they took from the trip. They will feel a sense of pride, while also reminding themselves of the knowledge they gained.

Revisiting the trip will also be a great tool for planning your next one. This sort of detailed recounting by children is an incredible window into what was meaningful, interesting, and enjoyable to them. Hopefully everyone is having a great time while you are away, and if you are fortunate enough to have everyone enjoying themselves constantly, then these recollections will help you to gauge what really sank in. Knowing not only what your children enjoyed, but what they remember, will be your best guide to planning the next trip. Look at each vacation as a chance to learn about a new place, as well as to learn about vacationing itself.

Travel is about more than just enjoying the time you spend away from home. It is about collecting experiences that you all share and can relate to. It is about setting precedents and opening doors that relate to daily life as well. It is about stepping out of the usual in order to expand your definition of what usual means.

If you try something new while away that your child is surprised to have liked, remind them of it. If any or all of you accomplished something you really doubted you would be able to do, remember it. By sharing reminders of these things at home, they become more than just fond memories of fun times, but principles that apply to their everyday lives. If you tried that and it was better than you thought, why not try this? If you trusted us to know you would be safe while we were away, don't you think you can trust us now? The excitement of vacation can push all of us to do and be things that seem impossible to us. Why have those feelings only on vacation? Carry it home with you and make it count.

Family vacation time should be just that: family time. Resist the urge to check in with work just for the sake of checking in, or use phones and other devices for anything other than important needs or as part of the trip itself. When teens and older children, who are big users of devices themselves, see you making an effort to be there in the moment, they are more likely to follow suit. Set an example and show, rather than tell, that this is family time. There are few other chances in life to be so utterly in the moment. Treasure them and leave home behind.

The opportunities afforded by the shedding of daily life, and the chance to try new things together, make family travel a truly special opportunity. Seize that chance and use it to really grow. Vacations provide unique windows into the growth of your family. Use them to check in on everyone, plant the seeds of new ideas, and nurture your children as well as your family. These are the times you will all remember, make them count.

Active, Engaged, Curious

One of the many benefits of family travel is the level of enthusiasm it builds. In an age where everything is online and children seem to grow up much faster, travel is a chance to get children who have "seen it all" really excited about something. Getting kids active, engaged, and curious about a new place and time shared with the family is both a means to great ends, and a reward in itself.

While the joy is in the journey, excitement and activity can (and should) start at home even before you leave. As parents, the logistics of getting yourselves there and preparing a trip that "works" is your charge and main role before the journey begins. The "job" for children is to get excited, and build their curiosity so that it can be unleashed in full force upon arrival.

A vacation that promotes growth and shares in the many benefits we have discussed (and will continue to build on) requires some forethought. There is an inevitable adjustment period transitioning from life at home, with its many responsibilities and obligations, to life on vacation. While parents and children spend their day to day lives multitasking and splitting focus between the present and the future, getting "in the moment" while on vacation does not happen at the drop of a hat. There are a few things you can do ahead of time to help get your children excited.

First, get them engaged and excited about the destination. Just as selecting a location to visit is the first step in planning a trip; it is the first step in building enthusiasm in children. Even if you have involved them in narrowing down the field, the moment you announce the destination for an upcoming family trip should be one of exuberance and the start of the fun. A little theater won't hurt, and showing your own excitement will go a long way in building theirs.

After recently deciding to book our next vacation to Thailand, a trip that is exciting and unusual even for veteran travelers, our youngest children were absolutely ecstatic. Even though they didn't yet understand what they will see or do while there, for the time being that was of less importance to them. Their enthusiasm for the simple *concept* of the trip was infectious, and will keep us all excited over the coming months as we plan it. This is just one of many examples in which the joy of a parent can feed a child, and vice versa. Start sharing in the enthusiasm for your trip early, to set yourselves up to share in the experience once you are there.

We took the children over to the large wall map we keep in our house. This is something we recommend for all families. Placing pins and tracking the places you have been is a fun reminder of past trips, a way to help determine future ones, and a great way to teach children geography and help them to gain context for their travels. Not only could the children use the map to see just how *far* away we will be going, but they could observe where Thailand is in relation to other countries in the region. They could spot other countries they have heard of, other countries they want to go, and other places we have already been. They could identify what areas we will fly over to get there, and see the location of countries that are the subject of current events.

At this point, for our younger children, the vacation boils down to a single word - the name of a country. Yet, the level of joy and elation that came from that simple word was delightful. Travel, like so many other things, gives us a chance to step back and observe our children, and remember those simpler times. The mirth and curiosity that came from that simple announcement were enough to keep them going for days.

At this point it is fitting to mention the next step of building excitement about an upcoming trip: asking questions. With nothing more than a destination in mind, especially when it is one that is mystical and faraway, children have the opportunity to explore their curiosity. When looking at a visit to another country, there are so many questions to be answered. Is it a monarchy? A democracy? What languages do they speak? What do they sound like? What is the currency? What do people wear? Eat? Do for fun? The list could go on and on.

The possibilities for answering these questions are almost as numerous as the questions themselves. You might want to equip yourselves with some knowledge about the country or city you are visiting and let the kids ask you what they want to know. You could supply your children with a list of questions like these and have them do research and report back to you. You might read an article or look things up together. You could have the kids look up things on their own and host a family quiz show where you ask questions and have the kids ring in to answer. There really are so many possibilities, limited only by your imagination.

After the destination is in hand, the next step is to continue building excitement up through the time you actually leave. Depending on how you plan, this could be week, or months of time. Try sharing media with your children related to the vacation to keep them excited and enthusiastic. After announcing the Thailand trip, we sat down with our kids to watch videos online. Some of them were just general videos from the area, including beautiful scenery and videos of elephant feedings. We also showed them some things that had initially caught our eye as possibilities. For Thailand, this included a hotel which is located on a river and can only be accessed by boat. We even shared some of the names of places we knew would be strange and funny sounding to them, like Phi Phi Island. Laughter and amusing facts can go a long way to building that excitement in children.

By starting soon after announcing the trip, and continuing the process until we leave, we will keep our kids excited and build anticipation for the vacation before it even begins. By making them laugh, think, and begin to have fun with the idea early in the process, we have set a tone that will continue through the time spent in-country.

There are plenty of ideas for media that can be shared over the course of the time leading up to a vacation. Find videos online, as well as longer-form pieces related to the destination. This could be a documentary about the place you are visiting, or a TV special about it, but also doesn't have to be. You might find a fictional piece from film or television set in the place you plan on going. The settings for scenes will provide material to get excited about, as you enjoy a leisurely family movie night watching something fun and also related to your upcoming vacation.

It is also a good idea to start following the news for your destination, and encouraging kids who are old enough to do the same. Keep track of what is developing in the place you are about to visit before you go. This not only informs you, but also allows everyone to begin to develop a stake in the place and an understanding of what is important to the people there. Share the news stories together, and note both the similarities and the differences between the lives of people there and where you live.

Spacing out the media, and keeping an eye on the news, provides opportunities to continue your building of enthusiasm for as long as you have until you leave.

The other great way to build enthusiasm as your trip approaches is to involve your children while you plan the actual itinerary. Once you set your destination, a whole new world of possibilities emerges to help get kids excited.

When you involve children in the planning process, it helps to increase their stake in the upcoming trip. By feeling some sense of personal contribution, they have that much more to think about and to feed their curiosity. Motivating and inspiring children about the things they will be doing, as well as the place that they are going to, makes for a much more positive and enthusiastic experience once you finally arrive.

The planning process opens up so many more possibilities for engaging activities that help children learn, grow, and build towards the trip. They also help set the tone for the vacation as a shared family activity, in which each person is important and where everything is communal.

Here are some of the things that have worked for us in the past:

Discussing and reading either with our kids (or to them) information obtained online regarding our destination. Important information we like to cover includes: background about the area, the local cultures, and the sites we will be visiting. This background will enable them to get more involved in the planning of the activities by giving them a basic understanding of what they will see and experience.

We like to assign our kids specific destinations within an upcoming trip. The children then create reports about the places we are going to visit. For a trip to another country that involves touring around, this might mean giving each of them one or two cities. For a trip to another city, we might have each one focus on an area. Allow them to be creative with their research and the facts they choose to focus on - you'll be surprised what they come up with. You may also learn about some new travel destinations you'll want to put on your itinerary. Children and teens often will find interesting, fun places you may have missed and which you may want to add to your itinerary to balance the trip.

After you prepare your itinerary; have your children create ads or "commercials" for the destinations in the cities they will be visiting. Another great way to get your kids involved and to offer hands-on experience is to have your children locate establishments that are on the itinerary. For example: one of our kids chose to map out the closest Starbucks to each of our stops (after all, dad needs his caffeine to stay energetic!).

Another great method we have tried is to have our kids get crafty with their involvement. One way we do this is by having our children and teens create detailed maps. The younger children will enjoy using crayons and colored pencils for this. It serves as a fun, educational art project which targets the various destinations on the itinerary.

- Another great method we use to get our children involved in our itinerary is to have them create videos about the destinations we will be traveling to. Kids get excited about creating videos and "being on television." We play the videos before our trips in the family room. A great time to do this would be after having a meal together, or during designated family game nights. Watch the videos your kids have made together as a family and then offer encouragement and discuss the attractions and culture of the places you will be visiting.

These are just some ideas that have worked in the past. Allow your kids to suggest projects, or come up with them yourself. Work together, or have them create things and present them to the family. While you plan the nitty gritty details of the trip and focus on "adult" issues like the budget, allow your children to contribute with their own creativity. Not only will it help them get excited about what is to come, but you will likely get a better trip out of the one planned by all of you working together.

It is important to note that Thailand is merely an example. Not all vacations will be quite so exotic. The same concepts will apply wherever your destination is. While taking a vacation that is down the road might have fewer differences from where you live, there are still things children can learn and report on. Even if you are not traveling internationally there is still the planning of the itinerary. There may even be more possibilities as children could know a friend who has visited a nearby or less exotic locale. Have them interview their friend and report back on the findings to your family.

Once again, the key words here are creativity and excitement. Hopefully at least some of these ideas are exciting for your family. If not, think of your own. The point is to involve children in the process as soon as possible; by doing so you set the tone for many positive things. Help get them situated to learn about a new place by engaging their curiosity from the beginning. Promote bonding by allowing them to be active in the process and a part of the vacation planning, rather than passive participants. Set yourselves up for fun by getting everyone engaged early on, rather than expecting children to suddenly snap into gear when you arrive.

This process of building enthusiasm helps to make for better vacations, and can allow your weeklong trip to bring months of closeness, and that is without even considering the memories and sharing after the fact. You should start thinking about your travels as a shared journey, one that is ongoing throughout your lives, rather than a series of isolated days and weeks.

Free Time and Options

An important component of any family vacation is building in some free time and leaving your options open as you go. While planning is critical, sometimes the things you didn't plan will end up being rewarding. On top of that, the realities of traveling with kids in tow mean that things can - and will - happen.

Different kinds of families plan different kinds of vacations. Some prefer a loose plan that hits a few highlights and leaves plenty of time for options. Some like to maximize time on the ground by packing in as many stops as possible and really taking in everything that can be reasonably accomplished in a given location. In our guidebooks and the itineraries suggested on RealFamilyTrips.com, we tend towards the latter. On vacation, our family typically gets up early, stays out really late, and tries to squeeze in as many things as possible - including zip lines, beaches, hikes, and museums.

While trying to see and to do as much as possible while away is great, even the most ambitious family needs to allow some padding in their schedule.

By leaving some wiggle room; you accomplish several positive things at once. The first is simply allowing for the unforeseen. Sometimes hailing a cab takes longer than expected, public transit has delays, a long line at an eatery or a store holds you up, a tour runs long, or an unexpected bathroom break adds time to your day. No one has to tell you that when moving around as a family, almost anything can happen.

On days with a series of general admission locations and stops with long hours of operation, it may be as simple as adding a half hour or an hour to your schedule that is "accounted for" beyond the stops you make. If you have timed tickets, a tour that leaves at a certain time, or a stop that closes early, you might need to add a few chunks of this padding to account for these and make sure you don't miss out.

We will speak more at length about the virtues of remaining flexible mentally, but for now it is safe to say that extra time in your schedule will help keep you calm and relaxed. In the end, skipping a stop or rushing a meal may not be ideal, but it is better than letting yourself be thrown by the change in plans. Children sense and emulate your mood. Protect yourself from frustration and the feeling of missing out, so that *you* don't end up being the thing that brings down your vacation. If the day runs more smoothly than expected, padding becomes "free time."

Free time is where your family gets to explore the things that are important to you. Shop for some souvenirs to bring home and remember the trip by. Pick up a unique and personal gift for that upcoming birthday or anniversary in your family. Stop for, or seek out, an extra photo opportunity. Find out if you can climb that tower, or walk up that hill, and stop for the picture that may end up being your favorite of the whole vacation.

Free time can also end up being your best chance to indulge in local culture. Stop in a shop or cafe without feeling rushed, and chat with an owner, waiter, or sales clerk. Learn a little about the area firsthand, and perhaps get a great recommendation for later.

Wander with your eyes open, and encourage your children to do the same. Did someone spot an ice cream shop, or a cafe that looks great to them? The extra time allows you to actually check it out. Depending on how much you pad a day, you might have to skip it for now, but keep track of the places that interest you and come back. Ideally you should be building this kind of extra or free time into each day of your schedule. Keep a running list of ideas, and discuss/add to it over meals, at night in the hotel, or in the morning on your way to your first stop.

We highly recommend building in extra wiggle room to the last day of your trip. This is the time for last minute shopping, or where you might need to stop and pick up something you placed on order or held at a store. It also provides that "last chance" opportunity to give family members an opportunity to visit that one place they have *really* been dying to go. Finally, extra padding on the last day ensures that you safely make your flight, train, or other means of getting home. If you are road tripping not far from your house this may be less important, but also allows for traffic. No one wants to end an amazing vacation with a harried dash to the airport, or a later-than-planned return trip home that starts everyone's first day back in the "real world" feeling sleepy and restless.

Free time provides you with another valuable opportunity to involve your children and make them feel like more active participants in the vacation. Just as it is important to involve them in the planning of your itinerary, letting them contribute some of the spontaneity is great for all of you. Children will have more fun and feel better about themselves when they feel empowered to make choices. They feel a real stake in their own vacation and are more likely to enjoy not only the stops they suggest, but the ones you do, because they can see the exchange as a back and forth. Also, children have a knack for finding some of the most fun and exciting stops. Listen to your children, their ideas might just end up making the vacation!

Part of being flexible will come from the planning process as well, and it pays to create an itinerary that doesn't just pad the schedule, but has its own options built in.

We find it is a good practice to pack days with plenty of activity, and then go further to allow a few options we likely will not get to. Don't think of it as overscheduling a day, as much as it is creating a day, plus a few potential extras or substitutions. Having a long list, and knowing before we even begin that we probably won't get to all of them, allows us to adapt our day on the fly.

Having too many stops that you are committed to seeing can sting when you have to cross some off, and having too few can leave you with the feeling of "what do we do now?" Your best bet is to have a long day with less that you absolutely "have to do." The extra stops on your list allow for things that don't go as expected. Maybe one stop ends up simply not being to your children's liking. Another may run way shorter than the expected, or recommended, time. The long (and flexible) list allows you to always have something to do next, or instead, when plans change on the go.

As much as it is important to have a positive attitude about losing a stop, or a backup plan for something that runs short, part of being flexible is also about savoring the moment.

Vacation will quickly start to feel like work if it is nothing more than a race to see as many things as possible, or a commitment to an itinerary that goes above the desire to enjoy. Remember, this is all about fun. If you and your kids find yourselves at a stop that is simply amazing, one that goes beyond expectations and finds you not wanting to leave…don't!

If you find yourself aching for more, or wanting to see the rest of a museum you had only planned to view one wing of, do it. A tour might offer an addendum, or have a Q&A you weren't planning on. Stay for it if you want. Don't be a slave to the itinerary at the expense of having fun and living in the moment.

Allowing for flexibility in the schedule means you may just discover the unexpected. On one day during a recent trip we had planned to go on a second hike, and we got lost and could not find the trail. As we were about to give up and head back to our cruise ship we rounded the corner and found ourselves by a beautiful, glacier-fed lake. Our kids decided to jump into the freezing cold water, clothes and all. We had a blast. This was one of the most memorable and fun parts of the vacation, and it was spontaneous. It is important to let those moments happen. Don't stress if something goes amiss with your plans, it may just lead to something better.

Allowing flexibility in your schedule will enable you to find these things you didn't know were there and could never have planned for. It is important to have a plan, but to also feel free not to stick with it. There would be no point in asking locals for ideas if you were so married to your itinerary that you wouldn't be open to adding any of them.

The other simple fact is that not every location has a website, not everyone that does updates it, and no matter how hard you plan you could easily miss a great opportunity on the ground if you just stick to your itinerary. This means that the great place you selected may be unexpectedly closed, or that your best potential stop is one only the locals know about. Let yourselves feel free to add new possibilities and omit the planned ones. After all, the adventure of trying things together is half the fun.

Flexibility is more than just a good logistical practice; it is a frame of mind that will lead to new and better experiences. Whether it be keeping you from losing your cool, allowing yourselves to enjoy more time at a stop you love, or skipping one that doesn't appeal to you - the benefits of flexibility are just too many to name. If travel is about being present, and enjoying that "vacation frame of mind," then allowing yourself to remain adaptable is one of your best tools for getting there.

Balance the Activities

When planning your trip beforehand, it is important to aspire to an itinerary that includes a wide array of activities. Vacation offers so many different kinds of opportunities, as well as benefits. The best way to arrive at them all is to mix things up. You can't expect that doing the same thing every day, or even every vacation, will net you the same family gains we cover in this book.

Educational, active, fun, cultural, relaxing, cool, and different - these are just some of the types of activities that a great vacation should include. In order to reap all the benefits of family togetherness, knowledge, worldliness, enjoyment, inspiration, adaptability, and more - that vacation can (and should) offer - you need to find and include activities to match.

Educational activities are the ones with the most to offer as far as new knowledge. Some are obvious, like museums, historical sites, guided tours, zoos, aquariums, and the like. Others might be subtler, like a workshop or even a particular performance. The point is to seek out locations and activities with something to teach you, whatever it may be.

Active stops and activities help get your hearts pounding. These can be more "traditional" like a ski slope, snorkeling time, enjoying a park, or something similar. They can be extreme and different for you, like rappelling, zip lining, ropes courses, or rock climbing. All that matters is that you create an opportunity to do something that gets you engaged through activity, preferably that you can all share in together.

Fun varies a lot from family to family, or even person to person. We spent a whole chapter talking about it. Any of the activities in your day can and should be fun. More importantly, if you decide that there are one or more stops that are "important" to do (like a landmark, a memorial, or anything that is more somber and serious), often you should balance it out with something purely fun.

Cultural activities take you inside the local scene and expose you to how another group of people live. An entire upcoming chapter will be devoted to this, but for now think of cultural centers, tours by local guides, art, and even indulging in some local food or drink.

Relaxing is an important part of any family vacation. You don't need to run yourselves ragged. This could be time by the pool or at the beach. It could be as simple as taking cabs over walking, or taking some time to enjoy a sit down lunch over an on-the-go bite. Your family may need days or minutes of it, but relaxing time helps balance things out.

Cool locations and activities are the ones that make you say "oh, wow!" Again, this will vary from family to family. If your kids are of different ages, it may also be very different for a teenager than a preschooler. Try to seek out things that are "cool" for each member of the family. Go beyond the expected and the important to the things that are neat in and of themselves.

Different stops offer unique opportunities. Find the things that are more unique within your destination and not easily available elsewhere. Seek out a regional specialty or something representative of the area. If in Hawaii, visit a volcano. Swim with dolphins in the Caribbean. Visit Mayan ruins in Cozumel. Make sure to seek out and enjoy the special offerings of a given location. They take you out of your ordinary and may just provide some of the most treasured memories.

Seek out opportunities for activities that tick multiple boxes. If you want to take a walking tour of an old city, hire a local guide to escort you. Now, a stop that got you active with some walking and would have been mildly educational, is highly informative as well as culturally immersive because of what the guide can bring to the table. By asking about fun and different things to do in the area, you set yourselves up for an afternoon with even more varied experiences.

You will not always be able to foresee all the benefits, or predict exactly what a location has to offer. Furthermore, some of the greatest benefits of family travel are the hardest ones to create yourselves. Family bonding and unity aren't things that can be forced. That moment where you discover a whole new level of connection with your children may be in a museum, looking at a great piece of art, or it may be meeting them at the bottom of a massive zip line. It may also be that these moments vary from child to child, and between spouses. By having a varied itinerary you maximize the opportunity to have these moments, and set yourselves up for the types of memories and experiences that matter to each of you.

Balancing the activities also helps prevent against things getting stale while you are away. Too many of the same things in a row can get boring, or at the very least, predictable. When we talk about engaging children (and adults for that matter) it is important to keep yourselves on your toes. Even when you all know what is coming next, the excitement of changing up the pace will keep everything fresh.

Make sure that days utilize both your body and your mind. Too much physical activity risks burning you out, while too little can leave you bored or restless. It may seem simple enough to say that you want to focus on educational gains, so you'll include more educational stops. However, without a variety of activities, you may lose out on many of the planned benefits. As illogical as it may seem, you may need that hike to have a hope of absorbing much of anything educational, because without keeping everyone engaged certain stops will just be lost.

It is also important to note that almost any stop can be augmented with additional factors to help it cover more bases for your family. Get a book or pamphlet about that mountain before you hike it, and point out plants, wildlife, and history as you make the trek. Suddenly a stop that was primarily active becomes an educational experience.

Even the time in between stops can be utilized to maximum effect. For mealtime, choose a really authentic local place for a cultural experience, or that crazy theme restaurant for something fun. Take a rickshaw or a pedicab between nearby stops rather than a taxi, and savor the local culture as you travel. Go to a hot springs instead of a pool for your relaxing time, and see something totally different from the usual. When you look at your day as a series of opportunities to insert new and exciting opportunities for activity, the possibilities for fun are endless.

Balancing the types of activities also helps to ensure you are seeing as much of what a destination has to offer as possible. This practice helps give you a better overview than you would get by focusing on one type of activity. If you spend your entire time in a given city touring museums and landmarks, you may be maximizing the number of facts you hear about it, at the expense of *feeling* it and really taking in what the city means. With a balance of activities, you can come closer to a representative slice of life in a different place. Vary the activities and the experiences and go home with a better sense of what life there is all about.

Varying activities accounts for different ages and tastes, as well as different moods on a given day. Your 4 year old and your 13 year old probably like very different things. While there should be options that will delight them both, chances are that to really hit home, you will have to try different things to accommodate them individually. You might have children a year apart, but if they have different tastes, the same notion will apply. We also know that none of us are the same every day. This is especially true after a long week of touring with tiredness catching up, or at the beginning of a trip while adjusting to a new climate or time zone. For this reason it is best to vary activities within each day of your trip, as well as over the longer course of it. Try not to build only one "active day" where every activity is about working up a sweat, followed by slower activities for days on end. Try your best to mix up each day with a variety of activities, and try to alternate days of the trip accordingly.

Build some of this variation into your alternate ideas as well. Having different types of alternate activities will help a great deal and allow for your backup plan to be as varied as your original idea. If the goal is to be flexible, there is nothing that shows more of a willingness to adapt than a day that ends in options to go on a hike or relax on the beach. Have a variety of activity types in both your plan and your backup plan, and you'll hopefully keep everyone engaged, and if you start to lose someone, be able to switch things up to get them back in the game.

Another of the primary reasons that it pays to have some solid backup plans is weather. This is one of the single most unpredictable factors when traveling, and can make your original plans fly out the window without much warning. Being able to switch things up or change to another plan will be key in making sure that weather doesn't cause you to *lose* a day of vacation, but simply force your hand to consider your other options.

Variety is also important with respect to the types of vacations you choose. When looking at a lifetime of trips, and the entire catalog of your family's travel experiences, variety can be just as important there as within a given vacation. In the chapter on discovering ordinary as well as extraordinary places, we mentioned the value of different kinds of destinations. While variety within a trip and within a day is important, some destinations will naturally lean heavily in one direction. You should find things to learn in a ski destination, but recognize that you will likely spend most of your time on physical activities. Seek out the chance to get active in Europe, but embrace the fact that cultural and educational opportunities will probably be more predominant.

After a vacation that has you running around every day, consider slowing things down for the next. The same is true in reverse. The idea that you have a lifetime to travel together is important, and over that course of time you can build a well-rounded travel life for yourselves.

Watch the Pace

A vacation is a marathon, not a sprint. Even when taking a long weekend away, or a similarly short jaunt, it is important to pace yourselves in order to ensure you are getting the most out of your time. Sometimes less is more, especially if it means that you will better appreciate the time you have.

Pacing your vacation is another way to add variety and keep things engaging. A well-paced day is another gateway to the same benefits that come from varying the activities. Just as the active excursions will help you appreciate the educational ones and vice versa, the lulls in your trip will help you tackle the busy times and the packed days will make you appreciate the slower ones.

Arriving in a new destination is sure to generate a lot of excitement. Your first day in a new country or city will be full of temptations to dive right in with both feet and try to see everything in the first day or hours. Take advantage of this natural boost in momentum but don't allow it to burn you out too early in your stay.

Also keep in mind that this temptation to overdo things can happen within a trip that changes up locations. A week spent touring a country may take you city to city, and the more exciting destinations can see you pushing yourselves too far at the expense of what comes after. If you have a day at a theme park, out on the water, or hitting the slopes - that day with increased physical activity may tire you out for a day or two following. It is important to let yourselves enjoy the moment, but also to make some decisions beforehand about how much you feel your family (kids especially) can honestly handle without suffering for it afterwards.

The best vacations enjoy a balanced pace that keeps up a fairly regular level of activity. Some days will necessarily pack in more than others, but it is important to not go too far overboard.

If you do take a particularly busy day, try to slow down the pace for the next day, build in a relaxing stop like some time at a beach or pool, and give yourselves a chance to catch your breath and relax.

Try not to go too far in the other direction. In the same way you do not want to run yourselves ragged with a day that runs for 12 hours of time spent on your feet, you may not want to waste a day in an exciting new location by sleeping until noon. Abrupt changes in schedule can wreak havoc on your sense of time and ability to enjoy and appreciate the things you do. This is especially true of children. Some days will be busier and others lighter, but aim to keep everything in the middle, with minor variations rather than drastic swings.

Remember that there is more than one way to burn yourselves out. The easiest to see and to feel is the physical sense, but pacing doesn't begin and end with level of physical activity. In addition to how much energy your body expends, you need to keep an eye on pacing your mental and emotional energies. An entire day spent taking in museums, or seeing heavier things like memorials, can take a lot out of you and your children.

In this way, pacing yourselves goes hand in hand with providing variety in activities. You need to pace mental and emotional outings by intermixing them with fun and exciting activities. Remember that seeing something powerful like a war memorial or museum can be just as draining as a morning spent running around, and treat it as such. Think about your family and once again be flexible. If you have a busy afternoon planned and notice everyone starting to slow down by lunch, be willing to change things up. After an overdone day you will find yourselves working harder and harder to catch up, and may never have the same level of energy back during that vacation.

Pace is important on both any given day, as well as over course of the trip. You should avoid packing too many activities into the morning, afternoon, or evening of a given day while away, just as you shouldn't load up one part of the week at the expense of others. Once again, the first bit of work to accomplish this will come in planning. You know your own family well enough to make estimates of what you think they can handle and what a nice vacation looks like for you. The second part comes on the ground and at your destination. Your commitment to flexibility and being adaptable will allow you to either add things to recapture a family member who has lost interest, or cut things back to save a group that is starting to fail.

The goal is to have days that each create different experiences in terms of the things done and the fun had, but that *feel* similar in terms of the energy expended. Keep your family on their toes in terms of what is coming next by varying the kinds activities, but provide a sense of comfort by keeping the *level* of activity fairly similar. This way you get the best of both worlds, and you increase the chances of your family staying engaged and excited.

Watching the pace can be a challenge for some. You may feel like you are doing your family a disservice by not packing in every possible activity, and taking advantage of every possible opportunity while in a new place. This risk runs especially high in more expensive, exotic, and faraway locations. The feeling that this may be your only chance to visit a given place may tempt you to run around taking it all in. While keeping a busy schedule is one thing, once the fine line between busy and extreme is crossed, your family suffers. Once children get tired, they start to lose their ability to absorb anything. Packing in three stops when one was enough to tire them out doesn't help anybody; the time is ultimately wasted.

It is worth sacrificing a stop or two to make the other ones really count. Sometimes less is more and really keeping kids engaged is far more important than covering more ground. If fun, happiness and togetherness are at the top of your list, then your ability to keep an eye on these things should dictate the pace of your trip.

The art of mastering this balance will come with time. Look at your past vacations and think about what worked and what didn't. Sure there are a lot of variables, including the interest of the destination and the age of the kids, but you learn more about your family with each vacation. Don't expect that you'll get it perfect. The goal is that over time, your itinerary begins to mirror your actual vacation more and more. As you develop this skill, you will do a lot more improvising in the beginning, adding and eliminating more stops. Over time you will be able to predict your family better, but you can start having better vacations today by committing yourselves to this principle.

Keep in mind that the pace at which your family moves will often be dictated, at least in part, by your youngest child/children. While you cannot run a four year old ragged by trying to keep up with teenagers, it is also important to allow older kids to flourish rather than planning everything to conform to the needs of your youngest. There are a few simple approaches to consider:

The first is to split up. Parents can go separate ways and have one take the youngest child or children to a "lower impact" activity to meet them on their level. This could be for a half an hour or a half a day. We don't advise overdoing this, as family vacation time should really be about spending time with all of you together. If you do choose to, make the most of the time. Work in one or two activities that really only appeal to the very young or that only the teens can do. Take your toddler to the kid's exhibit and your teens on the bungee jump. Take advantage of a chance to really excite and/or really tire out older kids so that the sacrifice made in splitting up lasts longer and goes further to satisfying unique needs.

Find ways to have older kids get more actively involved with your younger kids. If you visit a children's museum aimed at 3-12 year olds and let everyone explore on their own, older kids will burn through the things that interest them in short order and quickly switch over to "bored" mode. If, however, your teens are "in charge" of making sure your toddler has fun, it forces them to slow down, think of their siblings, and savor an opportunity to enjoy things on another level. Getting your kids to "team up" in this manner keeps them involved and engaged, while promoting family bonding at the same time.

Get creative with "break time." The free time we talked about building into the schedule can mean something different when it comes to evening out the pace. While a much younger kid may need this time to nap and literally recharge themselves, the extra energy older kids have can be put to other uses. Let older kids do their shopping while younger siblings sleep. If kids have reading to do for school, or exercises to keep up with for sports, they can burn off their excess energy while other kids (or parents!) rest up. Try to locate places like parks and malls on your busy days to either include in your itinerary or list of options. These types of locations offer the ability for you to spread out while sticking together. A midday stop in a park can see one child napping, another reading, and others running around, all while dad enjoys a coffee and mom a snack. These quick breaks can be invaluable.

Sometimes the best way to wake up a child's body is by engaging their mind. Seek out activities and options that engage children with hands-on fun. While running around may perk a kid up, taking a nap later isn't always an option. Rather than simply looking at sleep to help perk up restless children, consider crafts and activities as a means of producing a "second wind." In fact, too much sitting still, or an extended stretch of time in which they must "keep it down" can also make children antsy and wear them down in much the same way physical exertion can. Sometimes the best cure for both the "too tired" and the "too quiet" is to give children something to accomplish. If you can't find an activity in your location that allows for this, bring one with you. Provide a craft or an engaging activity for your youngest during the aforementioned park time, or during the period of transit between stops, and perk them up by getting them involved in something.

Finally, and perhaps most importantly, *do* plan things around your youngest children but *don't* plan things around what you think your youngest children can handle. By this we mean, don't make assumptions about what your children are capable of. You may end up selling them, and your vacation, short. Young children are capable of doing much more than we sometimes give them credit for. Test their limits (carefully of course) and find out where their actual barriers lie as opposed to imagined (or assumed) ones. While there is something to be said for a "one for us, one for them" strategy when selecting stops that delight children and then adults, your children (even the youngest ones) may develop interests in things you didn't expect. If part of the goal of a great vacation is to help your children learn and grow, as you learn about your children and grow closer, you need to push things from time to time. Without a challenge, children will take much longer to show you where they stand.

Listen to the needs of your family and encourage an open dialogue. Rather than acting as the omnipotent vacation master who dictates what is to be done at a given time, check in with your kids and encourage them to speak up when they are feeling too challenged, or not challenged enough. Use mealtimes as a chance to touch base and get a solid idea of how everyone feels. Don't fall into the trap of letting someone push themselves too far because they want to keep up or please the rest of the family. In the end, this can end up backfiring. The chance to open a dialogue will also help to build family unity and bring you closer to each other.

This would also be a good place to note that some great things happen at night as well as during the day. The idea of pacing yourself and keeping your schedule adaptable will also be key in enjoying these times. Your family may be the type to wake up very early and get going right away. This is great, but beginning and ending each day at 6 might limit you from enjoying some very special opportunities at night.

On a recent trip to Israel we booked a night of stargazing, as well as a unique caving adventure that took place late at night. In our New York City book we mention the joys of taking your family to the theater at night to enjoy a play or a musical. A day that ends up tying things off at ten, eleven, or even midnight may seem impossible for some families, especially with younger children. Our solution is simple: adjust your sleep schedule. Sleep in later one morning to stay out later at night, or build in a nap time midday to break things up and prepare you for your evening. Don't push yourselves through a 16 hour day, but *do* switch up your schedule for the unique opportunity to enjoy your destination both before and after dark. Some locations change entirely at night, and the chance to see what this looks like is part of offering your family the full package. It also wouldn't do anyone any good to turn down a special activity that occurs only at night because you're afraid of losing some sleep. Make it up somewhere else, and reap the rewards by committing to adaptability.

Keeping a steady pace helps to balance both the benefits of your family vacation, as well as the expectations of your family members. Help prevent anxiousness, boredom, fatigue, and more, by letting children know what to expect.

The concept of pace works hand in hand with variety and adaptability to form a trifecta of vacation concepts that also carry into the real world. By keeping things even, interesting, and flexible, you give yourselves the best possible chance to keep things happy and rewarding.

Experience Different Cultures

Exposing your children to foreign cultures, and developing an appreciation of the rich variety of experiences the world has to offer, are some of the greatest joys of travel. The sense of worldliness will also become one of the greatest benefits, as children with a greater knowledge of the world grow up discerning, experienced, smarter, more open-minded, and better equipped to handle the world at large.

Beginning great travel - memorable and extraordinary travel - at a young age sets great precedents for children. It teaches them from an early age that the entire world, not just the part they see every day, is real and special. When children grow up seeing (and hopefully interacting with) peoples, cultures, and situations other than their own, they develop a deeper empathy and understanding of the world. Suddenly other countries and continents aren't just words in a book or a picture on a map, but real places with people they can identify. This later produces adults who value the entire world, and are more likely to care deeply about others.

This is another time when it pays to remind you that we believe "big trips" and wonderful getaways should not necessarily be "saved" until children are older. Even young children will get something out of the experience of seeing a faraway place, eating an exotic food, meeting people from another country, and interacting with a different cultural experience than their own. Start early, and continue as often as you can throughout your children's lives.

These experiences can grow with your children. At first it will be vaguer memories and a sense that people dressed differently and spoke in a manner that was strange. While a child around ages 2-5 may not absorb many of the details, there is still value in them developing a sense that the world has many different kinds of experiences to offer. This picture will sharpen as they grow older. By showing your children more of the world, they become aware that more of the world is real and valuable.

The sense of empathy that develops while visiting a foreign land is an important one to nurture after the fact. Just as we encouraged you to follow the news for a location you have visited leading up to it, the same practice is valuable after visiting. Keep an eye on developments in places you have traveled to, and relate them to your children during times of family discussion. This provides an opportunity not only to reinforce the importance of that place, but to relive your experiences there, together.

This is, of course, far easier to see when talking about international travel. At the same time, there are opportunities closer to home to provide your children with a wider cultural picture. When we talk about booking and the best techniques for finding vacation deals, we hope that you will see that really extraordinary and exotic trips are far more within reach than many people believe. However the simple reality is that for many families frequent international travel will still be out of the question.

You can still work to instill a sense of cultural awareness in your children when traveling domestically by being careful about choosing your destinations. Try to discover someplace different than where you live. If you live in a rural or suburban area, take your children to cities when you travel domestically. If you live in an urban environment, consider a national park, a dude ranch, or an opportunity to travel off-the-beaten-path and experience a bit of "country life." Travel to the far corners of the nation and see how different these areas can be from where and how you live.

Visiting larger metropolitan areas also offers a chance to experience many different cultures at once. New York City is perhaps the best example, and offers a real slice of the entire world within just a few square miles. If an international trip is out of the question for now, consider visiting a city like New York and focusing on cultural experiences. Eat ethnic meals and visit cultural museums, neighborhoods, and other sites to create a domestic trip that pays homage to other areas of the world.

There is no reason not to make cultural exploration a part of your vacation process. No matter your means or other limitations, with enough creativity and dedication, you can open up the world around you to your children, and reap the rewards.

Those rewards are plentiful. Besides the qualities of worldliness and empathy, the exposure to other peoples and places helps children to engage their curiosity and expand their horizons. A world of knowledge opens up when you look beyond your own day to day, and there are many things you can do as parents to help facilitate this.

Make a point to highlight the differences while traveling with your children. Even if they are young and you will be handling the financial transactions yourself, make a point to show them foreign currency and explain its value in relation to the money they use at home. Not only will this show them something new and different, but it will help them better understand the value of money, the global economy, and instill an appreciation for the things they have.

Help children to appreciate foreign language. This is one of the easiest ways to see how international experiences can vary and evolve greatly over the course of a child's life. For very young kids, start with the simplest of things. Teach them to say "thank you" in the native tongue of the place you are visiting. They will delight in the opportunity to express thanks to everyone from tour guides to waiters. Older children can handle a bit more, and you should encourage them to learn and adopt a few simple phrases. Trying these out will be fun and rewarding, and allow them to get a better feel for local life. As children become old enough to take a language in school, it may pay to visit a country where they can try out the language that they are studying. Budget minded families would do well to remember that Spanish speaking Mexico lies due south, and that there are French speaking parts of Canada that can allow for two of the most common foreign languages to be practiced without crossing an ocean.

Cultural exploration is also a chance for parents to "show off" a bit and expose their children to things important to them. Demonstrate your own skills with an applicable language to inspire your kids. Visit places you have been to yourself and revisit favorite locations. Expose your children to food, games, and activities that you have developed a taste for either earlier in life, on business, or through some other means. Not only is it a chance to impress your children, but the opportunity it opens to share about your own experiences will promote family bonding.

You may consider choosing accommodations that help aid in cultural exploration. Resorts and all inclusives are great, but given the option, the right choice for you may be staying in the heart of the city. Many websites have opened up the world of renting apartments and other places that help you to live more like a local. These are worth looking into, as they can help provide an even greater slice of local life for your family.

Take an interest in what the locals love. This is the time to indulge in all aspects of foreign life and seek out the activities that matter in the day to day of life in another place. Take in the favorite local sport, especially if it is something different than seen near home. Pick up a local newspaper even if it is in a language you can't read, just to leaf through and show children what other people read and enjoy. Eat local foods. Seek out where the "real people" are and while you can still enjoy the favorite tourist attractions, mixing in some more obscure stops will help develop an appreciation for a foreign place as not just a series of awesome sights, but a place that real people live, work, and play.

On that note, don't ignore things just because you think they don't directly apply to you. An outdoor produce market may seem like a waste of time, because you only want to eat out and have no means of cooking, or of bringing food back home. At the same time, this may be one of your best chances to interact with real locals and experience an important part of daily life for locals. This is just one example. You may limit your time and make it a quick stop, but don't shy away from things that seem a little different for you. Only by exploring do you get to really see the value of new things.

Besides pointing out and enjoying the differences, you should also make a point to demonstrate the similarities. This too can take many forms. Even if you don't go in, children will enjoy seeing that yes, they have American fast food chains there as well. Visit little shops and see brands you know from home alongside local fare that is totally new. If you have something you particularly enjoy doing together at home, seek it out while traveling as well. See a foreign movie, visit a local park, or make a point to surf channels on the hotel TV and watch a few minutes of news. Point out the similarities and help children understand that the place you are visiting isn't all about vacation, but a place where similar people lead lives not *that* unlike their own.

The exposure to different places is one of the most concrete examples of real and immediate benefits for children while traveling. Each new place and new experience will expand your children's minds and open them up to new possibilities. When viewed in the long run, the course of your family's travels will continue to grow these benefits exponentially. While the first new country will be exciting, the next one and the one after will aid children in forming connections and color in their image of the world. Keep pushing your children, asking them questions as well as answering theirs. Encourage curiosity and promote tolerance. The result will be children who care and understand more, and who will carry these feelings with them through their daily lives at home, as well as the course of their growth on through adulthood.

It may require a little effort, and some proactive measures to make exotic destinations possible. It can also mean spending extra time during the planning of the trip and while on the ground to find the most culturally rewarding activities and locations. The reward is more than worth the effort.

If Things Go Wrong (They Often Do)...

To think that even the most diligent planning, or the most seasoned family travelers could go away for any length of time without a single hiccup would simply be unrealistic. You can do the best with the things that are under your control, but there are many variables that are not.

We choose the word "hiccup" here for a reason. We encourage you to see many of the types of problems that develop while away as just this - something bothersome and not really welcome, but also not devastating. A hiccup is annoying, but it passes in time. You don't stop your life for a case of the hiccups, and often laughing them off is the best medicine.

Remember that by its very nature, travel puts you in strange new surroundings. This may be most obvious when exploring the far reaches of the globe together, surrounded by different languages, dress, and money. At the same time, just crossing state lines or moving from the city to the country will throw off your sense of normal. This is particularly true for children, and the change of pace can just as easily be jarring as refreshing.

Keep in mind that it isn't just the "big changes" that can get in the way. The change of continent may go unnoticed while a change in bedtime becomes an issue. Stepping outside of your routine will provide a certain degree of unpredictability. Do your best to prepare for this beforehand by talking with your children, but accept that even the best preparation is not a guarantee that things will run smoothly.

One key is to understand the difference between things you can control and things you cannot.

Maybe you booked a charter sail around a local harbor at your destination. You made the reservation early, and even confirmed it a week out from your vacation by email. When you arrive, it turns out that a new staff member misfiled your reservation and had it for next week. The boat is gone and your family is out of luck. You did your part, you can't control what happened. Getting upset won't fix things, the best action you can take is to move on and find something new.

If in that same scenario, your boat is ready to leave but you are running late because someone lost their sunglasses - now you have a problem which is within your control. As annoying as it may be, you can buy a new pair. Find someplace on the way and pick up something inexpensive. You may not like that you have to, but you decide that not missing the boat is more important.

The difference between things you can impact and things you can't is important. It helps you to embrace the concept of "going with the flow" and letting your vacation unfold in its own way. Trying to force issues you have no control over will only get you frustrated. It won't make your vacation any better to fight tooth and nail for something that didn't really matter in the first place. This is about fun, relaxation, and togetherness - not perfection.

Try hard not to let your children see you get upset or frustrated. Nothing can have a more negative experience on your vacation than this. Children are sensitive, constantly looking to their parents for strength and guidance. At the same time, you are trying to impart lessons and set a good model for them to live by. If you let them see you upset, especially over something ultimately frivolous, it not only damages your vacation but can teach them bad behavior in the future. One angry family member can spread their negativity through the group and throw everyone off balance. If it does happen (we are all human) try to fix it as quickly as you can.

On the other hand, the chance to see you handle issues with grace and dignity can actually be a blessing for your vacation. Demonstrating flexibility will provide a very positive example for your children. While a lost booking or a missed stop may not be your ideal image for how the vacation was going to pan out, the chance to teach your children good behavior should have been part of the goal from the beginning. An unexpected setback can provide an unplanned teaching moment. Turn lemons into lemonade by providing a positive example and set children up for a life in which they let things roll off their back and meet challenges with solutions, rather than frustration.

Variations in the plan and other disturbances will arise. Children may get upset, frustrated, or act out. The busy schedule of a trip may not allow you to employ some of the techniques that you use at home to address frustrations. There are rarely chances for "time outs" and the like while away. This is where communication will be key.

Prepare your children before the trip. While you discuss the many fun things you plan on doing, remind them that they are just plans, and that plans may change. Places close, people get sick, and bad weather happens. Help keep them in the loop as you check in with locations and vendors before you leave. Let them know if something is uncertain, and that you are trying your best to get to particular places, but that nothing is guaranteed. Remind your children that the opportunities you are about to enjoy are amazing, whatever form they take.

Keep this communication up during the trip. Check in with your kids often. Transportation between stops, meal times, and the beginning and end of the day at your accommodations are ideal times to check in and see how everyone is doing. If a child gets upset about a cancelled stop, a lost item, or another issue - let them express their frustration in a constructive manner.

The most important things to manage on a vacation are expectations - both yours and your children's. Planning a great trip is also about the willingness to make changes to plans on the fly. We have spoken at length about flexibility, and this is where it comes into play.

By all means, you should have not only plans, but backup plans, and plans to backup the backups. Things can and will change shape over the course of your vacation. When you can walk into a trip with your expectations in check you have already won. A great vacation is a combination of planning and attitude. If you decide that it is going to be great, it will be. If you are so married to the plan that any change will "ruin everything" then things likely will get "ruined" - even though this never has to be the case.

If things don't go according to plan, they are not "ruined" - just different. You aren't trying to have a perfect vacation, but a great one. Nothing runs perfectly in this life, and while we can logically accept this in our home lives, there can be a tendency to see vacation as special and different. Vacation *is* quite special, and quite different, but because it is a fun and rewarding time, not because you are guaranteed to have everything go your way.

On our recent trip to Israel, we had an opportunity to practice these principles ourselves. During an evening drive of about two hours through the desert, on our way to meet a guide who was to take us spelunking at sunset; our rental car got a flat tire. It was frustrating to say the least.

We piled out of the car and assessed the damage, then began making calls. While trying to answer questions from the rental company, and simultaneously searching for a spare tire that we just couldn't seem to locate - something fantastic happened. A passing car slowed down and stopped, the couple inside got out and asked what they could do to help. They went on to offer not only advice, but support as well, as they helped us to deal with our rental company, even getting on the phone to speak in Hebrew with the operator on the other end. Then another car passed by and its three passengers got out to try and help us locate the spare tire (which oddly, was nowhere to be found) and offer assistance.

They stayed with us for what must have been about forty five minute to an hour, helping us to feel a sense of kinship rather than frustration. Everyone was relaxed and friendly, and the people who stopped and tried to help us were warm and gracious. Once it was clear that the rental car company was sending a replacement vehicle, the people who stopped to help had to move on, and our guide started to make his own way up to meet us where we had broken down. At this point the sun had set, and in the desert, far away from civilization, this meant *pitch* black and a rather eerie environment. We had nothing for light save a few headlamps for our upcoming caving adventure but we made the best of it while we waited on the deserted road, on a bluff overlooking the Dead Sea.

Eventually our guide arrived, now two hours past when we were supposed to meet him. At this point we assumed that our excursion was off, and that we were out of luck on this particular adventure. When he arrived he said that despite having to adapt his own schedule and stay out later than expected, he was happy to push on with us and make it work. We had an amazing time, and not just because we still got to go.

For our children, and our family, it was an adventure. Truly an unplanned adventure, and one that we probably could have done without, but we enjoyed it nonetheless. Of course we were helped by the kindness of strangers and the resilience of our guide, but it was also about sharing the experience together and doing our best with the hand we were dealt. We could have easily gotten frustrated, as far as vacation snags go this was one of the bigger ones we have ever had to deal with, but instead we committed ourselves to just seeing what happened next and running with it. We hiked and went spelunking from 10 PM to 2 AM, and returned back to our lodging at about 5 AM. All things considered, it was a terrific night, one of our favorites of the trip, despite the flat tire.

Just as things will always go wrong, once they do they typically find a way of working themselves out. Having some faith in the process and staying in the moment goes a long way to letting a problem become an experience as opposed to a mounting frustration. Vacation should be fun, not stressful. Accept that some things will go wrong, but you can still make them work for you.

Vacation IS a Vacation

If you are reading this book, you obviously care a great deal about your vacations and the time you spend with family. Many are content to simply show up somewhere and enjoy the time off. Those who put too much time and effort into making their trips the best possible experience run the risk of falling into the trap of seeing vacation as work.

There is a fine line here, and you need to do your best to stay on the side of it that allows your vacation to be a break. Your travels should be fun, and while a great trip isn't just going to happen, it doesn't need to be an ordeal either.

Traveling well requires planning, being informed, and making the most of your experience. At the same time, we hope we have showed you over the course of these explanations and thoughts that there is a lot to be gained from every step of the process.

Vacation and travel need to be seen as an ongoing process, not just a week here or there. The fun isn't just to be had from check-in to check-out, or from wheels up to return flight. The joy is in both the physical journey - whether it is a road trip, cruise, or international adventure - as well as in the journey of planning, anticipating, and reflecting on your time away.

By involving children in planning, incorporating creative activities, and building anticipation, the process of crafting a trip can be just as fun as the trip itself. Of course, poring over booking sites for flights and hotels isn't most people's idea of a good time, but the rewards can be great. Let your children's involvement in the process make the more mundane aspects fun. While you try to make a budget work, hearing the new things that your kids are learning about your upcoming vacation will turn something you *have* to do into something you *want* to do. Let each other's excitement fuel you and remember that your vacation is something that everyone is excited to be a part of.

It may seem like there are an overwhelming number of things to keep track of and consider. We have presented you with the importance of varying activities, pacing your days, keeping kids engaged, seeking out fun, and many other considerations for great vacations. When you sit down to research a trip and plan an itinerary, how do you keep all of this straight!?

The key is to recognize that it isn't about being perfect; the effort is its own reward. The fact that you are trying to make vacation better and more meaningful will in itself give more power to the experience. Remember that you are looking at the big picture. Experiences you don't pack into a particular trip can be enjoyed on another. You and your family are enjoying your lives together, not just for that given week or so of vacation. As you and your family grow, your continued dedication to providing them with the best possible experiences will show over years, not days.

The principles we have laid out in these chapters have accumulated over years of experience and numerous trips around the country and around the globe. The fact that you are even considering these ideas puts you ahead of the game. We have chosen to share these thoughts so that other families could get a leg up on things that took us a lot of time to learn. Don't think of them as things that you need to "get right," but rather as ideas that can enhance your experience while you do what you were planning to from the start - enjoy yourselves.

With the potentially stressful aspects of planning and anticipating a vacation addressed, it is important to talk about the trip itself.

Every family travels differently. If you like to take things slower, and pack less in, simply making careful choices with the activities you do participate in will go a long way to enhance the quality of your vacation. If relaxing is what you like, your vacation will only feel like a vacation when you include enough downtime. Do that, and savor the benefits of traveling with an attitude and plan that also has an eye on the big picture of your family.

If you are anything like us, or want to maximize the benefits of your time away, vacation is going to be quite a bit busier. Making sure you experience as much of a destination as possible takes a lot of stops, and some long, busy days. Mixing in the right dose of active, educational, cultural, and unique activities to ensure the benefits of each of these experiences can mean trading off some sleep or idle time for maximum activity.

While it is true that a given vacation may not be exactly restful, it can (and should) be an exciting, amazing, and wonderful experience. Walk in with both eyes open and embrace it for what it is. You may well find yourselves busier than you are when you are at home. Remember what you are trying to accomplish, and the preciousness of this time together, and embrace the busy.

A busy vacation can be wonderful when you consider how much you get to enjoy together. Waking up early, staying up late, or trekking across a city to pack in another exciting adventure should be about the joy of the adventure, not a sense of obligation. If it is starting to feel like work, then step back, cool off, and reassess.

You know your family, and over the course of your travels you will get to know each other even better. We encourage you to push yourselves, because that is where growth happens. At the same time, watch for the fine line between something extra and too much. If and when you cross that line, pare back, and make sure that what you are doing is still fun for all involved.

We hope that together we can dispel the notion that vacation is work, and that planning or taking a great one is a hassle.

We hope that by learning more about the process of planning and booking, and with some tips and tricks of the trade, we can show that the "before" of a trip is less mystifying (and difficult) than many imagine it to be.

The many considerations of making a vacation better are not meant to "add to the load" and overwhelm, but to offer hope and opportunities for a better experience. Don't look at them as things you have to do, but as things that you may want to, because they will make vacation more rewarding. The idea isn't to force anything on you or your family, but to see that you may want to do more because there is so much fun to be had in all of it.

Set your expectations aside and don't let yourself get stressed before you even begin. Family travel is a wonderful process. Your family will adapt and develop your own style over time. Don't add work to the experience; simply expand your mind to the possibilities and let new ideas about how to travel become a natural part of your journey.

Great Experiences to Treasure for a Lifetime

The end goal of great travel is to enjoy the experiences and the lessons, and to treasure them throughout your lives. Travel should inspire you; it should touch and enhance your lives, both while away and after you return.

One of your goals should be to enjoy experiences that move you. This may seem like a lofty goal, but these moving experiences will emerge on their own. They may come when you least expect them to, just as easily as they can emerge from the highlights of your vacation.

A moving experience may be the result of an activity or location of great power. You may be moved by a piece of history, a memorial, or an incredible tour. Many of these experiences may also come out of your time together. You may be moved by how your children react to a certain location, just as they may be moved by seeing you go out of your way to create a memory for them.

Rest and rejuvenation are great and should certainly be a part of your trip, but these moving experiences are the ones that will last a lifetime. Have an eye on your family's immediate needs as well as the long term ones. Rest when you need to, visit with friends and relatives, and show children that place that will help them with their school report or enhance their understanding of a favorite hobby. Also seek out the experiences that will help teach them life skills and shape their view of the world. Take your preteens to do preteen things, but also expose them to information that they can utilize when they have families of their own. Having both feet in the present moment, with an eye on the future, will help you to vacation in a way that will outlive the relatively short time you spend at a given destination.

Also take the time to savor these moments as they happen. You may not always recognize them while they are going on, but when you do, stop and enjoy the experience. When you see your children's smiles widen, and their eyes light up, nurture that feeling. Stop and look, take a picture, talk about how great it is, and let the memory sink in and start to take root. More than the souvenirs you collect on your journeys, these precious moments of family togetherness are the real treasures accumulated over years of shared journeys.

The memory that will truly last a lifetime could be anywhere. The story that you will tell each other, and anyone else who will listen, over and over throughout the years could be hidden at the top of a mountain or deep below the sea. You may create an amazing experience out of nothing more than a beautiful backdrop and a well-timed line from one of your children. The more places you go, and the more things you are open to, the better your chances of finding these special times and forever capturing them in your shared lives.

So get out there! The world is waiting for you and your family. We hope these views on the value of travel, and the best means to go about improving your vacations, have helped spark new ideas in you. In the coming sections we will move past the "why" and delve into the when, where, and how of traveling better. With the bigger concepts penciled in, it is time to color in the details of just how to go about making this kind of extraordinary travel simpler and more effective for you and your family.

Part II

Location, Location, Location

Expand Your Vision on Where You Can Go

Everyone knows the old standbys for family vacations. We wouldn't disparage any of them, and there is a good reason that there are a handful of places "everyone goes" - because they do have many things to offer. Some destinations are popular with good reason; others are popular because they are convenient. Just about any place on Earth deserves your consideration, and the tried and true favorites both domestic and abroad deserve your attention.

But...we would strongly encourage you not to stop there...

Think outside of the box and expand your scope of what is possible for you and your family. The usual destinations are likely to get you the usual results, and you are going to have to push your comfort zone a little bit to get all of the benefits we have discussed.

While family travel is far more about the company than the destination, the destination certainly can't hurt. It is also true that any location can be done bigger, better, and with greater reward by traveling smartly. Don't feel that you have to go *too* far to get anything important out of it, but you do need to challenge yourself.

Start by pushing yourselves to go a little farther, a little more off-the-beaten-path, a little more exotic than you are used to. For some families this could mean looking past a Florida resort to a Caribbean island. For others it could mean passing on the beach house at the shore to take a road trip to a national park. For others it may mean flying to Asia instead of Europe. Resist the urge to follow other families and do the same thing that everyone else is doing. On the same note, don't try to keep up with the exploits and adventures of another family if what they do simply wouldn't work for you. Start expanding your own vision, and exploring the world as it fits for your family.

The first step of planning any vacation is selecting a destination. In this section of the book, we will take a look at our "bucket list" of great spots that we one day dream of seeing ourselves, as well as some of our favorite past vacation spots. We will talk about why they interest us, and what they have to offer families.

Use this section of the book to equip yourselves with some information you may not have known, but also to ignite your own imaginations. Get inspired and take this list not as an end, but as a beginning. Let one family's views of what (and where) is fun, help to start your own.

A Follow-Up Note About Budget. When considering where to travel, budget is one of the first and main considerations for many families. While it is true that you certainly don't want to take a great trip at the cost of putting your family in a tight spot, we encourage you to read on before jumping to any conclusions.

Too many families make assumptions about the high costs of travel, only to sell themselves short. There is a difference between traveling on a budget and limiting yourself based on misconceptions about budget. Armed with more knowledge about good booking practices, and great places to look, more things become possible. Similarly, when you make a commitment to traveling better and become willing to put in a little effort, that time can be rewarded by big savings.

Our family's upcoming, 10-day trip to Thailand, wasn't something that was chosen blindly, and we did work within a pre-set budget. Thailand was on a list of locations (which will follow in the coming pages) that we had our eye on. When pricing out the trip based on exact dates of travel for an upcoming school break, we looked over the possibilities. After looking at weeklong cruises for the same window of time, we were as surprised (and delighted!) as anyone to see that the week and a half Thailand trip would be the same price as the weeklong cruise that we had our eye on.

Some careful comparison shopping, setting alerts on your computer and other techniques can save you a lot of money, and open up destinations that would not have otherwise been within your budget. There are sites that literally put the world at your fingertips, and help you see what continents and regions are cheaper at a particular time than others. The resources in Part IV of this book will lay out many of these, and equip you to do better research and become informed consumers.

Another important thing to note is that any destination can be expensive at a given time, while considerably more affordable during others. This is true for times of year (read: holidays and summer) as well as year to year. While Europe or Asia may have a seller's market one spring, by the next fall, economic realities may have cooled off prices and made the time ripe for a dream vacation that you have been waiting for. The key is to watch and wait, as some patience can pay off in a big way. Trying to force a particular vacation at a particular time may be a bank-breaking proposition, while waiting a bit and being open to traveling to the place that presents itself as affordable at a given time will open up the world to you and your family.

The key is to research, research, and research some more...then JUMP! We will speak more about booking at length later in the book, but for now, this is simply some food for thought to help you see what can be possible with a little effort, a healthy dose of knowledge, and the ability to move quickly.

A few summers ago, an airfare alert that we had set came through, showing that we could buy tickets for the entire family from New York to Honolulu for about $200 per person (round trip). After a few minutes of hesitation, we quickly scooped up the tickets right away. Of course, the deal was gone shortly after that. Just for kicks, we immediately checked to see what a single seat on the same flight would cost after we had booked our family's seats. The cost of a single ticket had risen to nearly $800 within minutes. This just goes to show that amazing deals do come along, but if they are part of a flash sale such as this one was, you need to be ready to act quickly if you hope to take advantage of them.

More than anything, we hope that you will not sell yourself short before you take the time to get informed. Don't limit yourself up front. Dream big, and then find a way to make that dream vacation a reality - whether it be in four months or four years.

Great travel can be much more affordable than you may think, if you commit to traveling smart.

Our Family's Vacation Wish List

Call it a "wish list" or a "bucket list" or whatever makes most sense to you. For our family, with nearly two decades of experience traveling with our children, spanning age groups and experiencing the world - these are the places we want to be.

While the places tend more towards the exotic, the faraway, and the extreme, there are also a mix of some more "usual" or accessible options mixed in. This has more to do with our own tastes than any "right" or "wrong" way to travel. We are not saying these are the best places in the world to go (how could we say, we haven't been there!) but they are ones that have piqued our interest.

For each we will give a brief overview, some things to note, some things to do, and our reasons for wanting to visit. The information is meant to expand your understanding of them, and to help give you reasons to consider them yourselves.

The other reason is to offer insight into the way we operate and to aid you in thinking more critically, and creatively, about how you travel and where you might want to go.

You may find yourselves with tastes very similar to ours, in which case we welcome you to borrow our "bucket list" and travel through it yourselves.

The real value of this list however, for most families, will be to help you get started on your own.

Read about the places we want to go, why we want to go there, and think about your own views. Start your own list. Work as a couple, work as a family, have everyone come up with their own ideas and then combine them.

If there is anything we want you to gain from this list it is to help expand and challenge your view of what is possible. Start thinking outside of the box, and stop crossing off places as "too expensive" or "unrealistic" before really researching and seeing ways to make it work.

We hope that throughout this section we can help to inspire you to think differently, so that you can travel differently, and enjoy more. Travel big and dream bigger, that way there is always another trip to look forward to!

Thailand

About:

Thailand is a major highlight of Southeast Asia's Indochina Peninsula. Enjoy sweeping beach areas juxtaposed against the modern cityscapes of Bangkok and other urban centers. Thailand offers quintessentially Asian experiences mixed with a fun-loving attitude. The nation holds tourism in high regard and opens its doors to foreign exploration, with a growing emphasis on families.

Bordered by Myanmar, Laos, Cambodia, Malaysia, Indonesia, and India - Thailand stands at an Asian crossroads that offers a truly unique intersection of varying cultures. The Gulf of Thailand and Andaman Sea also offer stunning waterfront areas that make for great vacationing.

Why Visit?

Ancient ruins, stunning temples, and rich local culture all offer a lot to show and to teach children. Besides local Thai history and people, the major cities offer a unique slice of pan-Asian life. While an Asian vacation counts as exotic enough for many families, those who have visited China or Japan - or those who are simply interested in making their first visit to the world's largest continent count - would do well to consider Thailand. Families can enjoy the chance to see and do more in a relatively short time and with less ground to cover and money spent, by exploring Thailand.

Thailand offers the kind of diversity that makes for great vacations. Relaxing and luxurious beaches allow you to kick back; while vibrant cities let you explore culture and enjoy modern conveniences with infrastructure to help make the transition less daunting. Mix in opportunities to go off the beaten path and explore nature, commune with wildlife, or get involved in some extreme activities - and Thailand quickly becomes a place where a family can enjoy several different vacations in one.

Some Exciting Highlights:

Cities to see with kids:
- Bangkok
- Phuket
- Hua Hin
- Chiang Mai
- Kanchanaburi
- Koh Samui
- Railay

Sites and activities on our "to research" list:
- Wat Phra Kaew
- Grand Palace
- Ride elephants (taking into consideration how the elephants are treated)
- Rock climbing, hiking, and waterfall swims
- Beaches, snorkeling, water parks and amusement facilities
- Erawan Shrine
- The bridge over the River Kwai
- Dusit Zoo
- Doi Suthep-Pui National Park
- Siam Park City
- Ko Poda

Things to Note:

The "high season" for tourism here runs from December to February. If traveling during this time, plan ahead and book as early as possible as things fill up. The summer is considered monsoon season in certain areas, so be mindful of this in planning your trip. Also note that your passport must be valid for a period of time before visiting, and special inoculations will be required to enter. More about both of these in Part III.

Guatemala

About:

Guatemala offers some of the best of Central America in a country just modern enough to make travel comfortable, while offering unique opportunities and authentic culture just south of Mexico. This is the most populous of the nations in Central America, and enjoys a rich history dating back to its status as the center of the Mayan Empire.

The history of native and Spanish influences creates a unique cultural melting pot with a lot to offer. The country also enjoys a special blend of biologically significant and unique ecosystems, which result in a great opportunity to explore a variety of different ecological experiences and native species. Travel a world of culture and span ocean, forest, jungle, and mountain regions in just a few short miles on a vacation that puts so much at your fingertips.

Why Visit?

Guatemala is great for the active family, who is willing to shed the big cities and focus on outdoor adventures that get you pulse pounding and set your eyes on amazing sights. Experience towering volcanoes, lush rainforest, and ancient Mayan ruins that offer you a chance to step out of bounds and become real-life explorers. The marriage of eco-tourism and ancient sites unites science with history, and allows your family to learn about a wide variety of material.

This Spanish-speaking country has some of the same great food and culture as you would come to expect from other countries in the region, coupled with a chance to practice your (or your children's) language skills. Camp out overnight in the shadow of a volcano, zoom through the rainforest canopy, and tour a coffee plantation on adventures that show children the natural world and local industry in exciting and accessible ways.

Guatemala is still a developing country in many ways. Safety concerns should be carefully considered when planning your trip. It is also worth noting that a trip to Guatemala can provide opportunities for service in travel. Volunteer to build a house for part of a day that will benefit the local population, and help create meaningful memories for your family.

Some Exciting Highlights:

Cities to see with kids:

- Guatemala City
- Antigua Guatemala
- Petén
- Panajachel

Sites and activities on our "to research" list:

- Tikal
- Lake Atitlán
- Pacaya
- Dulce River
- Rainforest zip lining
- Antigua Textile Museum
- Bella Vista coffee plantation (with tour)
- National Palace of Culture
- National Museum of Archaeology and Ethnology

Things to Note:

Public transportation is much harder to come by, and on a trip to Guatemala we would likely opt to hire a driver. Antimalarials may be required for certain areas. You will also want to look into which cities, and neighborhoods, are considered safe before visiting. Stick to well established areas and avoid travel at night.

Amazon River Houseboat

About:

The giant, snaking Amazon River represents one of the world's most majestic aquatic features, and possesses the largest drainage basin of any river in the world. With a length of about 4,000 miles, the river that begins in the Andes Mountains also offers a beautiful natural tour of the continent of South America.

The Amazon passes through the nations of Peru, Bolivia, Venezuela, Colombia, Ecuador, and Brazil before releasing into the Atlantic Ocean. The mighty Amazon has served as a cradle of South American civilization back through the pre-colonial era. Many ancient agrarian societies relied on the river to provide water for their crops, and some of the oldest life and history in the region can trace its roots to the banks of the Amazon.

To follow the river is to follow some of the region's greatest resources to the doorsteps of great places and fascinating people.

Why Visit?

By taking advantage of the river to guide you, any family can enjoy a sort of "best of" tour of South America from the comfort of a single base. The simplicity of a cruise meets the unique opportunities of a houseboat as you are brought to your destinations rather than making the trek on your own. As compared to a cruise, many of the typical amenities will be different (it will likely be much more rugged and basic), but the special experience will allow you to share a memory fewer families get to enjoy.

With a river cruise on a houseboat you get to enjoy hop-on, hop-off excursions into the jungle and various towns on your route. You can also enjoy the simplicity of booking a single experience (though you can always add on your own shore excursions) while still enjoying a variety of experiences.

Be sure to book through a reputable company, who will also pair you with a guide (or guides) to help ensure you get the most educational value and excitement (with safety always in mind) out of your journey. Just sit back, relax, and let the world of South America come to your new doorstep!

Some Exciting Highlights:

NOTE: With so many possible starting points, there are an incredible number of possibilities for these types of tours. These are just some possibilities to get you dreaming of your own possibilities...

Possible cities to see with kids:

- Manaus
- Pará
- Amazonas
- Tabatinga
- Belém
- Porto Velho
- Tocantins
- Palmas

Sites and activities on our "to research" list:

- Mundo Amazónico
- Estação das Docas
- Centro Cultural dos Povos da Amazônia
- Encontro das Águas
- Fish for piranhas, peacock bass, and other exotic fish
- Canoe through a flooded forest area
- See monkeys, wild birds, and other exotic wildlife
- Bosque da Ciência (INPA)
- Praia da Lua
- Serra do Aracá State Park

Things to Note:

Antimalarials and various inoculations may be necessary before your trip, depending on where you plan on going.

Costa Rica

About:

Stunning Costa Rica is a glittering jewel in Central America and one of the area's most popular tourist destinations. The capital, San Jose, has had a rich history and enjoys a variety of artistic and cultural institutions; while the outlying areas of the country include beautiful rainforest, stunning volcanoes, and rich wildlife to delight families. One of the most biodiverse areas in the world, Costa Rica affords an incredible natural education in a breathtaking setting. Because Costa Rica is wedged between the Caribbean Sea and the Pacific Ocean, it also offers opportunities to relax on pristine white beaches next to azure blue waters, in between wild adventures.

Roughly one quarter of Costa Rica is comprised of protected forest areas, keeping its beauty intact and ready to explore. The area was only sparsely inhabited during the precolonial era, with land too rugged for indigenous peoples to take advantage of. While Spanish rule brought some development, much of Costa Rica's natural beauty remains intact. Since its independence in 1847, it has a progressive and stable national culture. Enjoy Costa Rica on its own, or visit nearby Nicaragua to the North, or Ecuador and Panama to the South. Its position on the western edge of the Caribbean also offers opportunities to arrive or explore by boat.

Why Visit?

Costa Rica's stability makes it a smart choice, while the popularity of tourism makes package deals and special offers easier to come by than other parts of the region. This is a great way to "ease into" more exotic locales, with just enough infrastructure and established tourism to make you feel comfortable off the beaten path.

Serving as Central America's playground, this is a great place for more active adventures like horseback riding, ATV tours, zip lining, and breathtaking hikes. You can also relax on the beach, and explore some incredible examples of natural beauty as well as the unique opportunity to explore an active volcano. There is even unique lodging, as you can choose a beachfront cabin or a luxury resort in the rainforest as just some of the exciting options to stay differently.

Some Exciting Highlights:

Cities to see with kids:

- San Jose
- Arenal
- Tortuguero
- Turrialba

Sites and activities on our "to research" list:

- Pre-Columbian Gold Museum
- Hike La Selva Biological Station (and plant a tree there!)
- San Luis Canopy Tour (includes rainforest zip lining)
- Baldi Hot Springs
- Hanging Bridge Tours/Walks of the Jungle
- Go Horseback Riding
- Doka Estate Coffee Plantation Tour
- Poas Volcano National Park
- La Paz Waterfall Gardens
- Plaza Real Cariari
- ATV Tour of the Area
- Listen to a Classical Guitar Concert and Other Local Music
- Drive the Escazu Mountains (bonus points for a beautiful night trip)

Things to Note:

Health concerns are fewer here than most Central American or developing nations. The water is mainly safe to drink (but you should still check first) and you don't *need* antimalarials or other inoculations to visit. You will still want to exercise caution and use good judgement. If you rent a car, be aware that there are few to no street signs, and drivers sort of "take things as they come" - so exercise caution. Also, the country may be small but rugged terrain, including mountains and forest, can make travel times longer than expected within the country.

Ireland

About:

With a rich history dating back to the Mesolithic period, Ireland has long fascinated tourists and been a point of pride for locals. The sweeping green fields and rolling hills, all encased by steep cliffs that keep the Atlantic Ocean at bay, provide views for miles and a quaint charm that is hard to match.

The North Channel, the Irish Sea, and St. George's Channel separate this "Emerald Isle" from Great Britain. The history of colonialism and ensuing friction between these nations led to the splitting off of the Republic of Ireland (officially named Ireland) to the south, from the smaller Northern Ireland. Northern Ireland is a part of Great Britain.

The oceanic climate is mild, avoiding extremes of temperature in either direction, though rain here is frequent and can be quite heavy.

Why Visit?

Ireland is rife with opportunities for exploration of cultural and historical significance. Explore the history of British rule, Celtic Tribes, and more as you see a variety of stunning and ancient locales.

Enjoy the natural beauty of the countryside as you hike or drive the rolling hills. You can stay in the city, country, or both - and mix up opportunities for established tourism in populated areas with quaint and charming local life. Take part in crafts, enjoy local food and music, and experience a great Irish play or a local football (read: soccer) match to enjoy yourselves like the Irish do. This is a land with a lot to see and do, and many ways to experience it. This makes for a very adaptable destination, that can be something different to each family who visits.

Some Exciting Highlights:

Cities to see with kids:

- Dublin
- Belfast
- Killarney
- Galway
- Westport
- Cork
- Donegal Town

Sites and activities on our "to research" list:

- Brú na Bóinne
- Skellig Michael
- Giant's Causeway
- Bunratty Castle
- Tour a Farm
- Rock of Cashel
- Cliffs of Moher
- Holy Cross Abbey
- Blarney Castle (home of the eponymous stone, kissed to bestow "the gift of gab")
- Glendalough
- Book of Kells

Things to Note:

The mild climate can vary from chilly to warm, and rain can come and go even over the course of hours. Layers and keeping rain gear on hand will be key.

Iceland

About:

The history of Iceland is a relatively short one for a European nation, with cold climate and vast stretches of water keeping it isolated and untouched by humans for many years. Add to that a volcanically and geologically active climate, and Iceland presents as a truly unique place, continuing to emerge on the world stage.

Despite what the name might have you think, there is a lot more to Iceland than a snowy plain. Yes, the glaciers in Vatnajökull and Snæfellsnes national parks make for great ice climbing and hiking, but the interior plain opens up a much more diverse climate. A plateau of sand and lava fields enable you to see amazing features such as geysers, hot springs, waterfalls, and black-sand beaches. Parts of Iceland will have you feeling like you are on another planet, while the relatively small size of the country means that you are never far from modern European amenities and friendly citizens.

Why Visit?

A burgeoning tourism industry has more of the world turning to Iceland as a great destination with new and exciting features. While the growth in popular nightlife may not apply to families, the influx in luxury accommodations and great food that come with it are a welcome addition. Use these new facilities to enjoy old favorites among the locals. Take in a geothermal spa and relax in volcanically warmed waters while swimming at the foot of a glacier.

History is also alive and well in Iceland. While it may not go back quite as far as other parts of Europe, the history of Viking and Nordic peoples will be especially interesting to kids. See big ships and learn about great explorers in between adventurous jaunts into the countryside.

The fact that swimming is one of the top pastimes here (outdoor swimming at that) shows that Iceland is an often misunderstood and underestimated destination with a lot to offer families willing to think differently about where they go.

Some Exciting Highlights:

Cities to see with kids:
- Reykjavik
- Hofn
- Egilsstadir
- Husavik

Sites and activities on our "to research" list:
- Hallgrimskirkja
- The Golden Circle
- Ice Fishing
- Snowmobiling (try Langjokull Snowfields)
- Geysir Hot Spring
- Jökulsárlón (lagoon offering duck boat tours)
- Gulfoss Waterfall
- Geysers of Haukadalur
- Pingvellir National Park
- Blue Lagoon
- Whale Watching

Things to Note:

If you rent a car, do not try driving at night. Roads in Iceland are unlit, steep, narrow, and sometimes even unpaved. Climate changes can be extreme. Shifting elevation or even moving from the sun to the shade can cause temperatures to change steeply. Bring warm clothes and dress in layers to keep kids comfortable. Besides temperatures, also be aware that daylight hours change drastically here with the seasons. In the summer, the sun literally never sets.

Grand Canyon, and Other US National Parks

About:

To lump all these wonderful places together into one paragraph is not very fair, but the idea is to get you thinking about national parks as destinations worth going out of your way for. The Grand Canyon is one of those totally unique and memorable experiences, hence its status at the top of our list. Places like Arches in Utah, Sequoia in California, and many others offer similarly terrific opportunities, while other parks are simply great examples of wonderful landscapes. The point is that none are worth overlooking.

Why Visit?

Chances are you will have to fly to experience many of them, but they are certainly worth the journey. Once there you have all sorts of fun options. Many offer on-site camping (varies by park and with season, check online to confirm and reserve space), while others have nearby lodging that ranges from affordable to more upscale. Park entrance is free, and activities that come with an additional charge start in the very affordable range and go up from there. National parks bring the most stunning and magnificent parts of the United States to the public, offering amazing vacations for all - just as they were intended.

National parks are also great for their blend of education, relaxation, and adventure. While the opportunities vary greatly from park to park, some opportunities exist in all of them. Ranger led tours and visitor centers come packed with information that explains geological features, wildlife, history, and more. The freedom to explore at your own pace, and enjoy beautiful vistas, campgrounds, and even beaches make national parks a great choice for all ages and families of any speed. Park activities can include things like snowshoes, cross country skiing, hiking, white water rafting, snorkeling, and beyond.

Whether you choose it as the "adventure vacation closer to home" or simply because, at any price, the attractions are hard to beat - start considering national parks as travel worthy destinations today.

Some Top Parks to Highlight:

Top Parks On Our List:
- Grand Canyon (Arizona)
- Arches (Utah)
- Yosemite (California)
- Shenandoah (Virginia)
- Acadia (Maine)
- Haleakalā (Hawaii)
- Mammoth Cave (Kentucky)
- Zion (Utah)
- Joshua Tree (California)
- Hot Springs (Arkansas)
- Glacier Bay (Alaska)

Especially Great in Winter:
- Voyageurs (Minnesota)
- Everglades (Florida)
- Virgin Islands
- Sequoia (California)
- Big Bend (Texas)
- Crater Lake (Oregon)
- Bryce Canyon (Utah)
- Yellowstone (Wyoming, Idaho, and Montana)
- Rock Mountain (Colorado)

Things to Note:

Operating hours tend to vary by season, and changes in weather may close parts of a park or entire facilities. Check each park's website for details on hours, seasons, facilities, and up-to-date information about closures and safety information. Most also have information about camping (when applicable) which varies by season and is given out on a first come, first served basis. In many cases you can reserve space online. While park admission is free of charge, there may be charges for parking, equipment rentals, and activities. Visit NPS.gov to begin exploring park options and to plan your visit.

Tuscany

About:

This gorgeous region of Italy packs rich culture and charming countryside into an idyllic retreat within one of Europe's most popular countries for tourism. While many families head straight to Rome, Naples, or one of the other major cities (though Tuscany boasts the wonders of Florence and Pisa), Tuscany is filled with old world charm and educational opportunities.

Tuscany, located on the northwest of Italy's boot-shaped peninsula, boasts some of the most recognizable examples of Renaissance art and architecture in the world. The diverse landscape also spans a great variety of locations, from the Apennine Mountains to the fields, olive groves, and vineyards of Chianti. There are even the beautiful beaches of Elba, overlooking the Tyrrhenian Sea, rounding out an area rich in natural beauty and variety.

Why Visit?

While many try to pack in as much of Italy as possible, a country with *so* much to see and do may be better tackled in small chunks. For those making a first visit to Italy, or who have experienced Rome or another area and are looking to change things up, a vacation in Tuscany has a lot to offer.

The art, architecture, and influence of the Renaissance are alive and well in Tuscany. Florence has some of the most famous and breathtaking examples of this golden age. They exist in museums, monasteries, and even public spaces. Be sure to mix in plenty of time to relax and soak in the natural beauty of Tuscany. Stay in a luxury hotel, rent an apartment, or experience the wonders of a country villa; there are simply so many ways to enjoy every aspect of Tuscany.

Some Exciting Highlights:

Cities to see with kids:

- Florence
- Pisa
- Livorno
- Arezzo
- Siena

Sites and activities on our "to research" list:

- Uffizi Museum
- Siena Cathedral
- Leaning Tower of Pisa
- Tour a Vineyard, Olive Grove, or Farm
- Shop the High Fashions and Great Textiles of Florence
- Ponte Vecchio
- Palazzo Vecchio
- Santa Maria della Scala
- Piazza Del Campo
- Basilica of Santa Croce
- Boboli Gardens
- Museum of Metropolitan Institution
- Bargello

Things to Note:

The popularity of travel to Italy, and Tuscany in particular, means that you may be able to find good package deals and other discounts to help you book smarter. Florence is literally covered in amazing art and architecture, filling city squares and sitting wide out in the open. Find a good guidebook before your visit to help you appreciate everything you see, even the art in public spaces with no plaque to accompany it.

Spain

About:

Spain is Western Europe's second largest country, behind France. This great country offers a wide array of pursuits for most any family. The nation is actually comprised of 17 autonomous regions, each with its own geography and culture (similar to the city-states of ancient Greece). Spain has grown from a host of independent peoples, who later united under imperial force. The result is a wonderful patchwork of language, food, art, music, history, and experiences almost as diverse as Europe itself.

From the beautiful port of Barcelona, teeming with youthful energy and exciting art, to the regal capital of Madrid and the beautiful Balearic Islands - in truth, there are many Spains. The country shares a border with Portugal to the west, France and Monaco to the North, as well as a connection to Africa via Gibraltar to the South. Thus, it is easy to see how Spain has not only served as a crossroads for its own unique cultures, but for a variety of regional experiences.

Why Visit?

The diversity of Spain means that you can enjoy any number of interesting pursuits here. You can relax on a beautiful Spanish beach, tour museums and galleries, visit monuments and great buildings, eat wonderful food, hear beautiful music, and so much more. Spain has a history as old as any in Europe, and a culture that runs just as deep.

For a unique way to stay, consider bunking up in a monastery. Many of these older structures have been rescued by the Spanish government and converted into "paradors," or grand hotels. These old monasteries, and in some cases, castles, offer a chance to experience old-world culture as part of your lodging.

It is probably best to focus on a particular region, or even city, to break down this great country into smaller pieces and give you a chance to soak it all in. Also note that Mediterranean cruises from many providers offer another chance to sample a slice of Spain.

Some Exciting Highlights:

Cities to see with kids:

- Barcelona
- Madrid
- Majorca
- Seville
- Valencia
- Ibiza
- Málaga
- Toledo
- Córdoba

Sites and activities on our "to research" list:

- Sagrada Familia
- Dine on Tapas
- Ibiza
- Alhambra
- Prado Museum
- Parque Güell
- Guggenheim Museum, Bilbao
- Montserrat
- La Rambla
- Santiago de Compostela
- Picasso Museum

Things to Note:

The post-Franco period has brought a resurgence in regional dialects to Spain. Catalan, Gallego (which more resembles Portuguese), Babel, and Basque are just a few. While most signs and menus will be at least bilingual with Spanish (if not trilingual with English as well), be aware of the differences and don't get upset when your Spanish doesn't go as far as you think it will. Mealtimes are also very different in Spain. Lunch doesn't really begin until 2 PM and dinner comes after 10 PM. While you can eat at more regular times (in most areas), if you want to eat like a local, you will have to adjust your schedule.

Morocco

About:

Just south of Spain, on the Northern coast of Africa, lies one of the continent's most cosmopolitan and fascinating destinations. A confluence of different cultures, including Arabic, Berber, and European, have shaped this land over the years to create a cultural melting pot and an important piece of history.

The rugged interior is mostly mountains and desert, and many families will stick to the coastal areas. This is one of few countries in the world to enjoy ports on both the Atlantic Ocean and Mediterranean Sea, with great beaches and the exciting culture that comes from a lively nation abounding in trade.

With the sixth largest economy in Africa, this relatively small nation is more established than many of its neighbors. The official languages are Arabic and Berber, and the majority of citizens practice Islam. As such, certain observances should be made to pay respect to local culture, and you can expect amazing food as well as stunning art and architecture.

Why Visit?

Morocco's location makes it a great way to experience Africa as part of a pan-Mediterranean vacation, or using Europe as a jumping-off point. The diverse culture and rich history here make it a unique place, long at the crossroads of two continents and reflecting some of the best of both, while also enjoying a number of uniquely Moroccan pursuits.

This is one of those countries where a good local guide can be of great benefit to your vacation (see more information on sources to research them in Part IV). You will need to put in the paces to make sure you find someone knowledgeable and with more to offer than a flashy website. A solid guide will make this experience all the more illuminating. Language barriers, finding the best food and deals, and other potential issues may prove a little challenging, but are well worth the effort.

Some Exciting Highlights:

Cities to see with kids:

- Marrakech
- Fes
- Casablanca
- Agadir
- Rabat

Sites and activities on our "to research" list:

- Djemaa el-Fna square
- Marrakech's Medieval Quarter
- Visit a Local Souk (marketplace) for Unique Shopping with Bartering
- Volubilis
- Enjoy a Hammam (steam bath)
- Hassan II Mosque
- Majorelle Garden
- Jemaa el-Fnaa
- Bahia Palace
- Marrakech Museum
- Rabat Archaeological Museum
- Bab Agnaou

Things to Note:

While Morocco does not *require* any vaccinations before entering the country, families (especially those traveling to certain areas) may choose to get some of the more standard ones. Appropriate (read: modest, with head coverings for women) dress is required for many areas, as a sign of respect to locals and their customs. Also, never show the bottom of your feet to anyone. This can be a good opportunity to teach children about other customs and being deferential. Be cautious about water (drink bottled), ice, and only eating cooked foods to protect your health and better enjoy your trip. Also look into when Ramadan falls if planning a visit, as the month-long holiday (generally sometime in June-July) will have a big impact on business hours and the like.

China

About:

China, sprawling and massive, is another instance in which it almost seems inaccurate to simply lump it all together. China is as rich in different cultures and regional identities as it is in area - resulting in a gigantic country that more closely resembles a hundred smaller entities. Language, culture, lifestyle, and more can vary greatly from one region to the next. Geographically, China also spans just about every terrain you can imagine. From deserts and mountains, to seaside villages, dense forests and sprawling urban centers - China is nothing if not a world of possibilities.

With some of the oldest recorded history on Earth, and a growing presence on the world stage, China represents a connection to the past, present, and future for everyone who visits.

Why Visit?

When we talk about sharing world news related to destinations you have visited with children, China is a prime example. With the growing importance of this country on an international level, visiting with your kids and making it "real" for them will help them to better understand and feel close to many of the events that unfold over the course of their lives. It is also a great chance to experience a wide array of cultures, and to explore Asia on almost any budget. Once you swallow the airfare, the sheer variety that China has to offer means there are a hundred ways to experience this great nation. You can stay in the lap of luxury or backpack remote regions and stay with locals. China has something to offer any style of travel and price-point.

The unique experiences of China are ones that will leave an indelible mark on any family. From grand temples and ancient statues, to idyllic gardens and mountain retreats, China transports you to different times in history with is commitment to preserving its history. You can span thousands of years in a week, and see things wholly different from their Western counterparts.

Go modern with great amusement parks and forward thinking cities, step into the past with ancient shrines, or preferably - do both. A vacation to China requires careful planning and tough choices, but once you find the right area for you the fun can begin!

Some Exciting Highlights:

Cities to see with kids:

- Hong Kong
- Beijing
- Shanghai
- Macau
- Xi'an
- Chengdu
- Shenzhen
- Luoyang

Sites and activities on our "to research" list:

- The Great Wall of China
- The Terracotta Warriors of Xi'an

- Take a Yangtze River Cruise
- See Panda Bears and Other Wildlife (see Chengdu Research Base)
- The Forbidden City
- Summer Palace
- Tiananmen Square
- Yu Garden
- The Buddhist Temple and Cliffside Carvings of Luoyang (Longmen Grottoes)
- Reed Flute Cave
- Hong Kong Disneyland
- Cheung Chau
- Elephant Trunk Hill

Things to Note:

The difference in alphabet as well as spoken language means it is a good idea to equip each family member with a piece of paper that has where you are staying written in Chinese characters in case of separation. China is one country that actually makes getting a cellphone (or international SIM card) fairly affordable, so this may make sense to help you get around, make plans, and be equipped for emergencies. Cars have the right of way, not pedestrians, so cross streets carefully. Taxis are open to haggling, and driving is tricky for foreigners so you may wish to look into a local guide or driver.

Vietnam

About:

This Southeast Asian country has come a long way since the embattled nation the United States deployed troops to in the 1960's and 70's. Following this sad period in history, the country has undergone a major rebuilding. Over two thirds of the current population was born after 1975, and American tourists are said to receive a particularly warm welcome here.

Vietnamese is a particularly interesting culture, with its own unique language, art, food and way of life. The most popular religion is Buddhism, and Confucianism underlies much of the national thought. As a longtime tributary of Southern China, the country adopts many elements from Chinese culture, while also adopting elements from a period of French colonial presence, and from neighboring Hindu communities. This unique blend is augmented by a number of smaller ethnic groups within the country.

Bordering Laos, Cambodia, and China, Vietnam has a long, skinny land area with an abundance of coastline. Over 2,000 miles of Vietnam borders the South China Sea or the Gulf of Tonkin, presenting wonderful beaches and coastal fishing villages full of charm and opportunities for exploration. The dense jungle is not to be explored on your own, but tours take families inside to interact with local wildlife, and to enjoy the natural beauty of a rich and diverse ecosystem.

Why Visit?

Vietnam's history has been plagued by tumultuous foreign relations and internal struggle, but relatively recent stability over the last 40 or so years sees the country finally coming into its own. The new boom in tourism makes it a great time to visit, with a warm welcome and exciting opportunities awaiting any family that makes the trip - not to mention affordability, after making the flight of course.

The unique culture of Vietnam, coupled with its natural beauty, opens many doors for traveling families. This is a great opportunity to see and to do more with your kids. Explore adventurous opportunities in the jungle and on the water. Stay in innovative lodging, and mix big cities with rural communities for a vacation that packs in more.

Some Exciting Highlights:

Cities to see with kids:

- Ho Chi Minh City
- Hanoi
- Nha Trang

- Da Nang
- Phan Thiet
- Haiphong

Sites and activities on our "to research" list:

- Mui Ne Beach
- Cu Chi Tunnels
- Cuc Phuong National Park
- Kontum
- Mỹ Sơn
- Phong Nha-Ke Bang
- Ha Long Bay
- Hanoi Water Park
- See a Vietnamese Circus
- Shop a Local Market
- Ride a Boat on the Mekong Delta
- War Remnants Museum
- Saigon Notre-Dame Basilica

Things to Note:

You need a visa to enter Vietnam. Sort this out before you go and make sure everything is in order to avoid delays. Haggling is a way of life here. Be ready to negotiate prices, and be vigilant about things like counting change and having people repeat prices back to you. People aren't looking to rip you off (for the most part) but prices are more fluid here and some attention is required on your part. Drink bottled water, avoid ice and make sure foods are cooked and water is boiling when you order soup. Health concerns can be real here, especially in more rural areas.

Tanzania

About:

Tanzania, located in East Africa, is largely known as a big game and safari destination among tourists. Vast wilderness areas, virtually untouched by humans and accessible by jeep or other off-road vehicle, offer families the opportunity to commune with nature and enjoy exotic animals in their natural habitat.

As one of the oldest continuously inhabited locations on the planet, Tanzania is rich in history, though more of the natural sort, and is still largely undeveloped.

Why Visit?

Two main types of vacations exist here, though you can feel free to mix and match aspects of them, or to seek out your own unique experiences. Many families come here to safari. You can stay in unique lodgings like treetop hotels or camp out on the plains, then spend your days exploring the wilderness with guides and seeing magnificent animals up close and personal. The location on the Indian Ocean also provides great beach opportunities, and a number of waterfront resort areas.

A rich national park system preserves the natural world of Tanzania and makes it accessible to your family. The country possesses both the highest point (Mount Kilimanjaro) and lowest point (the lake bed of Lake Tanganyika) in all of Africa. Add to that a portion of the continent's largest lake (Lake Victoria) and you have a bevy of natural sights to see and extraordinary locations to visit.

Tanzania's accessibility to tourists makes it a great way to experience what most of us picture when we picture Africa. See the animals, enjoy the land, and enjoy some local culture from the relative safety of one of Africa's most stable and secure countries.

Some Exciting Highlights:

Cities/Areas to see with kids:
- Dar es Salaam
- Arusha
- The island of Mafia Marine Park
- The Island of Zanzibar

Sites and activities on our "to research" list:
- Mount Kilimanjaro
- Serengeti National Park
- Ngorongoro Conservation Area
- Tarangire National Park
- Mahale Mountains National Park
- Stone Town

Things to Note:

Tanzania's tropical climate comes with the usual international health concerns. You will need certain vaccinations and antimalarials. You should also be careful about water (drink bottled, avoid ice and uncooked food) while there. Visas are required for Tanzania and should be secured in advance. The Tanzanian shilling is the local unit of currency and no smaller denomination exists (no "cents"). Consider using a bureau de change in any major city as opposed to a bank to change currency (only some locations will accept cards). These bureaus offer a flat exchange rate and are quicker (sometimes cheaper) than a bank, at least in Tanzania (this is not the advice we typically give when traveling internationally). The "long rains" period runs from March to May. Flooding in the lowland areas during this time can affect hours of operation, and close some national parks and other locations completely. Keep this in mind when booking.

South Africa

About:

The southernmost nation in Africa, this is a fantastic country to visit. South Africa features Cape Agulhas, where the Indian and Atlantic Oceans meet and there is no more land until you hit Antarctica. This is just one of the stunning vantage points offered by this richly diverse nation, full of natural beauty and equipped with modern amenities.

South Africa's history as a valuable colonial outpost has helped shape its history. While the Bushmen may have made their marks on the rocks of South Africa 3,000 years ago, it was the Portuguese, Dutch, and later British settlers who most quickly and drastically changed this nation and made it what it is today. With the strongest economy in Africa, and a major player in continental politics, this cosmopolitan melting pot of different African and European cultures marries thousands of years of history from multiple continents to produce a unique destination with a lot to offer.

Why Visit?

The strong economy, ample infrastructure, and European influences make this a great "starter" location from which to explore Africa. Families with less experience off the beaten path, or outside of the familiar haunts of North America and Europe, would do well to consider beginning here as a way to see more of the world without shocking their systems too much.

South Africa also enjoys incredible diversity. You can go from the jungle to the desert in one day. Mountains actually offer downhill skiing, even in summer. Finally, the coast offers beachfront excursions and incredible snorkeling as well as scuba diving. You can choose to focus exclusively on natural pursuits, but unlike many other African nations, you can also mix in more modern and developed conveniences and a dose of city time. There are museums and cultural centers, resorts, sporting events (if the 2010 World Cup is any indication, soccer is alive and well here), and more.

Don't think of it as "Africa lite" - but rather, as a chance to experience some of the best parts of Africa while still feeling the comforts of home.

Some Exciting Highlights:

Cities to see with kids:

- Cape Town
- Pretoria
- Durban
- Newcastle
- Johannesburg
- Port Elizabeth

Sites and activities on our "to research" list:

- Kgalagadi Transfrontier Park
- The Cradle of Humankind
- Kruger National Park
- Robben Island
- Mapungubwe Kingdom
- Vredefort Dome
- Cape Agulhas
- Table Mountain
- Apartheid Museum
- Kirstenbosch National Botanical Garden
- Gold Reef City
- Boulder Beach
- Lion Park

Things to Note:

Since the end of Apartheid, many places have changed names, a process that is ongoing to this day. This can be confusing, as some may not recognize an old or a new name for a place you would like to see. For this reason, it may be easier to book as much transportation in advance as possible, as a driver/guide is useful for other reasons while exploring South Africa anyway. South Africa spans desert and tropical climates, and temperatures and weather vary greatly from region to region, as well as season to season. Put in the time to research in advance. Don't assume you'll get away with shorts everywhere, you may even see snow during your time. Also note that some areas are not safe to visit, so careful research will be needed when you create your itinerary.

The Galápagos Islands

About:

The Galápagos Islands are a volcanic archipelago off the coast of Ecuador, lying about 600 miles off the coast. This lonely spot in the Pacific Ocean maintains some of the richest and most important biodiversity in the world. With unique opportunities afforded by the islands' proximity to each other, and distance from the mainland, unique species have been discovered and studied here, increasing our understanding of the natural world.

It was here that Charles Darwin wrote "The Origin of Species," his famous work that revolutionized modern science. Now the same islands that he spent so much time are open to families, and represent some of the most incredible opportunities for ecotourism and exploration of the natural world that exist today.

Why Visit?

The unique ecological conditions have given rise to many species that only exist here. A local dedication to preservation dictates that specimens never leave the islands. Thus, for nature lovers and wildlife enthusiasts, the Galápagos are home to truly "once in a lifetime" experiences.

The lack of natural predators and abundance of "fun" animals like giant tortoises and sea lions also make this a perfect nature viewing locale for children. You can get up close and personal with animals that are both exotic and friendly, letting children safely enjoy the ultimate in natural bucket list locations.

The diversity doesn't end at the animals, as unique geological and natural features make each island its own distinct landscape. Traverse black volcanic rocks and white sand beaches in the same vacation, all set along a backdrop of azure blue waters in some of the most beautiful vistas imaginable.

Just half of the fun exists on land, as those pristine waters hold their own host of wildlife and opportunities for snorkeling and diving that people travel the whole world to experience. Nurse a love for science and nature in one of the world's most unique locations in the Galápagos.

Some Exciting Highlights:

Some of the Key Islands of the Galápagos:

- Santa Cruz Island
- Isabela Island
- Floreana Island
- San Cristóbal Island
- Española Island
- Fernandina Island
- Baltra Island
- Santiago Island
- Genovesa Island

Sites and activities on our "to research" list:

- Charles Darwin Research Station
- Galápagos National Park
- Tortuga Bay
- Hiking
- Kayaking
- Diving/Scuba
- Volunteer to Help Protect and Preserve Wildlife (while learning along the way)

Things to Note:

The busiest season runs during the summer months, as well as December - January (also key school break periods). Prices may be higher during these times, and bookings should be made well in advance. Most islands and areas cannot be visited without a licensed guide, due to preservation concerns. Booking guided tours is not only a good idea, here it is a must. In addition to flights, tours, lodging, and other regular vacation expenses, note that there is a fee (about $100 for adults, $50 for children) to enter the national park. Keep in mind that this type of trip will generally be quite costly, as it is not easy to locate deals or discounts for the Galapagos.

Peru

About:

One of South America's most sought-after destinations, Peru has long been a cradle of civilization and a home to natural beauty. Once the center of the Inca Empire, this country located on the western edge of the continent marries ancient ruins and culture with stunning South Pacific beaches. Bordered by Ecuador and Colombia to the north, Brazil and Bolivia to the east, and Chile to the south, Peru also enjoys mountainous regions thanks to a portion of the Andes. The diversity of environments creates a great vacation destination.

The city areas tend to be well established and modern, while rural communities can lack infrastructure. Tourism is a big part of the local economy, and tourists are treated well; however it is best to stick to established areas for the most comfortable experience.

Why Visit?

The single biggest draw here would have to be the ancient ruins of the Inca civilization. Machu Picchu is world renowned for its incredible preservation of ancient architecture, and the opportunity to experience it in its natural setting lends context and a definite "wow-factor" for families. Most traveling to Peru will (rightly) plan the trip around a visit to the ancient ruins.

They combine an incredible living piece of history with the natural beauty of their surroundings, and the adventure of hiking and getting active as a family. You really cannot go wrong with that combination. Children will also enjoy the fun fact that American Explorer Hiram Bingham would never have discovered the site without the help of an 11 year old Quechua Indian boy who served as one of his guides. Ruins discovered by children, for children.

A great Peru trip will make use of a local guide of your own, and can include plenty of other great active pursuits. The cities also offer further chances to explore history, as well as the local culture as you enjoy art, food, song, and dance. Thousands of years come together in Peru with jaw-dropping visuals, and the fact that you can end your day on the beach certainly doesn't hurt.

Some Exciting Highlights:

Cities to see with kids:

- Lima
- Cuzco
- Arequipa
- Iquitos

Sites and activities on our "to research" list:

- Machu Picchu
- Miraflores District, Lima
- Saksaywaman
- Sacred Valley
- Cusco Cathedral
- Qurikancha
- Moray
- Huaca Del Sol
- Paracas National Reserve
- Huanchaco

Things to Note:

Carrying cash isn't just a good idea; in many places it will be necessary. Don't expect everyone to take your credit card, and ideally carry plenty of small bills so you don't have to rely on locals to make change. The altitude adjustment in the mountains is something to be taken seriously. Don't push yourselves too hard, and allow for breaks if someone feels lightheaded. Be sure to eat enough and drink plenty of (bottled) water. The Inca trail is very difficult and requires patience and endurance. It is best not to assume your 4 year old can handle it. At the same time, an experienced porter can and will help ease your burden, carrying bags and even kids for the right fee. Peru is rife with unlicensed taxis. while many are harmless individuals looking to make extra money, play it safe and look for registration before you get in.

Maine

About:

Like a jewel adorning the northeast corner of the United States, Maine's tucked away location preserves its beauty, while hiding it from many who have yet to discover its wonders. The long maritime tradition of the state permeates thought here, which marries the best of the sea and the land.

In practice, many would say that there are two Maines - that of the coastal areas and that of inland Maine. The rugged, rocky coast is home to all manner of seaward activities, with famous waterfronts, sailing, and charming towns. Inland Maine enjoys lush forests and an abundance of parks and reserves. Camping is a favorite retreat within the granite and spruce tree forests. The chance to observe animals including moose in their natural habitat reflects the local desire to live *with* the land, rather than simply on it.

Besides possessing the northernmost point on the east coast, Maine also enjoys the northern extreme of the Appalachian Trail. If you choose not to explore the Atlantic coast, take in a stunning lake or river view. Maine has a very friendly local population, and they will enhance any trip, whether it be with helpful suggestions about which landmarks to see, or simply greeting you with a smile.

Why Visit?

While so many look to the northeast corner of New England as a ski mecca (Maine does have some great skiing), people often fail to push past Vermont and New Hampshire's resort mountains to enjoy the unique taste of Maine.

Part of the beauty of Maine lies in the options available to family travelers - you can stick to the coast, and enjoy great food, sailing, beachfront areas, and the charming shops of the more metropolitan areas. A trip inland will result in some amazing camping, a stay at a quaint lodge, and a chance to mingle even more with locals in between some adventurous hikes or climbs. Maine seems to be on the rise for nearly everything. A burgeoning food scene in the major cities offers a lot, and there is adventure for everyone. If you look hard enough you can find unique places to stay, fun activities to enjoy, and great memories waiting to be made.

Some Exciting Highlights:

Cities to see with kids:

- Portland
- Bangor
- Augusta
- Bar Harbor
- Rockland
- Brunswick
- Bath

Sites and activities on our "to research" list:

- Acadia National Park
- Casco Bay
- Go Kayaking or Canoeing as a Family
- Charter a Sailboat and take to the Ocean or Bay

- Victoria Mansion
- Portland Museum of Art
- Visit a Local Flea Market or Farmer's Market
- Two Lights State Park
- Fort Western
- Go Fishing, Crabbing, or Periwinkle Picking (a great choice for younger kids)
- Tate House
- Bailey Island Bridge

Things to Note:

State and national parks get busy during the peak season of summer. Be sure to make arrangements in advance if you plan on camping. Winter is much slower here, and great deals can be had. Part of the reason for this is that Maine gets *impressive* amounts of snow. While Mainers do a great job of clearing necessary areas, don't expect everything to be open or new snow to be cleared very quickly. If you plan to visit in winter, allow extra time on every stop to account for weather.

Northern California

About:

Another sort of catchall designation, in order to further promote the idea of thinking creatively when it comes to domestic travel, we urge you to consider the beauty of northern California. For many families considering a US destination, the first thoughts run to major cities, or theme parks and the like. California usually sees people jumping to Los Angeles, or another city like San Diego or San Francisco.

Northern California is a world apart from its southern component, a world with a slower pace, a different kind of natural beauty, and a land seemingly built for road trips. While cities like San Diego and San Francisco are great, also consider lesser appreciated beauties like Sacramento or Santa Cruz. Use bigger cities as beginning or end points for a trip in order to allow you and your family to see more of the state by packing up the car, and finding the places that interest you.

Why Visit?

With multiple, stunning national parks, there is a lot to see in Northern California. Explore wine country, which is fun even for children as the beautiful vineyards and the process are just as interesting to children as the beverage is to adults. Dart back and forth between the shore for beach time, and the woods for camping. Enjoy the best of the "other California."

Depending on where you live you may need to fly to start and end your journey, but once here, you can get by without spending too much. The well-established area makes using apartment and space renting sites a solid choice, and national/state park camping sites allow for cheap and effective lodging. Rent a car and live like California nomads, exploring at your own pace and blending active, educational, and relaxing pursuits.

Get some sun, enjoy the fresh air, seek out unique experiences and enjoy some amazing photo opportunities. From the stunning coastline to the giant redwood trees - northern California shouldn't be overlooked as a great way to do more for less.

Some Exciting Highlights:

Cities to see with kids:

- San Francisco
- Fresno
- Sacramento
- Eureka
- Chico

Sites and activities on our "to research" list:

- Point Reyes National Seashore
- The Napa Valley
- UC Berkeley Botanical Garden

- The Many Museums of San Francisco
- UC Davis Arboretum
- Farmer's Markets and Great Local Food/Produce
- Bird Watching
- Lake Tahoe
- Yosemite National Park
- Muir Woods
- Redwood National Park
- Lava Beds National Monument

Things to Note:

Much of Northern California is warm and sunny...most of the time. However, even in summer, evenings can actually get quite cool and you will want to dress in layers. In the winter don't expect to be running around in shorts and in the mountains it will snow (in fact, you can ski!). Look into the cities and locations you want to visit beforehand, check the weather and pack accordingly. Don't make assumptions based on a perception of the state as a whole.

Niagara Falls (USA or Canada)

About:

Niagara Falls is actually a collective name for three major waterfalls that straddle the border between Ontario, Canada and New York State. This treasure shared by two countries makes for a great family destination, with impressive visuals and fun surrounding attractions.

The three waterfalls are called Bridal Veil Falls, American Falls, and Horseshoe Falls, in order from smallest to largest. Horseshoe Falls lies mainly on the Canadian side, while American and Bridal falls are on the American side. The group derives its name from the Niagara River, which drains one of the great lakes (Lake Erie) into another (Lake Ontario). The highest flow rate makes them the strongest in the world, with powerful, surging waters sure to impress any visitors.

On the American side, visitors can take in the view from Prospect Point Park and its accompanying observation tower. Queen Victoria Park on the Canadian side offers beautiful gardens, great park facilities, and stunning views from the observation deck of Skylon Tower.

Why Visit?

One of the best features here is the shared aspect of the falls, allowing it to be enjoyed entirely from the United States, Canada, or as a shared vacation that enjoys both countries. The ease of passing back and forth between the two areas makes for a great way to expose children to another country, but in a safe and simple way that still retains elements of home.

Many fall prey to the misconception that there is nothing to do here but view the falls and move on. This couldn't be further from the truth. The impressive display of the falls has long established the site as a meeting place and tourist hotspot, resulting in the growth of a lively area for natural exploration, entertainment, and family fun.

Some Exciting Highlights:

Nearby cities to combine with your visit:

- Buffalo, New York
- Rochester, New York
- Hamilton, Canada
- Toronto Canada

Sites and activities on our "to research" list (with indications as to which country they are in):

- Explore the Niagara River Recreational Trail (Canada)
- Whirlpool Aero Car (Canada)
- Cave of the Winds (USA)
- The Journey Behind the Falls (Canada)
- Niagara Falls State Park (USA)
- Goat Island (USA)

- Fallsview Tourist Area and adjacent Clifton Hill (Canada)
- *Maid of the Mist* (boats operate from both sides)
- Nearby (on the American side) there are theme parks, canal cruises, jet boats and the history of Old Fort Niagara.

Things to Note:

US citizens will still need passports (even for children) to complete a round trip into Canada. See more information in Part III of this book upcoming, in case you are first-time or passport renewal candidates. The peak season is in the summer. Lights on the Canadian side make this both a day and night attraction during this time, and booking in advance will be more important during summer.

Our Family's Favorite Vacations and Destinations

As important as the hopes and dreams of future vacations are, we would be remiss not to share some of the places we *know* to be great. Over the years, with children of all ages (from infants to teens) in tow, these are the locations that have brought us the most joy and offered incredible opportunities to grow.

These are places that we have learned from and that have provided all sorts of fun and excitement. These are solid bets for just about any family. If you are a new family looking to strike out for the first time, or more low-key travelers looking to ramp up to new experiences - we recommend you start here.

Similar to the last section, for each place we will give a brief overview, some things to note, some of the best things we did, and some other advice for travelers. For these locations we can provide more in the way of practical advice, as well as concrete opinions about activities that have worked for us. While we won't run through the full vacation for each, rest assured that the things we chose to mention here are among the best.

Just as we shared our wish list to help inspire you to start your own, these locations are meant to aid you in starting to think outside the box. Some may be "expected" while others are a bit more obscure. The point is that we have gained something from each of them, and can share with you a bit of just what that means.

Continue to challenge your conceptions of what *can* be done, and begin considering what you *want* to do together. Selecting your destination is about dreaming first, and figuring out the logistics later. See how it has worked for one family, and draw inspiration from the experience.

For even more of the places we (and other real families) have gone, and what has been done there, visit RealFamilyTrips.com and check out both the "Itineraries" and "Spot-"Spotlight" sections. Our growing collection of guidebooks also highlights specific vacation values and practical information from some of the locations we describe in the following section.

Here is our list of the "best of the best" for family vacations…so far.

Israel

About:

Israel is one of the most magical places to travel with family, so much so that we keep going back. Israel offers significance in every area that makes for a great vacation. Culture and history both abound here in truly unique ways. As a holy place for Jews, Muslims, and Christians - Israel has been a place of significance throughout recorded history. Perhaps no place else on Earth is such a melting pot of peoples and cultures. The opportunities to educate children here are extraordinary, spanning an incredible stretch of time and all manner of experiences. So much of this education is hand-on, allowing you to visit the places where incredible things happened and to interact with unique, interactive exhibits and people from all walks of life. Modernity and antiquity unite in Israel, bringing a progressive attitude to a land of history and making for a well-rounded experience.

The geography of Israel is as diverse as its people, and the climate spans deserts, mountains, forests, and more. These features play into another great aspect of an Israeli vacation - activity. Far from being a nation with nothing to do but visit holy sites and museums, we have found that Israel abounds in exciting adventures and some of the best active ventures we have ever encountered.

The Value of Visiting:

Israel is a chance to explore a location that has long served as a crossroads for the world. So many people have passed through here over centuries and millennia. The peoples of Africa, Europe, Asia, and beyond have all turned to Israel over the years. Each of these groups has left its own mark, and the opportunities to not just learn *about*, but to *experience* other cultures is invaluable.

There are so many different ways to experience Israel that by varying the stops, a vacation here never gets boring. Amazing museums, important sites, great food, fantastic wildlife, nature preserves, active adventures like hiking, spelunking, and rappelling, and some of the great guides of the world come together to create opportunities for family touring that really do have it all. This kind of vacation also facilitates bonding on a wonderful level. Seeing such important things and having such incredible fun is a real shot in the arm to any family. It is hard to leave a place like this and not feel changed - for the better.

Some Exciting Highlights:

Cities/Areas we have enjoyed with kids:

- **Jerusalem** - One of history's most important cities, a true melting pot of culture, and home to some of the most incredible sites in the world. A great place to start, Jerusalem is a city that will never get old if you need to choose one.

- **Tel Aviv** - Demonstrates that Israel is not frozen in time. Here, the modern flourishes and progressive thought unites with amazing beach life to show the contemporary nation of Israel at its best.

- **Acco** - This ancient city turned modern metropolis, also known as Acre, sits on the Mediterranean and brings together the history of Crusader knights, Arab traders, and Jewish residents. Experience the old city and market for a blast from the past and a number of other important sites.

- **Galil/Golan** - Israel's rocky northern region boasts incredible mountains and lush farmland. Experience great opportunities for active excursions, and a slower pace.

- **Mitzpe Ramon** - To the south, the sprawling Negev desert dominates the landscape. This region shows how innovative Israel has been in carving a life out of these arid parts, and you will see stunning natural features.

Great sites and activities not to be missed:

- **The Kotel** - Also known as "The Wailing Wall" this most sacred of sites is a powerful visit and a great opportunity to experience peoples from all walks of life, and corners of the world, coming together. Be sure to dress and act with respect, and enjoy the chance to take in this amazing location with your family.
- **Chizkiyahu Tunnel Tours** - A unique blend of history and adventure, the chance to explore these former water channels from an ancient siege will let you feel like explorers as you celebrate the past.
- **Mahane Yehuda** - This celebrated souk, or marketplace, has a history that goes back hundreds of years and offers a true taste of the region. Enjoy great food and shopping in a unique setting.
- **Museums** - There are so many great museums in Israel, here are a few to get you started: Israel Museum (Jerusalem), Palmach Museum (Tel Aviv), Herzl Museum (Jerusalem), Museum of the Underground Prisoner (Jerusalem), Golani Museum (Galil/Golan).
- **Rappelling, Swinging, and Spelunking** - The caves, cliffs, and mountains of Israel present very special opportunities to get active. Go beyond museums and even hikes, enjoying amazing views that lend context to the area while getting your pulse pounding and creating a unique family memory.
- **Beach Time** - Tel Aviv has the most famous beaches in Israel.
- **Dead Sea** - This famous body of water may have beaches but falls into a category all its own. The salty

waters serve as a natural spa, and the location has long been a place of historical and cultural significance.

- **Yad Vashem** - Israel's official memorial to the victims of the Holocaust is an incredibly moving and important site. For children and teens who are up for it, this powerful location can offer a key lesson for you all to share.
- **Special Ways to Travel** - get off your feet and ride a camel, hop in a Jeep, or drive in an ATV through the desert. Enjoy fun and exciting travel that helps you to not only enjoy yourselves, but see more as well.

Things to Note:

Israeli summers get quite hot, and a boom in tourism presents a dual concern. Do your best to book early, and plan for warm days and cooler nights (in some areas) by packing accordingly. Certain areas of Jerusalem, including important sites like the Kotel and various houses of worship require special dress. Even if you plan on spending more time running, swimming, or climbing - bring a set of modest clothes to enjoy these areas.

Israel is a prime area to hire an experienced guide, especially for first time visitors. Read more about how to find them in Part IV, in our guidebook, and on our website.

We have written extensively about Israel in our guidebook **"Israel for Families: An Adventure in 12 Days."** More information about it follows at the end of this book, as well as on RealFamilyTrips.com.

Finland

About:

Adjacent to Estonia and Latvia, and sharing borders with Russia, Sweden, and Norway, the great Nordic nation of Finland is an often overlooked treat within Europe. Most families focus on the southern and western areas of the continent, never turning their eyes north for the fun and adventure to be had on the Baltic Sea. We have found Finland to offer a variety of family activities, a fascinating history (made all the better by being less familiar with it before visiting), and a new culture to explore and share both during the trip and upon returning.

The modern nation of Finland is a Euro-zone country, with all the comforts and amenities of its European neighbors. Its location makes it great for hopping around to nearby countries, either by sea, land, or air. There are a number of ways to experience it, and the modern cities are augmented by areas of great natural beauty. This is one of just a few places in the world where you can take in the Northern Lights, as well as home to some world-class ski resorts.

The Value of Visiting:

With everything from cutting edge art and great shopping, to a great family amusement park in Helsinki, and historic saunas, Finland is another location that lets you do just about anything you can imagine.

Our visit came as part of a Baltic Sea cruise, which is a fantastic way to experience Finland while adding in some of the neighboring areas. We also got to experience cities in other nearby countries, including places like Copenhagen, St. Petersburg, and Stockholm (more on this below). For families looking to sample the northern part of Europe, a cruise can open up new horizons.

Finland is a great way to expand your view of what Europe means, and see that more exists than just the most popular tourist destinations. There is a lot of value in taking a unique and extraordinary vacation that will help your family to enjoy a place many others overlook. The chance to be more educated about our world, and share special memories with your family, will bring you closer and expand your worldview.

Some Exciting Highlights:

We spent our time in Finland touring **Helsinki**. This capital city of the nation features a great mix of things to experience. Here, culture, art, food, history, and fun come together to provide a great slice of Finnish life. If you are looking to take a similar cruise to the one we enjoyed (several lines offer them) or create your own tour of the Baltic region, we recommend the following:

Other cities we enjoyed on our Baltic tour:
- Copenhagen, Denmark
- Tallinn, Estonia
- St. Petersburg, Russia
- Stockholm, Sweden
- Berlin, Germany

Sites and activities to think about when visiting Helsinki:
- **National Museum of Finland** - Gain context for your visit to the area with exhibits that span Finnish history from the Stone Age through modern times. There are guided tours, English language plaques, and even an interactive area to help engage children. This is a great way to gain a foundation for other sites along your visit.
- **Fortress of Suomenlinna** - This UNESCO World Heritage Site pays homage to Finland's military past while providing amazing views of the surrounding area. Tour the ancient fort on a guided tour, and enjoy the opportunity to enjoy children's activities, historical interpreters, and a decommissioned submarine.
- **Linnanmaki Amusement Park** - Over 60 years old, this national treasure represents a great historic amusement park that has reinvented itself just enough to maintain its effortless cool factor. This clean park, with courteous and professional staff, provides a lot of fun and a chance to cut loose and enjoy after or in between more educational pursuits. Our kids really loved this park.
- **Museum of Contemporary Art Kiasma** - This ultra-modern facility encapsulates the forward-thinking city of Helsinki with a collection of some of the most cutting-edge art around. Engaging activities like the opportunity to contribute a "postcard from Kiasma" to a

wall in the museum will help keep children happy as they explore modern art with a healthy mix of fun.

- **Enjoy a Finnish Sauna** - An important part of the local culture, sweating out in gender-separate saunas is a favorite local pastime. There are a variety of spas and other facilities where you can indulge in a bit of relaxation. Just put in the time to research beforehand: prices can vary from affordable to astronomical, and some facilities are wary about children.
- **Rock Church (Temppeliaukio Kirkko)** - Carved into the side of an actual mountain, this feat of art and engineering is a must-see and one of the most unique structures in the world. Not only is it a jaw-dropping site and a great photo-op, it is free of charge to visit.

Things to Note:

Tipping is not a part of the culture in Finland, so don't be surprised when a bill comes without a line for gratuity. You can still leave something if you like, just round up to the nearest whole number. If you plan to take in a sauna, be aware that they do separate by gender and you will need to make sure this works for you keeping an eye on your kids. Also note that the Finns are not shy about nudity in their spas, and so if this is a concern you might want to skip over a stop involving a sweat. Finally, Finland's geographic placement means that extremes in temperature and even hours of daylight are a part of life. Summer sees warm weather and almost perpetual daylight, a fun phenomenon but also one that can be difficult to adjust to for visitors. The winters can be bitterly cold, and see little to no daylight for long stretches. Be aware of the differences, pack and plan accordingly, and be sure to double check hours of operation for your exact dates of travel.

Hawaii

About:

The 50th United State feels like a world away from the rest. An idyllic destination in the Pacific, Hawaii boasts warm temperatures with low humidity, year round. It's unique and special culture blends elements of Polynesian, Asian and European heritage for an experience like none other. Hawaii has something to offer every family - whether you want to be beach bums on some of the world's most beautiful sand, or get actively involved in educational and enriching pursuits.

The Value of Visiting:

Want to lay on the beach? Not a problem. You can even choose what color of sand you want. Want to explore museums? Shops? National parks? Hawaii has you covered. You can eat anywhere from five-star to food truck, and stay in a luxury resort or a bed and breakfast. Hawaii has such an array of active ventures, from jet skis and parasailing, to world class golf that a family never has to sit still if they don't want to. There are few things you *can't* find in Hawaii. The weather, the infrastructure and the booming tourism industry make most any dream possible. Find exactly the right vacation to suit your family's pace.

Hawaii also manages to feel like any of the most luxurious and alluring island locales. It has the weather, the food, the culture and the stunning landscapes to match or beat any island getaway in the world. At the same time, US citizens can enjoy it without the need for a passport, and English speakers won't have to worry about a language barrier. Visitors from anywhere in the world can know that they are enjoying the safety, security and comforts of a vacation in the United States, while feeling like they are anyplace but. This is a fantastic way for families to explore the wonders of an exotic island getaway in a more accessible manner.

The 8 islands provide unique experiences, as well as some common threads. Depending on the amount of time you have and your personal desire, you and your family can tackle one, or jump around. You'll find it easier logistically than bouncing around the Caribbean (once again you never change countries), but also isn't necessary unless you have very specific landmarks you want to see.

Some Exciting Highlights:

Some of the Hawaiian Islands to explore with highlights:

- **The Big Island** - Home to Hilo, Kona, and other great cities, the largest island has some of the best known attractions. Enjoy Hawaii Volcano National Park, opportunities for shopping, and great beach parks. We have not visited the Big Island, it is on our bucket list.
- **Oahu** - Visit important sites such as Pearl Harbor, the USS Arizona Memorial, Battleship Missouri, and famous Waikiki beach, to name a few favorites.
- **Kaua'i** - This often overlooked island features the stunning Na Pali Coast, beautiful Waimea Canyon and Rainforest, multiple waterfalls, and opportunities for activities like horseback riding. Kaua'i is our family's favorite of the Hawaiian islands.
- **Maui** - One of the most popular islands, with good reason. Enjoy Waimea Bay, Haleakala National Park, humpback whale watching, and a great launching point to explore the islands of Molokai and Lanai.

Great sites and activities not to be missed:

- **Adventure Tour** (ours was on Kaua'i) - Hawaii is the perfect setting for active pursuits, including (but not limited to) zip lining, kayaking, hiking and waterfall swimming. Several tour companies can set you up to create a package that will include every member of your family, and help work up a sweat while you tackle fun challenges together.
- **O'heo Gulch Pools** (Maui) - Known as the Seven Sacred Pools, this place of great natural beauty is an ideal spot for a dip and to slow things down. There are no shortage of beaches in Hawaii, but look beyond the sands just outside your hotel and do something special like experiencing this lush tropical setting, replete with relaxing pools and numerous waterfalls. This was a favorite for our family and a highly recommended excursion. It is a long (though very scenic) drive to get here.
- **Jagger Museum** (The Big Island) - Augment opportunities to see actual volcanoes with this museum to

volcanology. Named for famed scientist Thomas A. Jagger, this is a great way for a family to better understand the things they see on their vacation. Teach children that it is important to appreciate the sights and experiences of a great trip, rather than simply blowing through them without context.

- **Experience a Luau** (ours was on Kaua'i) - There are multiple options on all the islands (just be sure to read reviews) that allow you to enjoy Hawaiian culture at it's very best, including traditional music, dances, games, and other forms of entertainment. While some may view this as inauthentic and touristy (some are), many of these events offer authentic flame dancers and other forms of traditional excitement and are worthwhile.

- **Pearl Harbor** (Oahu) - Experience an important piece of US history. The museum strikes the kind of balance parents should strive for in exploring difficult issues from the past, holding reverence for those who made the ultimate sacrifice, while educating and allowing them to enjoy a great setting. Round out this stop with another exciting Honolulu opportunity, like a chartered sail, shopping, beach time, or even an Elvis impersonator!

- **Submarine Tour** - For something really different, try taking an underwater excursion in a submarine. There are tours run out of Kona on the Big Island, though you can likely find similar companies operating elsewhere. Enjoy the opportunity to savor the underwater sights rather than rush them, to talk with your children while you observe fish, and to level the playing field for children young and old alike.

Things to Note:

Hawaiian tourist sites and "real Hawaii" are quite different. You can choose to spend your whole vacation within the comforts of an all-inclusive resort, or venture beyond to mix with the locals. Almost anything you can do in a resort may be enjoyed for cheaper in local facilities - from swimming and surfing, to golf and food. This is especially true as compared to other island locales considering the lack of a language barrier. Also keep in mind that while you won't have to change your money, things will cost more here. The island location means that many essentials need to be flown or shipped in, and cost a lot more than they do at home, including gas for your rental car. Budget accordingly.

England

About:

Merry old England, in the United Kingdom, offers a great European nation with a rich history and a spot of that great British class. Familiar sights like Parliament, Big Ben, and the Tower of London will allow families to experience the familiar in a new and exciting way.

The connection between the United States and Great Britain has led to an ongoing cultural exchange that makes it feel like a home away from home - while still offering fun and excitement in a new setting.

The Value of Visiting:

England is a great way to launch a family's first foray into international travel. The omnipresence of the English language and familiar customs will make the transition easier for kids, while many decidedly European elements will help it feel different enough to be special. From the moment you step off the plane, new sites, a rich history, and British culture will embrace you - opening up the world to a family that wants to ease into the waters of faraway places.

England's culture is accessible to children, with activities like high tea that feel familiar while still being different enough. Even driving on the "wrong" side of the road will create a memorable experience that cements the fact that you are in a new place, while keeping your children from being too overwhelmed.

England's cultural opportunities run deep, with an incredible wealth of art, theater, music and sport to enjoy. See the places and works that have made England great, as well as a treasure trove of great pieces from around the world. Britain's colonial history has resulted in the consolidation of ideas from around the world making their way back to the motherland.

Some Exciting Highlights:

Our experience in England has been limited to **London**. This is not because the rest of England (and the other parts of Great Britain including Wales, Scotland, and Northern Ireland) doesn't have anything to offer. In fact, we encourage other families to see London, while taking the time to push further into surrounding areas, and the rest of the nation. We have just not had the opportunity to push further out than London yet.

Other cities to enjoy *outside* of London:

- **Manchester** - Experience a wealth of 19th century history, the home of famed football club Manchester United, and The Lowry.

- **Windsor** - An easy day trip from London, Windsor Castle is an amazing exploration of the past and a charming town.

- **Stratford-upon-Avon** - The birthplace of Shakespeare also houses stunning gardens, canals, and yes, theater.

- **Glastonbury** - Dive into medieval times and mythology in the home of King Arthur, with a famous abbey and cathedrals.

- **Keswick** - A famous lake presents great opportunities for camping and outdoor pursuits.

- **Dover** - Brimming with history, the famous Cliffs of Dover are accompanied by great castles and lighthouses.

- **Bristol** - A younger presence encourages street art, music, great cycling, and opportunities for night activities.

- **Brighton** - Beaches and seaside resorts offer opportunities to relax, while music and theater keep it interesting.

- **Chester** - This centerpiece of the Roman Empire offers chances to explore the history of that era, explore canals, and enjoy some top-notch shopping.

Great sites and activities to enjoy in London:

- **The Tower of London** - This one time prison is now a major tourist attraction, and a great one to visit with kids. Engaging tour guides help the past come to life. The Crown Jewels are another great feature here, and sure to delight children of all ages.

- **Oompa Loompa Tea at the Chesterfield Hotel** - This twist on the classic British high tea will offer an engaging option for children, and provide fun mixed with tradition. We recommend this option, where kids not into the tea can opt for milkshakes and the like. This activity features a healthy selection of sweets to make sure that tea time is something everyone can get excited about.

- **Buckingham Palace** - While it may seem like an obvious choice, it needs to be said that this is simply a great choice for anyone of any age. The State Rooms are beautiful, and you should go with the optional audio tour to make sure you get the most out of the experience. The full tour may take over 2 hours, but is well worth the time. Pay attention to their website to see if certain areas are closed for state functions, and plan around these closures.

- **The British Museum** - This famous museum has an *extensive* collection including over 8 million pieces. This is a place that the vast reach of the British Empire, and its longstanding commitment to history and tradition, really shines. Experience art and antiquities from across the world and the entire span of mankind. This place is huge, and popular exhibits like the Rosetta Stone can have long lines. We recommend researching on their website and choosing a few exhibits (and a few backups) in advance and tackling this sprawling facility with a definite plan to maximize your time.

- **See a Show** - The rich tradition of theater is alive and well throughout the country. London has a number of great venues, and shows are a great way to enjoy something fun and different with your kids. Whether you go for an authentic Shakespearean production at the famous Globe Theater, or something more like a Broadway experience at one of the modern venues - this is a great way to wind down a busy day.

Things to Note:

Driving on the other side of the road is one of those things that vary a lot from person to person. Some see it as no big deal, and others struggle with it for some time. If your trip is short, the time spent adjusting might occupy the entire vacation and interfere with your ability to enjoy yourself. This will be hardest in London and other major cities. Have a backup plan if you rent a car, so as to not waste your vacation feeling trapped and uncomfortable with your transportation situation. In London, the underground (subway) is a great way to get around. Service is frequent, and signs are easy to follow. It is also worth noting that England is modern enough that your credit card will work just about anywhere, with street fairs and other cash-only operations being the only place you are likely to *need* cash. This option to use credit can save the time, cost, and hassle of exchanging currency (save a small emergency amount) if you plan on sticking to the cities.

Italy

About:

Italy is one of Europe's most popular tourist destinations. The center of the Roman Empire, a major force in Mediterranean trading, and the home of some of the greatest artists of all time - Italy offers a window into some of the greatest history and culture in the world.

Italy is a large country for Europe, and its development from a collection of city-states means that everything from language to customs vary greatly from one place to another. There are many Italys to visit, and one can choose to focus on a certain city, region, or to create their own "best of" tour that spans from north to south. While we have already spoken about Tuscany, Italy has other great places to see and visit both north and south of this famed home to renaissance art.

The Value of Visiting:

Italy not only has a wealth of history and a unique cross-section of culture - it has the kind that are easy to get kids excited about. The fact that familiar foods like pizza and pasta are king here makes an easy bridge to push children further to explore new and exciting options. Similarly, while sites like the Colosseum or St. Peter's may already be known to kids, their feeling of familiarity will make it easier to encourage them to expand their horizons and open up to new ideas. In short, Italy meets you halfway and allows the "job" of getting kids excited to quickly give way to family fun.

It is hard to walk 10 feet in Italy without bumping into something of artistic or historical significance.

It is also worth mentioning that a trip to Rome can result in an opportunity for a "bonus" country in the form of Vatican City. Home to an incredible collection of art and history, the idea that this walled enclave is its own country, likely smaller than your own home town, will fascinate children and allow you to rack up more locations on your list of places experienced together.

Some Exciting Highlights:

Our experiences in Italy have been limited to the city of **Rome**. We will share some real experiences from there, but also talk briefly about other great cities and what can be expected on a visit there. The cities of Tuscany (namely Florence and Pisa) have been omitted here, but information can be found in the earlier section on Tuscany.

Other cities to enjoy *outside* of Rome (and Tuscany):

- **Venice** - St Mark's Square is one of the best known locales in the city of picturesque canals, and relaxing gondola rides.

- **Milan** - One of the fashion capitols of the world (upscale shopping abounds) is also the home of the Duomo and the famous painting "The Last Supper."
- **Naples** - The birthplace of the pizza, also home to some amazing history and the Royal Palace of Naples.
- **Sorrento** - Perched on a hilltop overlooking the Bay of Naples, this stunning beach resort town offers relaxation and amazing views.
- **Amalfi** - Along the stunning coast of the same name, this charming area features an old-word feel, beaches, hiking, and historic cathedrals.
- **Pompeii** - Home of Mount Vesuvius and the famed volcanic eruption, the archaeological site is a fascinating look at the past. Any easy day trip from Naples.
- **Genoa** - Home of the Renzo Piano, a palace, great museums and rich history; all set on a beautiful harbor.
- **Palermo** - Churches, a palace, cathedrals, markets, art, and theater are all alive and well here.
- **Lake Como** - A great place to get active, with windsurfing, kayaking, hiking, swimming, and more - all set on beautiful lakes. Agritourism is also growing here for a different kind of trip.
- **Syracuse** - Explore the history of Ancient Greece with a great amphitheater, ancient temples, and more.

Great sites and activities to enjoy in Rome:

- **The Pantheon** - This fascinating look at the religious life of the ancient Romans offers a fun chance to explore not only the beliefs, but the actual construction of the site and all that it entailed.
- **Piazza Navona** - This location, which started out as a competition arena in ancient Rome, is now a popular city square. This is a great place to stop for some food, a sweet treat like gelato, and a little shopping. When indoor shopping malls can be substituted for outdoor

areas like this one, it allows for more of a cultural experience while you enjoy the things you need to do.

- **Basilica di San Clemente** - With three levels, each from a different time period, this site allows you to see the progression of Rome over the years in a unique way. On top of that, the experience is free of charge (or you can pay 5 Euros for a special tour) making it a great fun and affordable option in Rome.
- **Borghese Gallery** - One of Rome's premiere art galleries, the 22 room size of this venue make it a nice, manageable option for families. Rather than overwhelming yourself with too many options and not enough time, tackle this smaller museum for amazing art in a quainter setting.
- **The Colosseum** - No visit to Rome would be complete without it. This stunning site of ancient Roman games and events is simply amazing to behold. Any family interested in history and/or architecture will love this spot. It may get boring for very young children after a while, so plan accordingly.
- **The Jewish Ghetto** - Established in 1555 in the Rione Sant'Angelo, this enclave within the city was originally walled and had three gates locked at night. With a long history and great cultural significance to explore, this often overlooked stop is a great one for families.
- **The Trevi Fountain** - Designed by Italian architect Nicola Salvi and completed by Pietro Bracci, this famed fountain is one of Rome's most popular attractions (with good reason). Visit at night for a special treat (it is gorgeous all lit up), and enjoy a great spot for people watching and feeling the energy of the city (at any time).

Things to Note:

Cash is much more common in Italy than other places in the developed world. Don't assume that every place will take your credit card, and be sure to have plenty on hand to avoid an issue. Finally, Italy has one of the highest rates of petty crime in Europe. While not something to be overly concerned about, be careful with your wallet and protect yourself against pickpockets.

Italy can also be experienced on a cruise - either one with a focus on Italy, or a Mediterranean cruise that stops in other countries like France and Spain. This can be a great option for families who want the all-inclusive experience, and/or the convenience of touring Italy without having to worry about transporting yourself.

Greece

About:

Lying on the southeastern part of the European continent, the unique composition of Greece provides incredible variety, with islands large and small that each has their own special character, and preserves local culture and history in fascinating ways.

The history of Greece is long and storied. The ancient Greek empire gave birth to so many great ideas that helped shape the modern world. Some of the greatest ideas of philosophy, science, art, and literature can trace their roots back to Greece. This is also the home of the first Olympic Games, and a rich tradition of sport demonstrates the Greek commitment to excel at everything they do.

Modern Greece has seen its share of economic troubles and internal problems, but is still alive and well for tourists. With so many things to see and to do, an exploration of one of its great cities, or many of them, is sure to bring a lot to your family travel experience.

The Value of Visiting:

Greece enjoys the best of Mediterranean life, as well as its own body of water, the Aegean Sea. Throughout history, the water has allowed for the free exchange of ideas here, as well as the import and export of goods as well as culture. For a family vacation today, it means that the unique opportunity to island hop provides an extra fun way to see and to do more. Consider incorporating a cruise or chartered boat as either a part of, or a basis for your entire vacation. Many companies run Aegean cruises that help you to effortlessly tour some portion of the mainland and a collection of islands without having to make other arrangements. Of course, if you are willing to make your own way, boats and planes can be combined to create a unique tour that takes in some of the islands as well as the mainland stops.

All this water also means that Greece has amazing beaches, with stunning white sands and crystal blue waters. Spend time at the coast to enjoy great food and fun, in between your exploration of history and culture.

Some Exciting Highlights:

Our time in Greece involved a good amount of hopping around, another reason we recommend this as a format for your trip. Here are the places we went, and some highlights of what we enjoyed there:

Athens

- **The Acropolis** - With new archaeological discoveries still being made here, this ancient meeting place of Athens is a must-see for families. We recommend getting a guide to help get the most out of it. There is some climbing involved in the experience, something to be aware of with the very young or physically limited.
- **Evripidou Street Market** - A great option for those interested in less "touristy" and more local experiences. Shop where the locals shop and experience real and authentic wares.
- **Asteria Balux Beach** - A great place to wind down a busy day in Athens. Not nearly as stunning as some of the island beaches, but a clean and manageable beach.

Crete

- **Heraklion Archaeological Museum** - This museum spans over 5,500 years of Greek history, from the Neolithic period through Roman times, with a special focus on the important Minoan civilization. The exhibits are fascinating, and set you up to explore the important Palace of Knossos.

- **Aquaworld Aquarium** - For a nice change of pace on an island *packed* with history, have some fun at this modern aquarium that allows for fun and interactivity.

Delphi

- **Mount Parnassus** - 8,000 feet over Delphi, this mountain offers some of the most amazing views of the area, with scenic vistas of the countryside and olive groves north of the Gulf of Corinth. In the winter months, skiers and snowboarders often visit the two major ski centers, Kellaris and Fterolaka. In the warmer months, the broad network of trails makes this mountain a hiker's paradise.

- **Archaeological Museum of Delphi** - See the Delphic sanctuary, the site of the most famous ancient Greek oracle. The museum's collections include architectural sculptures and statues reflecting its religious, artistic, and political activities from the 8th century until the period of late antiquity.

Santorini

- **Lignos Folklore Museum** - The museum is housed in a traditional 1861 Santorini cave house that was untouched by the earthquake of 1956. Walk around the gallery to see works of famous artists inspired by Santorini and sit in the garden filled with beautiful trees and flowers. Visitors of all ages will enjoy picturing what life was like in Santorini during the 1800's.

- **Megaro Gyzi Museum** - Located in one of the few family mansions still standing from the 17th century. This museum includes painting and photography exhibitions, as well as concerts, recitals, theatrical performances, lectures and film showings. The museum's permanent collections include authentic engravings, historical manuscripts, paintings and old photographs of scenic Santorini, along with a collection of Santorini's volcanic rock strata.

Corfu

- **Main Market in the Old City** - Narrow, winding alleys lend old world charm to a bustling marketplace that sells authentic wares to locals and tourists alike. The location along the city wall allows you to climb steps for one of the best views of the surrounding area. Spend an hour or two wandering and shopping to immerse yourself.

- **Glyfada Beach** - West of the old city of Corfu, lays a beach enjoyed by tourists and locals alike. Intermingle with the population while cooling off - an especially useful stop if visiting during the busy (and hot) summer months.

Things to Note:

Because of its location and reliance on the sea, time can be somewhat relative in Greece. Plan on arriving early and be open to leaving late for excursions, especially those involving boats. Concerns like changing winds and weather mean that the chartered sale you booked might leave a few minutes early, or late, because the operator's primary concern is (or should be) safety and not sticking to the ticket. August is the busiest season for travel in Greece. If you plan on going during the end of summer, book early and have backups for your plans. For island hopping, consider overnight ferries as a way to get you from point to point without sacrificing daylight hours in transit.

New York City

About:

Known by some as the capital of the world, New York City is one of those places that brings so many people and ideas together into one place - and makes experiencing them all a lot of fun. It was the topic of our second book for good reason, a place within the United States that allows you to explore both local and international history. It has its own unique culture as well as reflections of those from across the globe.

New York City is so many things at once, and right at your doorstep if you live in the United States.

With one of the oldest histories in all of the US, New York City has long been a place of great importance. It served as the first capital of the United States. It houses the United Nations, two of the world's largest stock exchanges, as well as the glittering lights of Times Square, the fun of Broadway, and some of the world's most amazing museums.

New York City consists of five boroughs, and even many locals can get so caught up in Manhattan that they never look beyond to Queens, Brooklyn, Staten Island, and The Bronx. We have found tremendous value in all of them, and hope you will as well.

The Value of Visiting:

New York City is one of the most amazing places a family can visit without leaving the United States. It packs in so many activities and so much fun, while providing a very long list of opportunities for family excitement.

The five boroughs have their similarities, but also possess their own unique flavors. It is like 5 cities in one.

New York City is a place where you can expose your children to the history, food, art, and excitement. It is packed with the sort of unique experiences, cultural explorations, and good old fashioned fun that make for great family vacations. This is one of the best places to enjoy the sort of trip that this entire book is trying to promote.

Some Exciting Highlights:

The 5 boroughs and why they are fun with kids:

- **Manhattan** - The center of it all, so many possibilities, great museums, shopping, and more. Many of the locations you think of when you think "New York" are here - but many hidden gems as well.
- **The Bronx** - With more open space, this borough houses the city's most famous zoo, botanical garden, and much more.

- **Brooklyn** - Having totally reinvented itself in recent years, hip and exciting Brooklyn offers incredible cultural experiences and unique family-friendly venues.
- **Staten Island** - A long maritime history and stunning Victorian era past give way to some of the city's most underappreciated sights.
- **Queens** - One of New York City's most diverse boroughs, Queens has a little bit of everything. Enjoy great parks, rich history, and unique opportunities afforded by a sprawling amount of land and open space.

Great sites and activities to consider (and where they are):

- **Queens County Farm Museum** (Queens) - Who knew there was a working farm in Queens? We do, and this is one of many great activities we have discovered looking past the usual in NYC.
- **American Museum of Natural History** (Manhattan) - This old standby is popular for a reason. Put children toe to toe with dinosaurs, a life-size whale, and more attractions that amaze as well as educate.
- **Historic Richmond Town** (Staten Island) - This historical village pairs reenactors with well-preserved buildings and activities for kids.
- **New York Botanical Garden** (The Bronx) - Unique offerings for families help get kids excited about visiting a botanical garden. The annual Train Show each winter is an especially great way to enjoy the beauty here.
- **Brooklyn Heights Promenade** (Brooklyn) - This world-class view offers a small park and an easily accomplished stroll that allow families a chance to unwind and savor the city. Pair it with nearby historical neighborhoods and a great meal to round out a day.
- **National Museum of the American Indian** (Manhattan) - Down near Wall Street, this lesser known museum does a great job of telling the stories of the original New Yorkers.

- **Staten Island Ferry** (Staten Island-Manhattan) - This ride is some of the most fun you can have in New York City for free. Take in great views and enjoy the surrounding area the way New Yorkers have for ages.

- **Edgar Allan Poe Cottage** (The Bronx) - Explore the onetime home of this literary legend and simultaneously take a glimpse into New York City's past. A small and manageable stop, this unique opportunity is a fun lesser known NYC attraction.

- **"The Beast" Speedboat Ride** (Manhattan) - Take to the water and enjoy something truly different. Savor views of Liberty and Ellis islands as you zoom down the Hudson River. This will delight kids with a change of pace and offer views of the city that few get to enjoy.

- **Coney Island** (Brooklyn) - This onetime destination for the masses fell out of favor, but now it's back. Ride some rides visit the beach, and kick back in an amusement area that will inject some fun into your visit.

- **Sony Wonder Technology Lab** (Manhattan) - Near Central Park and other great NYC landmarks, lays this incredible interactive technology lab. Let kids explore science through robotics, motion capture technology, and more. Just be sure to reserve tickets in advance.

- **Trump Rink** (Manhattan) - Located within beautiful central park, this ice skating opportunity opens its gates from late October until late January. Rent skates, sip cocoa, and enjoy the ice while gazing up at some of NYC's most famous buildings.

Things to Note:

We find Manhattan to be a great "base of operations" and starting point, but don't sell your vacation short by limiting your time to only this popular island. The public transit system is an efficient and affordable way to get around. At the same time, it doesn't make sense for every day or every stop. Plan ahead and know which days to get around by bus and subway, and which will make more sense by cab. Each season offers incredibly different and exciting options. No single time of year is "better" than another, but look into seasonal offerings and take advantage of them.

We have written extensively about New York in our guidebook **"New York City for Families: 5 Boroughs in 7 Days."** More information about it follows at the end of this book, as well as on RealFamilyTrips.com.

Part III

Travel Tips And Hacks

Years of traveling have taught us a thing or two. While great vacations don't have to be as hard as some people make them out to be, they aren't necessarily simple. Travel, especially family travel, has its own set of rules, and its own concerns. It is a skill to be learned much like any other. The good news is that you can save time, effort, and frustration by borrowing from our experiences.

This is our travel almanac. We have packed this section with real, practical advice about some of the most necessary aspects and concerns regarding family travel. Here you will find answers to the big questions, as well as thoughts about certain intricacies of touring. This is our compendium to a great trip, intended to aid you in logistics related to both the before and during of any family adventure.

So far we have spoken about the philosophy of traveling with kids, as well as the fine art of choosing a destination. In this section of the book we compile information gained over years of actual travel, advice from experts, and close to two decades of family vacationing - to help you spend less time planning and more time doing.

Some of these chapters may contain information you already know, and others information you simply think you know. While you may have a perfectly workable knowledge of a given subject, we encourage you to read and explore the topic further. In many cases, we have discovered over time that while we knew *how* to do something, we learned a better, quicker, or more enjoyable way to travel by keeping our eyes, ears, and minds open.

Keep in mind that the travel landscape has shifted in recent years as a result of the Internet and the rise of the online travel industry. The main thing to be aware of is that a series of mergers, acquisitions and other business deals have led to a consolidation of sorts in the world of "travel deals" sites as well as the travel industry in general. These days the variations in prices may be slight, so it may not pay to spend hours browsing every travel deal site on the web. Many will have the same offerings or at least *very* similar offerings and prices. You might spend half a day searching and only end up saving about the cost of a cup of coffee. There *are* still deals to be had, but many may be last minute deals or very limited time offers. The real deals are usually time and/or location specific for the family who has a little more wiggle room in their schedule.

Some of the information here borrows from articles in the "Travel Tips" section of RealFamilyTrips.com. Some of the chapters here will provide fuel for future posts there. This section covers the bases of the most important information we have learned, and what we consider "need to know" in terms of vacationing both abroad and near home. If you are looking for more information on a given subject, or something not covered here, we recommend starting at RealFamilyTrips.com first for supplementary posts and other information.

From passports and money, to packing lists and gear - this section of our book is meant to cover information everyone needs to know. We also discuss things like apps, room upgrades, and what to do when your flight is cancelled. This information will have you feeling like an expert and better prepared for whatever comes your way. Borrow from what we have learned and become instant experts today.

Getting or Renewing a US Passport

Throughout the book so far, we have encouraged you to think bigger and better as far as your destinations. Stop thinking your children are too young for great international vacations and start thinking about how to make such trips possible. A passport is one of the first steps.

You NEED a Passport for International Travel

In almost all cases, passport and visas regulations vary by country. When you fly internationally the rule is simple, you absolutely need a passport. If you travel by land or sea, you may not *need* one, but it is the simplest option by far.

U.S. adults are expected to present at least a birth certificate or other proof of citizenship, plus a government-issued photo ID, such as a driver's license, to cross borders into Canada, Mexico, and certain islands in the Caribbean. Children traveling with accompanying adults can often get away with just a birth certificate. Some cruise lines will require you to carry a passport for the Caribbean, while others do not.

Another option for land and sea crossings is a passport card (more on this below). If you have a vacation coming up very soon and you do not have a passport for your children, you can visit http://travel.state.gov/content/passports/english/country.html and see if you can get away without having a passport (and find out what documents you will need to carry). Investing in passports is a good idea. It simplifies the process, will be good for years to come, and prepares you for new opportunities. As you begin to think about traveling better, it is a small amount of time and money relative to the benefit.

What is the Difference Between a Passport Book and a Passport Card?

Passport books are what most of us think of. The United States issues classic blue covered books, with either 28 or 52 pages that include your information and space for stamps from your destinations. Passport cards are a relatively new development.

These are identification that resembles a driver's license or other government issued cards. They are slightly cheaper than passport books both to obtain and renew, though they are valid for the same period (10 years for adults, 5 years for children under 16).

The big difference is what they can be used for. Passport cards are valid for passing between the United States and Canada, Mexico, the Caribbean, and Bermuda at land border crossings or sea ports-of-entry. They are **not valid for international travel by air.**

For families that know they will only be visiting these places for the foreseeable future, this may be a simpler and cheaper option. However, because a passport book can do everything a passport card can do and more, the traditional book is a better investment in the long run.

Do Children of Any Age Need a Passport?

Yes. Each member of your family needs their own passport, even infants. Once again, some land and sea crossings don't require one (and you can research requirements for your particular destination) but you should expect that for any international air travel, each of your children will require a passport.

Children's passports need to be renewed more often than adults ones, but also cost less. New rules have seen some cracking down on obtaining passports for children, requiring things like signatures from both parents. Don't be concerned as the process is still fairly straightforward, but plan ahead and start the process as soon as possible.

A Note About US Territories

Guam, Puerto Rico, the US Virgin Islands, and other US territories are some of the only places you can travel that do NOT require a US Passport, even if you fly. If you are looking for a more exotic trip you can take right away, consider these options.

Blank Pages, Valid Months, Visas, and Other Details

The fact that each country sets their own rules can lead to some confusion, however knowing a few simple things to look out for can save you for a lot of hassle. As much as a passport is your golden ticket to see the world, there are a few more stipulations some countries impose that mean simply having one may not be enough.

Some countries require your passport to be valid in advance of, and beyond your trip. While these rules vary greatly, the magic number is 6 months. Certain countries will not let you enter with a passport that has not been valid for at least 6 months before your date of entry, and some require it to be valid for at least 6 more months after your date of departure. For parents who already have a passport, check how long it is good for. For children or entire families looking to get your first passports, don't expect that you can necessarily use them for a particular trip right away. Check requirements for specific countries through the state department.

Similarly, having a single blank page left may not be enough.

Most countries you visit will stamp your passport on exit and entry. Some require only a single blank page to hold those stamps. Other countries may have a requirement that you have anywhere from 2-4 blank pages left before entering their country. For some time, one could obtain additional passport pages for a cost of $82 dollars, often getting same day turnaround. 2016 changes to the process will phase out this practice. If you are running out of space, check the State Department for a particular trip, but think about renewing your passport when you get to five remaining pages or less.

Standard passport books have 28 pages. If you are a frequent traveler, you can request a 52 page book for no additional charge.

Do I also need a travel visa to go abroad?

This also varies by country. Some will only require your passport, others require specialty visas. These visas cost money, can take time, and require an application. Don't assume that all you need is a passport, and check the state department website for specific information on particular destinations.

The US State Department makes finding requirements for different countries simple.

Visit www.travel.state.gov (click on "Country Specific Information," then choose your destination). You can type in a name or use a map to find your particular country. This searchable feature will tell you about visa requirements, passport specifics, and a wealth of other information, including real-time alerts. Policies change often, so check back close to your trip and plan ahead.

If you plan on driving abroad

You need to check if your US license is valid in the country you are visiting. You may need to apply for an International Driving Permit, and/or obtain a translation of your US license. Find more information at AAA's IDP website (www.aaa.com/vacation/idpf.html)

Getting a US Passport for the First Time

Where to Go

When applying for a passport for the first time, you have to apply in person. This can be done at any acceptance facility, usually a local passport authority or post office. **NOTE:** Some post office locations will require that you make an appointment, so do not assume that you can simply walk in. To find an acceptance facility near you, visit the US Department of State website (travel.state.gov).

What You Need

When you arrive at the acceptance facility, you'll need to present several documents. First, you'll need the application itself, which in almost all cases will be Form DS-11. You can print it out and hand-write your information, or fill it out online (https://pptform.state.gov/).

Then, you will need to confirm your identity and your citizenship with a piece of primary evidence (or several pieces of secondary evidence, if you can't provide primary evidence). You will also need photocopies of any identifying documents. Some documents can serve as evidence of both identity and citizenship, such as a previously issued U.S. passport or a naturalization certificate.

Also note that when it comes to passports for children, special rules apply. For children under 16 years of age, the child themselves must appear at the passport office, as well as both parents. If one parent cannot be present, then a special form is required that will need to be notarized. This consent to passport issuance, as well as documented proof of parental rights, are necessary safeguards that make getting passports for your kids a little more complicated, but far from difficult.

Here's a full list of documents that qualify as primary evidence:

- **US Citizenship**
- Previously Issued U.S. Passport
- Naturalization Certificate
- U.S. Birth Certificate
- Consular Report of Birth Abroad or Certification of Birth
- Certificate of Citizenship
- **Identification**
- Previously Issued U.S. Passport
- Naturalization Certificate
- Driver's License
- Government ID
- Military ID

Lastly, you'll need to get a passport photo taken. Technically, you can take it yourself, but there are several requirements for the picture's appearance and size, so the easiest way to get one is to go to any establishment that takes passport photos. This would include most major grocery stores or pharmacies.

How Long it Will Take

The normal turnaround is four to six weeks. But if you're in a rush, you can expedite the process for a $60 fee, and your passport should arrive within three weeks.

How Much it Will Cost

A new passport for adults costs $135. A passport for a child under 16 years old will only cost $105.

NOTE: There are some exceptions for minors, international applicants, and parents who are behind on child support.

Our Best Advice?

Plan ahead, start early, and don't let the passport be the thing that gets in the way of your trip.

How to Renew a US Passport

How long is my passport valid for?

A passport is valid for 10 years if issued when 16 years old or older, it is valid for 5 years when issued to one 15 years old and younger. Remember that because many countries require six months of validity beyond your travel dates, this means that your passport may only be effective for 9 1/2 and 4 1/2 years in the eyes of many destinations. A passport with no (or only 1-4) blank pages is a valid form of identification, but not for travel.

Renewing your passport by mail

The easiest way to renew is by mail; however you must meet certain requirements to be permitted to do so:

- Have an undamaged passport that can be submitted with your application.
- Received your passport within the past 15 years.

- You were at least 16 years old when you were issued the passport *(Children under 16 years of age must always renew in person)*.
- Passport has your current name, or you can provide legal documentation of your name change (for example, a marriage certificate).

Renewing your passport in person

If ANY of these requirements are not met, you will have to renew in person (also the procedure for children under 16 years of age and first time passport obtainers) by making an appointment with a local authorized organization. These include certain post offices, clerk of court offices, and select libraries.

Visit the State Department page to find the nearest location to you. Look at the above list of ID forms (in the first time passport section) for an idea of what to bring in terms of identification. In-person renewals and first time applications follow the same guidelines.

Procedure for regular and expedited renewals

Passport renewals by mail are available on a regular and an expedited track. For regular renewal (approximately 4-6 weeks) follow this procedure:

- Fill Out Form DS-82: Application For A U.S. Passport by Mail, available to complete by hand or to type in and print online.
- If completing by hand, be sure to use black ink. Also be sure to sign and date the form on the first page. This is a common mistake that can delay your application.
- Submit your current passport (you will get it back, sometimes shipped separately from new passport).
- Submit one new passport photo deemed acceptable by State Department standards (they also have an online tool for scanning your own photos). Most photo shops and places that develop film can do this for a small fee.

- Send the applicable fee (check made out to US Department of State or money order only, cash is not accepted by mail) double check to see current passport fees, however as of August 2015, you can expect to pay $110 for a regular passport renewal, $140 for both the passport card and book, and an additional $60 for expediting the process.
- Submit a certified copy of your marriage certificate or court order if your name has changed.
- Mail everything in a secure envelope. It is recommended not to fold the forms, so use a large, flat envelope and not a smaller, letter sized one. The envelope should be padded and waterproof.

Mail everything to:

National Passport Processing Center
P.O. Box 90155
Philadelphia, PA 19190-0155

NOTE: Renewals by mail can only be sent to US and Canadian addresses. If living abroad you must renew in person at the nearest U.S. Embassy or U.S. Consulate.

For those in a hurry, or with a trip coming up very soon, expedited passport renewal is available for an additional fee. **This can get you your passport in approximately 2-3 weeks.** All the instructions are the same as above, however you add an additional $60 fee for expediting, and clearly write "EXPEDITE" on the front of the envelope you mail in. The address is also different.

For expedited passport renewal, mail everything to:

National Passport Processing Center
P.O. Box 90955
Philadelphia, PA 19190-0955

You can check the status of your renewal online after submitting (https://passportstatus.state.gov) to make sure everything is on track.

Your lifeline

Have a question not answered here? Call **(877) 487-2778** to speak live with someone who can answer your questions about your passport renewal or first time application.

A Guide to Online Resources for Travel Advice

Part of being the best resource we can be is identifying other places where you can find information that will be worthwhile in planning your next vacation.

The following FREE online resources can help you to plan a trip, discover information about a particular destination, and much more. You should always take advantage of all the opportunities available to you, and the state department and other government agencies are happy to share great advice to help you travel smarter and safer.

Traveler's Checklist

Website:
http://travel.state.gov/content/passports/english/go/checklist.html

Provided by the US State Department, this handy guide covers issues related to health, safety, documentation, packing and more - to serve as a go-to final prep checklist for families before leaving on vacation. All the excitement of getting away can lead to forgetting that one important thing you need. This list will help you go beyond just packing everything, to remind you to make preparations for emergencies, as well as medical conditions and more.

The Traveler's Guide to Preparing, Maintaining and Securing Your Home

Website: www.mortgagecalculator.org/helpful-advice/home-security-while-traveling.php

Leaving the home for any length of time means certain preparations need to be made. This resource is a useful checklist for making sure your home is at its safest and most efficient while you are away. Locking doors, unplugging appliances, and other considerations are arranged in an easy to reference format. Make sure you have everything covered so that a great vacation isn't soured by returning home to realize you forgot something that will cost you time, money, or leave you scrambling to catch up.

Travel and Health: General Precautions

Website: www.who.int/ith/precautions/en/

The World Health Organization has prepared a comprehensive guide to things you should know before setting off on vacation. This guide is packed with great information, some of which you likely already know, and other facts that may surprise you. Learn about water safety, staying healthy, and looking out for easy to prevent illnesses while traveling (especially abroad).

Your Survival Guide to Safe and Healthy Travel

Website: wwwnc.cdc.gov/travel/page/survival-guide

The CDC is another organization that has put together a guide to protecting your family's health while traveling. Besides a great checklist and links to relevant articles, for the busy pre-traveler, they also have a podcast you can listen to while on your next commute. This will provide great tips on how to be proactive about keeping your family healthy while vacationing.

The Adventure Road Trip Planner

Website: www.nationalgeographic.com/adventure/road-trips/index.html

Actively planning, or at least considering, a road trip for your next family vacation? This great guide from the folks at National Geographic suggests some fantastic routes, has tips on how to find cheaper gas and food, as well as a number of other great resources for getting the most out of this exciting type of family vacation.

U.S. National Park Service: Park Locator

Website: www.nps.gov/findapark/index.htm

As we have already discussed, national parks make for exciting and educational family trips. There are more than you may be aware of, and a great park may be closer than you think - or on your way to another great destination. Whether it is a stop on a road trip, or your primary destination, this guide can help you start gathering information when a national park visit sounds appealing to your clan.

Find Free Wireless While Traveling

Website: www.scratchwireless.com/pad/free-wifi/

WiFi access can be important while traveling. Whether it is to stay in touch, upload photos, or plan your next day's adventure - staying connected is more important than ever. While more airports and other locations are offering installed tablet access, and more hotels are making their WiFi freely available, finding connectivity away from home is important. This handy resource will help you stay online when you need to.

Shots, Inoculations, Safety, and Insurance

Traveling with your children means that you have the best possible companions, but it also means you are touring around with your greatest resource in tow. Kids are precious, and travel can introduce risks and concerns that may not exist at home. Traveling to a new and different place simply means new and different concerns arise, and some planning for your health and safety needs to be part of your preparation.

Some of these issues will boil down to common sense, while others only become obvious after years of traveling and practical experience. Still other concerns become things you actually *need* to do in order to travel to certain countries, and knowing your options as well as the expectations will help you have a trip that runs as smoothly as possible.

You may need certain shots or inoculations to enter a given country

Much like passport and visa requirements, the need to get a particular vaccine is up to the country you are traveling to. In this case, if you fail to obtain the shot or produce documentation of the procedure, you could be denied entry even after making the long flight overseas.

Beyond the shots and inoculations *required* by the country you are visiting, strong recommendations may exist. You should also loop your family doctor in before an exotic trip, especially in regards to your younger children. For tropical environments, antimalarials are common. See what government and medical professionals recommend, and follow their advice - it is for your own good.

To check requirements for a specific country you plan on visiting, use the same US State Department resource that lets you check passport and visa requirements:

http://travel.state.gov/content/passports/english/country.html

You might also want to consider calling and checking with the embassy of the country you plan on visiting to confirm current entry requirements. These can change with time, and immigration officials won't care that you checked a single website. It is on you to be sure of required vaccines, so call ahead.

For parents looking to play it safe, and go beyond just required vaccines, check the websites for the CDC (wwwnc.cdc.gov/travel/page/vaccinations.htm) and WHO (www.who.int/en/) to see what they recommend for a given country.

Traveling with prescription medications

If you or your children take any prescription medications, you will need to do a little extra planning ahead. Obtain a letter from your physician, describing your medical condition and any medications taken, including generic names. Carry this with you, and be sure to travel with your medications in their original containers and with clear labels (don't just have an unmarked pill box). This will help you avoid issues where medications are confiscated because their need or natures are unidentifiable.

Some medications may be illegal in certain countries under their laws, even if your US doctor prescribed them legitimately. Be sure to double check with the embassy of the country you are visiting to be clear on the rules, and make other arrangements with your doctor in case of a problem. You don't want to run into issues in which your prescriptions are considered illegal narcotics, or you are unexpectedly without essential medication because of confusion.

Medical Insurance Abroad

Know *before* you go. Not all medical insurance policies cover care abroad. You may not be planning on seeing a doctor while away, but unexpected things happen. It could be an accident suffered during an activity, or catching a bug from something ingested or encountered.

Call your insurance company and see exactly what services are covered overseas. If you do have coverage, make sure to carry both insurance cards (as proof of coverage) and a printed claim form or two, as you cannot count on locals to know how to work with your foreign insurance.

If your insurance coverage doesn't work abroad, you may be able to arrange for a short period of extended coverage.

NOTE: Many health insurance companies will pay what they call "customary and reasonable" hospital costs abroad. At the same time, very few will pay for your medical evacuation back to the United States in case of a real emergency. Medical evacuation costs can be astronomical, depending on your location and what happened.

For this reason, and in case your insurance simply won't cover anything outside the US, we recommend the following:

The importance of family travel insurance

For serious travelers, and those serious about their family's health and safety, purchasing travel insurance can be a great idea. Policies exist that cover health and emergency care, as well as bookings and other concerns. Travel insurance can be a comprehensive way to hedge your bets and protect your family at the same time.

While often overlooked by many families, buying insurance for your trip may be one of the most important things you can do. It may help save you money and even a life, by covering you for many worst case as well as common occurrences, depending on the terms of the policy you buy.

Logistics

The fact is, things happen. Travel insurance may provide reimbursement for bookings if you have to cancel (or come home early) because a family member becomes ill, the State Department advises that a destination is unsafe, or you unexpectedly lose a job. Besides specific provisions like the ones mentioned, you may consider purchasing "cancel for any reason" coverage, though it is more costly and you'll see far less of your money back. In any event, travel insurance may be the best, or only, way you see *any* of your money again if the unexpected forces you to change your travel plans.

Illness/Injury

While it is every parent's worst nightmare that something should happen to a family member while on vacation, or any time for that matter, things do happen. While medical expenses can cost a pretty penny back home, when traveling abroad they can be significantly more. If you're in a remote enough area you may need helicopter extraction to get to an appropriately equipped hospital, and air ambulance bills can easily run in the $100,000 range. To avoid very large medical bills, insurance may be your best friend when traveling to places where the nearest hospital is more than a cab ride away.

How To Obtain Travel Insurance

There are three main ways to get covered: through certain credit cards, with an annual policy, and through package policies purchased for individual trips.

- **Credit cards** may cover a number of the more standard occurrences like lost bags and rental cars, as well as the most extreme situations like accidental death or dismemberment. This is one of many reasons to use your credit card, as opposed to a debit card, for booking trips.

- **Annual policies** may cover things like medical care and are especially valuable for covering gaps left by your home health insurance. Before leaving the country, check if your health insurance policy covers international care or not. If they do not, you can enroll in an annual travel insurance policy to fill in the blanks. This is also a great option for families who travel frequently, as you can simply renew your annual policy and eliminate one thing from your list of steps to take in planning each trip you take. NOTE: Annual policies are not typically meant for those who do not take a number of trips each year.

- **Packages** purchased directly from travel insurers and customized for individual trips are the best bet for the most comprehensive coverage. Besides the advantages of tailor-making a policy for your vacation and family, they offer coverage for a greater number of eventualities than the other options. Allianz Travel Insurance and Travel Guard are among the companies with competitive rates and years of experience.

This is One Place Not to Cut Corners

The latest statistics show only about 29% of travelers who could have used insurance had it. Don't let your family be in that group. Be sure to read all the terms of the policy, including the fine print, so you understand what is and is not covered by the policy you buy. Policies differ widely in their coverage, so be sure to ask rather than assume.

If you need a doctor abroad

If someone in your family has a medical condition that requires a physician, you can find a list of doctors abroad through the American Board of Medical Specialists.

Website: www.certificationmatters.org/is-your-doctor-board-certified.aspx

In case of almost any emergency overseas

It pays to have information for the local embassy and consulate. Embassies and consulates are different from one another in their general duties, but for the traveling family their roles are fairly interchangeable. An embassy is generally home to an ambassador, and concerned with diplomatic duties in addition to administrative ones. A consulate is more specifically concerned with the lives of citizens and procedural duties, though these issues can be addressed by both. As far as your family is concerned - go with whoever is closest.

For a guide to US embassies and consulates abroad, visit the Bureau of Consular Affairs online. You can find the lists under the "American Citizens Services" heading.

Website: www.usembassy.gov/

Depending on where you are traveling, we think it is a good idea to take the time to research in advance and have a phone number and address written down to pack with you.

Print out copies to give to your children, and explain to them that this is a place they can go for help if they get separated. An embassy or consulate is there to serve, and your primary resource for dealing with issues while away - don't be afraid to use them.

You should also register with the U.S. State Department before your trip, in order to make it easier for the U.S. government to help you in an emergency abroad.

<u>Website</u>: https://travelregistration.state.gov

Preventative care is still your best tool

With some of the bases regarding emergencies covered, it is important to note that the best thing you can do to keep your family safe and healthy abroad is to be proactive. Whether you are vacationing across the globe or near to home, for a day or a week, the nature of travel and changes in schedule can upset the body.

The good news is that much of this can be avoided by following these few simple tips. We know vacation is exciting, and a chance to change things up and indulge a little. However, by moderating and keeping an eye on a few key factors, you and your children will be better able to enjoy vacation, with less fear of spending it in bed with health issues.

8 Quick Tips to Protect Your Health While Traveling:

1. <u>Let Your Body Catch Up</u>: Your body needs rest. Whether exhausted from jet lag, or simply worn out after a long journey, you're at your most vulnerable when tired. Children are especially susceptible and need time to regroup.

2. <u>Keep Hydrated</u>: Water is immensely important when traveling. The actual trip will take a lot out of you. Active vacations demand more of your body, while relaxing on a beach may be low impact but heat will still deplete your body's stores of water. The excitement of traveling can make it easy to forget, but water is your friend. Keeping hydrated will also help combat the effects of jetlag.

3. <u>Mind Your Water</u>: For certain destinations it is well known not to drink the local tap water. You should always be cautious in any less developed areas. However, even if the water isn't flagged as dangerous, you may still do better staying with bottled. Local tap water may have elements your system isn't used to that don't upset locals but can interfere with your body's equilibrium.

4. <u>And Don't Forget</u>: Ice is made with local water, so you would do well to forgo ice outside of hotels and well known restaurants. It can also be easy to forget about water when brushing teeth. Even if you spit it out, in some locations using tap water while brushing can result in enough time in your mouth to upset stomachs.

5. <u>Ease Into New Food</u>: The excitement of a new locale and exotic food might have you clamoring to try everything in sight, but you'd do better to take your time. Start with restaurants and established locations for the first day as your body adjusts. Don't try too many new things at once as you don't know how your body will react to one, much less a combination of, new ingredients and flavors.

6. <u>Use Your Judgement</u>: While it is always important to keep an eye on what you feed yourself and your family, be especially vigilant while away from home. Stick to more reputable restaurants and ask hotel concierges for recommendations. If you choose to eat at a local food stall or street cart, look for things like proper storage of seafood and other ingredients, boiling water as opposed to simply warming it, cleanliness of the staff and clean knives/cutting surfaces. If it looks suspect, move on.

7. <u>Don't Overdo It</u>: While vacation is certainly a time to treat yourself and your family a bit, don't go overboard. You may choose to eat things you wouldn't normally eat, or to indulge with a bit more than usual, but do so within realistic boundaries. Choose a single meal to really splurge as opposed to simply overdoing all of

them. Also try to eat and drink more conservatively when trying new things.

8. <u>Prepare For The Simple Things</u>: You know your family better than anyone, and have the ability to anticipate common things. If someone is susceptible to motion sickness or fatigue, don't push them too far. It also pays to travel with some basic remedies like Dramamine for motion sickness, aspirin, and something for stomach related issues. Identify local pharmacies and hospitals early in the trip so that you are prepared in the case of real illness. Don't use any of the aforementioned products unless you are accustomed to them, and please consult with your doctor before using anything new.

Follow these simple tips and you'll be much less likely to have a family member down for the count and miss out on your great vacation. Look out for each other and you'll be taking family photos instead of being stuck in bed.

Some additional thoughts regarding cruises and the norovirus

NOTE: Many of these tips are also good ideas for all-around travel, and make good additions to the general checklist for illness prevention.

Cruise vacations are magical opportunities for fun-filled family travel and allow you to create lifelong memories. The last thing you want is for those memories to be of you or your children laid up in your stateroom bed turning green.

Whether you are cruising the Caribbean, touring Europe, Alaska, or really anywhere a ship may take you, certain common concerns ring true. Between the exotic food and foreign locales, and the nature of being at sea itself, gastrointestinal distress is a constant concern. Cruising is an incredible way for families to see the world, and a few simple and practical adjustments can help keep you healthier.

Here is a Handy Checklist for Staying Healthy at Sea:

- <u>Wash Your Hands</u> frequently, with warm and soapy water. This is both the simplest and the most important tip for remaining healthy at sea. Cruise ships have a lot of communal areas, as well as a lot of opportunities to enjoy food and beverage. You should wash your hands before and after meals (or snacks), as well as after touching public fixtures like doorknobs and using public facilities. Don't just rely on hand sanitizer, as it is not as effective as warm water and soap.

- Keep an Eye on the Buffet. Cruises often serve big meals buffet style and this can potentially cause problems. Be sure to keep an eye on foods that are grabbed by hand rather than utensils, as well as other passengers near you unnecessarily touching or getting close to food. You should also steer clear of anything seemingly room temperature that you know is meant to be served either hot or cold. While some foods may be exciting to see and to eat, play it safe and stick to things you know are safe in a buffet. Save foods better made to-order for sit down meals at other points in the trip.

- Do Some Research Ahead of leaving for the trip. Cruises require some additional considerations, considering that you are entrusting your lodging, food, and safety to a single company. You can find information on recent outbreaks of norovirus and similar concerns via the CDC's Vessel Sanitation Program (www.cdc.gov/nceh/vsp/). Check the history of a ship and a cruise line before you book and only stick to those with the most reputable track records. Different itineraries are no more germ-laden than others, but certain ships may be. Also, winter cruises may be more susceptible to outbreaks just as any on-land location sees more people sick with viruses during the winter months than the summer ones.

- Use Common Sense above all else. While a cruise vacation is extraordinary, most of the things you need to stay healthy aren't. Follow the same practices you would to keep you and your family healthy on dry land as you do at sea and you should be fine. Don't let excitement distract you from good personal health and hygiene.

A note about pool safety

While it may seem matter of fact, it is important to note: Not all pools are manned by lifeguards. Furthermore, in the event of an emergency, you cannot rely on the notion that other staff will possess the proper training to handle an emergency, especially of a medical nature.

Every once in a while a tragic story comes to our attention (no doubt you see them as well) that reminds us of this fact, and we felt the need to reiterate it here. Vacation is a time to relax and enjoy, however there is no "break" from us having to carefully observe our children, especially when they are involved in an activity with potential risks.

Keeping Children Safe When Swimming Without a Lifeguard

This general note can apply to a variety of locations including hotels, resorts, and cruise ships. If there is no lifeguard on duty, or a sign saying not to expect one, they mean it! It is also not good enough to assume that in the absence of a lifeguard, other staff will be able to cover their duties in an emergency. Just because someone is stationed at or near a pool does not mean they are trained in CPR or water rescue.

When there is no lifeguard or other supervisory staff, it is also important to be the one to ensure your children follow the applicable rules of the pool area. Make sure they are not running, jumping, or diving in areas where it is not allowed.

Don't assume that someone else will be able to take care of it, take responsibility for your children and their safety.

Your family should enjoy using pools, water features, playground equipment, or other facilities. But use discretion and keep a watchful eye on children as they play. Please be aware of the rules and the type of staff on hand.

Traveling with disabilities

Families with disabled children should be aware that there are a number of additional resources available to help plan a trip that allows you to participate in as much as possible, and travel with the peace of mind that considerations can and will be made to ensure maximum comfort.

Preparation will be especially critical here, and planning ahead will keep you from being left in the lurch. Speak with families who live with the same or similar disabilities for ideas on places to travel, and advice on what may be available as far as resources at a particular destination you have in mind. Also, consult your travel agent, hotel, airline, insurance agent, and anyone else important to your family and your trip, to understand the services available.

To find disabilities organizations overseas, visit MIUSA

Website: www.miusa.org/resource/tipsheet/disabilityresources

You can (and should) also reach out to the TSA and take advantage of their information and services designed to assist travelers with disabilities and medical conditions.

Website: www.tsa.gov/travelers/airtravel/disabilityandmedicalneeds/tsa_cares.shtm

Phone: 1-855-787-2227

Learn about policies, procedures, and what to expect at a security checkpoint, in order to facilitate the smoothest possible experience.

Tips on staying safe while traveling

Along with caring for your health and planning for the worst with travel insurance, you also want to make sure your trip goes uninterrupted by protecting the safety of your belongings and most importantly, your children.

Once again, a few simple tips and changes to your normal behavior will help prevent the worst, as well as provide a plan of attack in case something does happen, so that a bad situation doesn't get worse.

- Separate Your Sources of Money so that it is impossible to lose everything at once. Rather than put all of your cash and cards in your wallet, keep at least some emergency money and at least one card in a separate place, preferably stashed in a hotel safe or somewhere else on your person. While cards can be cancelled easily enough, securing a replacement while abroad isn't simple. Keeping a stash of backup money prepares you for the worst case in which you lose your wallet or it is stolen.

- <u>Keep Copies of Important Documents</u> in a safe place as well. Scan passports, visas, itineraries, and other important information and store it on your phone or tablet, and keep hard copies in a carry-on while traveling, then place them in your room safe once you arrive. Having copies ensures information isn't lost and can help in case you need an emergency replacement.

- <u>Be careful Who You Trust</u> and educate your children on the same. The world isn't some big scary place that is out to get you, but the fun of vacation may lower your inhibitions. After jumping off some cliff into the water during an adventurous outing, you may be feeling like you can take on the world. Be sure to slow down and exercise common sense. Be wary about who you accept food from outside of established restaurants (street food is fine, but use common sense and take a close look), don't follow someone down an alley in search of a deal, and don't buy tickets from someone on the street even if it is a deal. Once again, tell your children to do the same, as the excitement of a new place and unfamiliar settings may have them wanting to befriend everyone they meet. Exercise caution.

- <u>Don't Display Your Wealth</u> This is not about being paranoid, but the fact is that there is no need to wear your most expensive jewelry, wave around pricey electronics, or discuss money in the open. Leave big ticket items at home, or if you do bring them, at the hotel - unless they are really *needed* for the day's activities. Also be careful about giving money to the homeless or beggars on the street. It brings out your wallet at unnecessary times, and can be a way to identify those carrying cash and make you a target. If you want to help while away, find a place to volunteer or a reputable organization to donate to.

- **DON'T Leave Bags Unattended, DO Use Storage Lockers** if you need to set something down. When you get involved in active excursions, you may need to stow a bag or jacket to get involved. It is one thing to leave it with a guide or in a designated area within a facility, but in public places use common sense and lock up belongings if they can't stay on your person.

- **Have a Plan In Case of The Worst** for a few common situations. Set meeting places during each day and at each stop should anyone get separated. Designate a room in a museum to meet back at if a child gets lost. Identify embassies or consulates, or a route back to the hotel. At home, you may all have phones and be used to relying on them. Depending on where you go, none of you may be carrying cell phones, or it may only make sense to pay for a single phone for the whole family that you carry. It is important to have a plan for these situations, and in the case of a single phone, for your children to all have the number. Know the locations of nearby police stations, hospitals, and other safe places.

- **If You Get Mugged** or accosted, just give them what they want. This is a worst case scenario, and something that gets talked about far more than actually happens, but even on vacation, your wallet is not worth your life. Simply give up anything that is asked for.

- **Don't Assume Everything is the Same as Home** because different countries have different safety regulations than the US. Some examples include exposed wiring in a hotel room, lack of railings on stairs, and poison based traps for rodents and bugs. Do a check yourself when entering a new area before letting young children wander on their own, lest they encounter something unsafe before you do. When enjoying an activity like a boat ride, operators may allow young children to ride without a life jacket - while this may be the standard there, do what feels right to you, and request one.

- <u>Common Sense</u> is, once again, the key phrase here. Use your head, and do your best not to get too caught up in the excitement so as to overlook what matters most.

A quick note about jet lag

Those who have traveled across time zones themselves know how tough it may be to adjust to local time. This can weigh especially hard on children, and can make the first days of a trip a little more difficult.

When possible, begin adjusting your children's schedules a few days to a week ahead of time. Get them up in the morning and put them down at night just a little earlier or later, depending on the time difference at your destination. Shift by a half hour at a time, so that when you do finally arrive the switch isn't so jarring. You can save yourself a lost first day in country by planning ahead.

Sometimes it can be a good idea to plan a lighter first day of vacation when dealing with a big time difference. Don't try to pack in too many things on top of a big adjustment in schedule, as you may end up burning yourselves out and spoiling other days of the trip with tired kids (and parents!).

There's an App for That

In an age of ever-present technology, devices open up new possibilities for family travel. Vacation itself should be a time to put devices away as much as possible and be present with your family. At the same time, a bit of directed use of a phone or tablet, and the use of technology to help plan or book your trip, will make things simpler and perhaps even better.

We will speak a bit more about international cell phones and plans later in this section, but chances are you plan on at least having one phone on you if possible during a trip. Even if you opt to leave your cell phone behind, using WiFi at the hotel or at designated public spots means you can use a computer or tablet for apps and websites from time to time.

Another benefit of incorporating technology into your vacation to some small degree is the opportunity it affords you to involve your kids. Kids tend to be much more tech savvy and involved than parents, and bonding over the use of apps and devices can be a way to bridge the gap. It may be that kids help you to discover new possibilities and apps, or that a child is the designated navigator or photographer. Even if a particular app is not a strictly "need to use" proposition, if it helps get your kids more involved and excited, this is a good thing.

Apps and phones have their place in a family vacation. They can help you to do everything from take and organize photos, to provide background information while you tour, and help you navigate an unfamiliar area. Some aid in the planning or booking process, while others provide help "on the ground" and aid your touring process directly. Take advantage of all kinds, and find new ways to enhance your vacation.

The ever expanding nature of technology means that new apps are released literally every day. We won't pretend to be able to present a comprehensive list, and even if we could, soon after this book comes out, great new things will have hit the market.

The following list represents a "best of" current apps we are aware of and have experienced. Much like the locations of our vacation "bucket list," this is not meant to be an end, but a beginning. Read about the apps listed here and use them to jog your thought process, and learn about some of the things that are possible when using a smart device while traveling. Check often, involve your kids in the discovery of new apps, and try out things just for the fun of it. We hope this section will open your eyes and expand your possibilities - you just may find something here or at some point down the road that changes the way you travel for the better.

Our "Starting Place" Guide to Discovering the Power of Travel-Related Apps

The Smart Traveler app

What is it?

Created by the US State Department, this free app provides easy access to frequently updated official country information, U.S. embassy locations, travel warnings/alerts, maps, and more. Users can access entry and exit requirements and safety tips for countries all around the globe, right at their fingertips.

The information about visas, safety, and health discussed in the last chapter can all be at your fingertips with this simple app. As a fun feature, you can also shake your phone, to learn about a random country.

Inside you will also find a handy guide to travel alerts and warnings, with up to the minute updates, and a simple and easy way to enroll in the Smart Traveler Enrollment Program (STEP). STEP allows embassies to better assist you while traveling abroad, and registers your trip so someone knows if you don't show up for your return flight.

How does it work?

When the app is opened, you will be directed to an alphabetical list of countries and areas. Select a country or area you're interested in or type the name in the search bar at the top of the screen. After the country is chosen, you will be directed to a fact sheet. Here you will see all sorts of information about the country. Some of it is very specific and may not be of interest to many families, but for teens it offers an opportunity to learn a bit about international relations. At the bottom of the fact sheet are links with additional information about the country. These links include human rights reports, travel and business information, narcotics control reports, history of U.S. political relations with that country, and several other useful details that travelers might want to be aware of. This type of information is a great way to begin to educate your children about international relations, economics, and many other topics they may find interesting.

Where can I get it?

Available for FREE on iOS and Android devices.

GateGuru

What is it?

GateGuru puts airport information at your fingertips. Quickly and easily find day-of travel assistance with airport amenity information, security line wait times, airport tips, maps, and several other helpful services.

Learn if your flight is on time, what restaurants are in the terminal, how long security lines are, and more. This can be especially helpful with children, as airports can breed impatience in even the best behaved kids. Quickly answer their questions about wait times, and let the app tell you if you have time to grab a snack before takeoff.

Additionally, the app can allow you to book last-minute rental cars. Through their exclusive partnership with Avis, GateGuru allows you to reserve a rental car at the lowest available pricing, with discounts up to 35% compared with other leading travel sites.

How does it work?

When the app is opened, you will be directed to the home screen including a list of national and international airports. The most popular choices are shown, but you can type in any airport name or code in the search bar. When you choose an airport, you will be directed to the "Airport Card," a screen providing information on that specific location.

Along with the list of airports, the home screen also displays your current and future journeys. By clicking on the suitcase icon on the upper right corner of the home screen, you can add an upcoming trip. You can choose a flight by a flight number or by route. After your flight is chosen, you will see your upcoming journey. This is your "JourneyCard," where you can view or access any information you may need on your day of travel. Your JourneyCard will keep you posted in real-time on any updates to your flight, such as security wait times, flight delays, gate changes, or layover time adjustments.

Where can I get it?

Available for FREE on free for iOS, Android, and Windows Phone.

LoungeBuddy

What is it?

To further ease the potential stress of your time at the airport, consider spending some time at the airport lounge. In the past, if you wanted to enjoy the comforts and benefits of an airport lounge, you usually had to be a member of a particular airline's loyalty program. There weren't many options for those who wanted to enjoy lounge comforts, but who didn't hold the required status level within a particular airline, have the right credit card, or who weren't frequent enough travelers. Finding a lounge where that was accessible and affordable to the ordinary traveler was no easy feat - until recently.

LoungeBuddy has been developed for the precise purpose of making it easy for travelers to find a suitable and available airport lounge; including those traveling with children who previously may have found it difficult or impossible to locate one. After you find a lounge, LoungeBuddy helps you book so you can walk in minutes later. Don't spend another layover anxious, bored, or stressed while waiting outside the gate.

How does it work?

The app allows you to quickly search for all available lounges at a particular airport and then make a booking. The LoungeBuddy system has been set up to ensure that lounges do not become overbooked or too crowded. Anyone can use the app, whether they are part of a loyalty program or not. If you are a loyalty club member then you can enter those details into the app where they will be stored for easy recall.

In addition to helping you find a suitable lounge at your desired airport, the app provides extensive details on each lounge. This makes it easier to select one that will be suited for your needs; this is particularly important for families as your children's experience in the airport lounge can set the scene for how they'll handle the flight ahead. LoungeBuddy will show you pictures, details of amenities in the lounge, and perhaps most importantly, real reviews of each location. You'll be able to gain an insight into the type of experience you can expect.

Where can I get it?

Available for FREE on iOS and Android.

Entrain

What is it?

Having spoken briefly about the concept of jet lag and the effect it can have on a vacation, technology has stepped in to help ease the pain and solve your travel related sleep issues. This app was designed by academics at the University of Michigan and is backed by science. Studies prove that lighting is the primary driving factor of our sleep cycles, and the app creates lighting schemes for you to use based on your usual sleep schedule, average daytime light exposure, and the destination to which you will be traveling. By adjusting your light exposure before the trip, you can get your body closer to the rhythm of your destination before you even arrive. According to the developers of the app, the goal is to have you sleeping like a local from day one.

Accept some help in order to sync your circadian rhythms and get on local time - and feel rested - faster. Our natural cycles of asleep and awake are wired into our brains, but with greater understanding of how they function, we can work *with* our bodies to give them what they need to make us feel rested and let us enjoy our vacations.

How does it work?

The app makes recommendations for types and durations of light exposure based on the information you input. It will tell you to stay in the dark for certain hours, and get in the light for others. Recognizing that this may not match up with the requirements of your day (business meeting in the dark?) it simply asks that you update in real time as you go about your day, with the type of exposure you are actually getting. The more information the app has, the better it can make recommendations for you. They even have recommendations for ways to "cheat" the system, like wearing sunglasses to at least partially limit light intake for specified periods.

The app lets you customize how long you would like to spend preparing for a trip, as well as a number of other variables. The fact that the app allows you to customize settings for your particular schedule is great for families. Early to bed, early to rise types? Do the kids keep very specific hours? The customizable settings of the app allow you to dial in your family's exact needs for the best possible experience.

Where can I get it?

Available for FREE on iOS and Android

Findery

What is it?

This new website and app, allows you to create a "travel journal" in real time. It ties memories to places in an elegant interface that ensures the right balance between preserving the time away and actually enjoying your vacation.

One of the most rewarding parts of family travel can also be the most frustrating: cataloging the memories. When traveling with your kids, you are especially sensitive to the preciousness of this time, and the fact that they will, at some point, grow up. Photos, videos and other remembrances are an essential part of family vacationing as they preserve the experience you have shared. On the other hand, if you spend the whole time looking through a camera and organizing photos, you miss out on actually *being there* with your family. This service is about striking a balance.

How does it work?

Findery lets you attach notes in a variety of forms - text, photos, videos, and audio - to specific locations while you are traveling. It could be your family posed in front of a stunning fountain, the funny joke the waiter told you at that wonderful cafe, or a video of your daughter trying on the too-big-for-her hats at a street market. By tying these unique memories, whatever they may be, to locations, you and your family can return home to find a real life map of your trip and help recall how you spent your days touring and experiencing an area with each other.

With the option to simply use GPS coordinates, there is no time spent searching and fumbling for places from a long list of similar sounding names (perhaps in a foreign language) and the notes you add can be as many or as few as you want. Findery is about empowering you to preserve whatever memories are important to your family, and providing a simple and attractive way to do it - on the go.

Findery is different from other services in that it isn't about "checking in" at businesses, or rating restaurants. Findery is all about stories and memories. The service allows you to see other people's tags (you can choose to share or hide our own) but you won't be seeing notes about who overcooks their eggs or how long the lines are at a gallery. Findery shares memories in whatever form is important to the user. You likely spend enough time on your phone at home. When you are on vacation with the family, put away the distracting apps and simply allow yourself to make a few quick notes that help you reconstruct the experience over a family dinner when you return.

Where can I get it?

Available for FREE on iOS and Android. You can also access the service online, at their website (https://findery.com/).

Other Photo App Options

In order to allow you to organize vacation photos, but still be able to remain in the present and enjoy your vacation, we have included some other options in the same vein as "Findery." Try them out, see what works best for you, or opt for one that integrates best with technology you already use.

What are some of the best?

Journi

This app is a good alternative to a travel blog, and easier to maintain than a traditional site. This app allows you to add notes to your photos, and the location that you took the photo will also be saved even if you are not online. The app also allows easy sharing of photos with other people. This is an ideal way to caption photos and add your own personal stories to each one, and enjoy the sharable benefits of a photo blog without all the time and effort involved. Available FREE on iOS.

Google+ Stories

More and more people are using Google+ accounts, and this service is an extension of the social media site. Google has devised a way to automate your photo sorting and editing. Google+ Stories attempts to select your best photos, then proceeds to arrange them for presentation as a timeline, where you can add your own captions. This is ideal for people who really want a hands-off solution, or if you've taken thousands of photos (many of which might be similar) and have little time to sort through them all. Available FREE for Android.

HeyDay

If you're the type to take lots of photos complete with notes and status updates, and would like to have it all organized for you, HeyDay is a good option. It creates a visual timeline, including the location that the photos were taken. All the information that you provide for each photo is integrated into the timeline automatically. Available FREE for iOS and Android.

Groupon Getaways

What is it?

Getaways by Groupon represents an expanded territory for the trusted brand, as they provide travel savings, with a focus on flash sales and discount booking opportunities. Travel deals have long been a part of Groupon's offerings, but the standalone "Getaways" is more robust and represents a real commitment to grow and expand the travel sector of their deals program.

This is great news for vacationers, as smaller iterations of Groupon travel deals have had great savings, but traded off options for dollars saved. Now Groupon offers expanded destinations and a greater variety of opportunities, all with the same low prices.

How does it work?

With the rise of similar services like HotelTonight, one of the fastest growing portions of the travel industry is flash sales and last minute bookings. While Groupon may not be your best bet to plan that dream vacation that is two years out, about which you have very specific ideas, it may be just what the doctor ordered if you're still flip-flopping on spring break plans and are ready to book something for a few weeks out.

While Getaways may offer low prices, don't confuse that with "budget" vacationing. Using Groupon Getaways, you can find luxury accommodations and experiences, but with a slightly lower price tag. The app claims to be as good for a "staycation in your city" as it is for "all-inclusive resort in paradise, or a two-week tour with included airfare that whisks you around the capitals of Europe."

Additional features include same-day bookings, and a "cash back" program. Users can earn 5% back in Groupon Bucks on

"Market Pick Hotels." Book your vacation, save money, and then use the Groupon credit towards things to get ready for your trip, adventures after you return, or your next vacation.

Where can I get it?

Available for FREE on iOS and Android. You can also access the service online, at their website (www.groupon.com/Getaways).

Other Apps for Last Minute Travel Booking

As we have mentioned, the idea of booking at the last minute is a growing trend in the travel world. For families with busy schedules and unpredictable commitments, it may not just be your best, but only way to travel to exotic locations.

These apps can also be a great way to inspire future trips. Browse them from time to time, see what is possible, and expand your view of how and where you can go by seeing what kind of deals are out there.

Some focus on a particular niche, like hotels or flights. Others span multiple aspects of travel and even provide last minute packages. Some come from well-established travel brands and booking services, while others represent startups (and perhaps the next big thing in travel).

What are some of the best?

HotelTonight

This app is about empowering you to find great deals on established lodging once you have already arrived. Although most families will not want to arrive in a city with no hotel in mind (we wouldn't recommend it either) this app is great for the family who chooses to spend a spur of the moment night in a nearby city, take a quick weekend jaunt, or decides at the last minute to extend a vacation. Let your family join you at the end of a business trip, or find something last minute when visiting family and adding on an impromptu vacation. Book same day hotels (now available up to a week out) directly from the app and save big as hotels look to fill up extra rooms. Available for FREE on iOS and Android.

Jetsetter

This well established brand books not only hotel rooms, but flights, cruises and entire vacation packages. Booking last minute with them can net savings up to 60% off full price tags. They also have their own section of travel articles that help inspire vacations with a specific theme. Skiers can find a guide to great slope-side vacations, or read about the best beaches to take your family, then book directly through the app. Also exciting is a credit card scanning feature which auto fills your information to save even more time. Available for FREE on iOS.

Last Minute Travel

This last minute booking app has many possible bookings in one place. Book everything from hotels and flights to cars and activities. One of the best features is the robust set of filters, which allow you to organize information by price, stops, length of journey, preferred airline, hotel location, and more. Even if you don't use it to book, the insight into bookings it offers may help you make decisions about where to go or how long you can afford to stay. Available for FREE on iOS and Android.

TravelZoo

Another app that compiles a large number of bookings, TravelZoo's mobile app can help you book an entire vacation package from your phone. It can also help you find a great activity with steep discounts in a nearby city, which may be its greatest benefit to families. This app can be just as helpful for day trips and evening plans as for your summer vacation, and considering you are much more likely to be impulsive with your weekend than your week off, this is a great feature. Available for FREE on iOS and Android.

Tripnary

What is it?

Tripnary helps you find your dream vacation and make it a reality. While the app uses the term "bucket list," simply think of it as your family's wish list for must-visit destinations (like the one we shared earlier in this book).

How does it work?

Within each city or locale you can input destinations (like the ones from our itineraries). After you input them all, you can continuously track real time airfare rates for all the cities on your list and when one looks right, jump on it.

Where can I get it?

Available for FREE on iOS.

Scribd

What is it?

Keeping the kids engaged on long drives or flights, or any time during a vacation when you need a minute, can sometimes be a challenge. There is also the temptation to allow longer sessions of movies or gaming than you may be comfortable with for the sake of quiet time. Enter Scribd, the "Netflix of books" which allows easy access to a plethora of reading materials.

How does it work?

The service costs $8.99 per month for a subscription, but you can enjoy a free trial month to start. All ages can enjoy a fun read, while older children may find what they need for a school project or research report. The service includes print and audio books.

Where can I get it?

App is Available for FREE on iOS, Android, and Kindle. Service requires subscription.

WhatsApp

What is it?

This cross-platform messaging app is a great way to stay in touch while in a foreign country. Use it in lieu of your cell phone messaging and calling to stay in touch without an international plan. You can even create group messages (great for families) and share your location (perfect if you get separated) all while avoiding international SMS and calling fees.

How does it work?

WhatsApp uses your phone's Internet connection (rather than cell phone bands) to make calls, send messages, and even share photos and videos. It can take advantage of cell data (2G/3G/4G/EDGE) or WiFi when available, and avoid roaming charges by allowing you to communicate through local data. The app is free to download, and the service is free for the first year. Current (as of Fall, 2015) pricing for the service after your first year is $0.99 USD/yr.

Where can I get it?

App is Available for FREE on iOS, Android, Blackberry, and Windows Phone. Service requires subscription.

Waze

What is it?

Having maps available while traveling to a new place is one of the most important things we turn to our phones for. Navigating a foreign land can be tricky, and planning or printing out directions for an entire trip before you arrive is impractical (besides the fact that things often change on the fly). While we also use Google Maps and other more straightforward applications related to getting around, Waze goes a step further.

How does it work?

Waze crowdsources information to give you the most accurate possible picture of real-time traffic, closures, and other obstacles. While a physical map may show you the possible ways to get from point A to point B, this app factors in real-time updates from everyone else using it (by tracking GPS locations) to help. Get alerts about upcoming construction, accidents, hazards, and more. You can also share data with other users, sending along things like your ETA to family members (should you split up). If you are going to use a map (you probably will) you should choose one that offers you more information and enables you to save time and headaches while away.

Where can I get it?

App is Available for FREE on iOS, Android, and Windows Phone.

TripCase

What is it?

You spend a lot of time planning a great vacation, and then you need to go about actually taking it. Things change and there are a ton of variables. You also can't very well walk around with a file folder filled with your many plans and papers while still keeping track of the kids.

TripCase conveniently organizes all your travel plans and itineraries on your devices (smartphones, tablets, laptops, etc.) for easy reference and real time updates.

How does it work?

After downloading, you enter your upcoming trip into the app which is as simple as forwarding the itinerary to "trips@tripcase.com"), and the reservations automatically sync up with the app. The service then keeps you up-to-date in real-time on any flight changes delays, cancellations, gate changes and other forces that impact you and your family.

Where can I get it?

Available for FREE on iOS and Android.

AllergyFT

What is it?

Do you or any members of your family have food allergies? Concerned about staying and eating safe abroad? The Allergy FT iPhone app allows you to create multiple profiles, select up to 86 food allergies and then translate those with a warning message into French, Spanish and German (more languages to come soon).

How does it work?

You create your profiles and select a language for the country you are visiting. Then simply show your phone to the waiter or vendor so they can understand your food concerns. It's that simple.

Where can I get it?

Available for $3 on iOS.

WeatherBug

What is it?

Weather can make or break a vacation day, especially when traveling with kids. It pays to know what's coming next. This app makes tracking weather across an area simple so you can be empowered when packing, as well as before you set out each morning. Depending on where you go, following local news for weather alerts may not be a simple matter (especially when language differences are involved) so better not to rely on the outside, and take charge yourself.

How does it work?

Weatherbug is simple to use and allows you to pre-program and check weather for multiple cities. Going on a road trip? See what the weather will be like two states over on Thursday so you'll know what you're riding into. Mobile alerts will also keep you appraised of last minute changes.

Where can I get it?

Available for FREE on iOS, Android, Windows Phone, and a Desktop PC Client.

My TSA

What is it?

When you're home and packing for your trip, trying to remember which items are allowed (contact lens solution? baby formula? portable DVD players?) this app will remind you of what is and is not allowed through airport security. It also provides information for users who are eligible for the TSA precheck program, updates on which airports are experiencing significant delays, and approximate length of the check-in lines.

How does it work?

It's as simple as asking "Can I Bring?" and the name of an item in the field. The app yields instant answers for help packing and planning. Then you can browse a list of airports for information about TSA PreCheck, updates from the FAA, and approximate wait times. Wade through the dense and ever-changing set of restrictions with their guide to TSA rules for travelers. See a full list of features at TSA.gov.

Where can I get it?

Available for FREE on iOS and Android.

Glympse

What is it?

Sometimes when you spend time together while away, it will mean spending some time apart. If you choose to split up and head in different directions for part of the day, or allow teens to explore on their own, this app will help you feel secure about where they are. The real time tracking can also be helpful in finding the quickest and easiest way to link back up.

How does it work?

The app reads the GPS on your phone and uploads your location to a map you share with other users (in this case, the rest of your family). Track each other with the onscreen display and know where the rest of your family is, get ETAs to a given spot, and set locations to meet back up. The app only shares your location with those you choose to, and offers convenience and peace of mind in one simple to use package.

Where can I get it?

Available for FREE on iOS, Android, and Windows Phone.

Roadtrippers

What is it?

Taking a road trip can mean the need to research a number of different locations along your way. A particularly long one might also involve unplanned stops for food, bathrooms, and the like. A *great* roadtrip should also allow for unplanned stops that are about fun and excitement - finding great local flavor and interesting locations along the way. This app affords you a level of spontaneity previously difficult to achieve, not to mention a level of thoroughness without all the work.

How does it work?

Plug in your route and let the app help you to discover destinations, plan your trip, and find fun things to do along the way. You can use it before you go, and carefully comb your entire route for great stops, or use it while away to instantly call up what is around you at a given time. Discover scenic views, places to eat, hotels, attractions, and more. You can view photos, read reviews, and even book certain stops right from the app. NOTE: This app is currently only available for the United States.

Where can I get it?

Available for FREE on iOS and Android.

Hopper

What is it?

When it comes to booking travel, one of the hardest things can be deciding whether or not to pull the trigger on a particular airfare. With so many variables and fluctuations in price, knowing whether a deal is good, great or horrible is rarely as simple as it sounds. This is especially true when considering a location that you know little about. Enter Hopper.

How does it work?

The app compiles data from a vast number of sources, tracking years of airfares across a variety of vendors. Plug in the trip you want to take, and the app will tell you when the best time to book it is. Years of trends and industry data would take you forever to comb through and make sense of, but this app does all of that for you.

Where can I get it?

Available for FREE on iOS.

Tripit

What is it?

A sort of ultimate travel companion, this app can sync your calendar, track all your bookings, store your travel documents, and put everything you need at your fingertips. Rather than opening emails, saving notes, and leafing through elements spread out across your digital and physical worlds, Tripit puts everything together and helps you not only access it, but think smarter about your vacation.

How does it work?

The free version of the app is ad-supported, and allows you to compile all your documents in one place, sync your plans, and compose your itinerary for easy access. The paid version (currently $49 a year for a subscription) goes even further. With the full service, you not only lose the ads, but gain real-time alerts about your flights (to spot potential delays) and even provides fare refund notifications and tracks other data that can help save you money. The ability to set and forget your details, then have updated information delivered to you, is a great solution for busier travelers, and allows parents to spend more time thinking about, and talking to, their kids.

Where can I get it?

Available for FREE on iOS, Android, and Windows Phone. Full version requires subscription.

Seasonal Travel Concerns

Each season and time of year brings its own concerns and things to be aware of when it comes to travel. No season is inherently better than another, except perhaps when it comes to a very specific destination; this is the type of thing that will turn up in your research and preparation. Think of the seasons as different flavors, each with their own things to offer.

Traveling in different seasons will mean different things for each family. You may be the type that likes to embrace winter and hit the slopes or go someplace cold and enjoy the snow. You may like to escape and go someplace warm to defrost and really feel as if you "got away." Some of this will depend on where you live, what your budget is, and other factors specific to your family. In any event, we encourage you to mix things up.

The times available for travel will also largely be dictated by your personal schedules. Most families have the most opportunities during summer, when kids are off school for a long stretch. You may have a long winter break around the holidays, another in the spring, and your jobs may add other qualifiers that limit or dictate your schedule. The fact that these are the most available times for every other family as well means that peak seasons for most destinations are the mid-December to early January period, and summer. Rates are higher, and places book up to capacity quickly. This makes careful planning and consideration all the more important.

School schedules are another part of the reason that we encourage families to begin great travel as early as possible. The urge to delay extraordinary trips until children are "old enough" often means middle or high school in most parent's eyes. Children's schedules only get fuller as they grow, and teenage commitments to sports and activities can be more demanding, and shorten your window for available vacation time. Starting the college search process brings a whole different set of concerns. Start taking your great trips as soon as possible. Delaying just a little longer may put them out of reach.

Another consideration regarding "seasonal travel"

Most people are acutely aware of their own holiday schedules when booking trips, but you must also think about holidays at your destination. This can be both a hindrance and an opportunity, but something that is important to keep in mind.

On the one hand, visiting another country during their holidays can be an incredible cultural exchange. Especially if it is a holiday not widely celebrated in the United States. Why not see what Tet is like in Vietnam, or experience La Dia De Los Muertos in Mexico? These could be once in a lifetime opportunities to share with children.

This doesn't just apply to international travel either. Even within the United States, different people celebrate the holidays in a variety of ways. The family that runs off to the warm waters of the Caribbean every winter may want to consider taking one cold-weather winter vacation to see how winter holidays are celebrated in different parts of the US. Celebrating holidays on vacation can be a fun opportunity to bond with your family. You may have to give up some time with your extended clan, but the tradeoff is a special memory for just you and your children that will stick with you, if for no other reason than being different.

At the same time, you need to pay attention to calendars in other countries to avoid surprises. Just as the holidays can bring surge prices for airlines and hotels at home, they can result in higher prices or closed businesses overseas. You may think that June is a great time to visit Egypt because it fits your schedule, only to arrive and find many of the places you wanted to visit shut down for Ramadan.

Most countries have official tourism bureaus with websites that share local calendars. Use these and factor in local holidays, as well as your own, when considering the best time to take certain vacations.

Seasons can cost, or save you money

It is easy to think of how peak times bring higher prices to certain locations and flights, but easy to forget that the inverse is true. One great way to make that dream vacation that seems just out of reach more affordable is to make a point of visiting in the off season. This is all about making choices for your family. Visiting at the "right" time for you may be worth paying a little extra, or the bargain of getting a great deal may be sweeter than seeing the sights at the peak of the season.

Also always be sure to pay careful attention to blackout dates and exceptions. This is true of deals you find in your research, using airline miles and credit card rewards, as well as any number of promotions. Few things can be more disappointing than putting the effort into researching a trip, getting the whole family excited, and then suddenly going to book only to find that the dates you had picked return an error message or a twice-as-high price tag because a deal you had been counting on was blacked out. Check these first and foremost, to avoid lost time and frustrated family members.

Logistics change with the seasons

As we have said, vacations are not better or worse because they are in the spring or the summer, as opposed to the fall or the winter, but the same vacation can look very different depending on where you go.

The changes may be relatively small. Getting around by bus, which was your original plan because it was cheaper, may seem wholly unappealing when you switch your trip to winter and realize you'll have to wait for buses in the snow. In this case you decide to take cabs, and not much really changes, except your budget. This is only a potential problem if you don't realize it until you get there. When planning, always try to picture yourself actually there, doing the things as a family. Besides being a fun little bit of day-dreaming, you will be less likely to overlook details like this when you think about them in detail as opposed to in concept.

Logistics may also change in bigger ways, and new opportunities may open up with the seasons. In the "winter version" of a trip to a national park, you may have budgeted for hotels every night of your stay. Moving that same trip to the summer makes camping an option (if your family is into camping), and suddenly the trip costs less. Where you stay, how you get around, and what you do are the biggest aspects of planning a vacation and all of them can be very different from one season to the next. These changes can be good, bad, or neutral - and a lot of that has to do with your attitude. See changes as opportunities, rather than hindrances, and go with the flow.

Finally, don't assume that a location is open year round, but don't assume it closes in the "off season" either. For example: New York City's Central Park is home to the famous Trump Rink during the months of October to January. This is a magical opportunity for family ice skating in a gorgeous setting, and one of the season's best attractions. Obviously this rink isn't open for skating in June, but it isn't entirely closed either. The same space in Central Park becomes "Victorian Gardens" during summer months, with rides, games, and a fun carnival atmosphere for families. They are vastly different experiences, but both have a lot to offer. Ignoring one for the other would be a mistake, and you don't know unless you look.

Actually going on your trip

Once things are booked and planned with the seasons and holidays taken into account, there is still the actual execution of your trip to take care of. One season with a particular set of concerns in this regard is winter, and with good reason. Spring, summer and fall are pretty straightforward in most places.

That being said, certain parts of the world experience serious weather in monsoon or hurricane season, and this is something to look out for when researching a new locale. Much of this same advice will apply to these "harsh weather" seasons for a given part of the world.

Winter, in the locations that experience true winter, with its cold and snow, can bring challenges and changes to logistics.

Winter is also the time when most people are eager to get away. The trickiest aspect of winter is flying, so here are some tips we have learned over time:

7 Tips for Easier Winter Flights with Family

1. Build in Extra Time: While you may be able to cut it closer at other times, in winter you'll want to pad your schedule to account for weather and other delays. An extra hour or two up front may seem like a long time, but if it helps you avoid delaying your entire trip by a day because of a long security line and a missed flight, it was time well spent.

2. "Winterize" Your Schedule: You'll want to plan and book a little differently in the winter to account for extra variables. Avoid connecting flights and travel nonstop whenever possible, even if it costs a little extra. Delays and cancellations tend to domino into each other for airports, so book earlier flights when possible, as later options have a greater chance of being thrown by current or earlier weather.

3. Pick Winter-Friendly Hubs: If you can't get a direct flight and have to connect, at least try to do so through a hub city less prone to bad weather. A connecting flight in say, Phoenix, is less likely to be affected by winter weather than say, Denver.

4. Have a Backup Plan: Knowing that weather may be a factor, and you may not have an idea until the day of, don't wait for the airline to present you with a second option. Know what other flights and airports are available to you. The sooner you can act, the better your chances are of being one of the first out of a bad weather situation and able to avoid extended delays. If driving or taking a train is an option, you'll want to move quickly to jump on your backup before everyone else has the same idea.

5. Check in with the Airline: While many bad weather cancellations are last minute affairs, these days airlines also preemptively cancel flights in advance of big storms to avoid problems. They may begin waiving

fees for changing flights days in advance of a big storm and you can be one of the first to switch if you are proactive about keeping yourself informed.

6. <u>Check the Weather</u>: It may seem like a no-brainer, but many travelers are so focused on the weather where they are that they forget to look at the destination, or vice versa. While you may have dodged the blizzard in your hometown, your connecting city might not have, or your destination may be looking down the barrel of a storm. Actively keep up on the weather for all stages of your journey and you may be able to spot and anticipate delays before the airline calls them.

7. <u>Use a Travel Agent</u>: While you may be a savvy online booker, winter is a season where having the backing of a good travel agent can really pay off. If you face cancellations and need to make a last minute scramble to save your trip, having an experienced professional in your corner can more than make up for their modest fee.

Money and Travel

Travel can represent a serious financial commitment, especially when doing your best to seek out the most exciting experiences possible. It also raises questions about how to safely use your money in a foreign country, and how to make sure that hidden costs like foreign transaction fees and conversion rates don't let you unintentionally spend more than you bargained for.

The goal is to figure out as many as your financial questions and concerns before you leave as possible. Vacation should be about enjoying time with your children, not stressing over how much you have spent, running out of cash, or dealing with banks and credit card companies. Make arrangements and create a plan before you go, so that once you are at your destination you are savoring each moment with your family.

Planning and budgets

With appropriate resources and planning, even exotic destinations can be enjoyed for less than you may think. Accommodations, food, shopping, and activities can all be far more affordable in the far-flung corners of the world - but you need to put in the research.

Furthermore, be sure to take into account the exchange rate. We spent three summer vacations in Europe with a terrible exchange rate, which increased the cost of the trips significantly. Had we gone the summer of 2015, we could have saved a lot, but these things are difficult to predict.

This is one of many areas where your careful planning and research will show you its benefits. When you have put in the time to research where best to stay, what you want to do, and other details, you can have a relatively accurate idea of what things will cost once you arrive.

We also encourage you to discuss the concept of a budget with your children. The small and enclosed environment of a vacation can provide great lessons in budgeting, currency exchange, and smart spending. The single week or so at a time makes for a great reference point. You and your children can consider your time away as a microcosm of your real lives at home, and let this time teach lessons about how far money goes and choices that have to be made. There can be a desire to "let the good times roll" and splurge on your kids while away because of how much fun you are having. Splurge on them with great activities and the best accommodations you can afford - let the souvenir shopping be a time for them to learn the value of a dollar (or peso, or euro, or yen…).

Credit cards are your friend

When it comes to traveling, your credit card is going to be your best financial tool and a powerful ally for many reasons. Some of these tips only apply to international travel (where a credit card, or two, is positively invaluable) but many apply to domestic travel as well. Your credit card, or cards, will provide many benefits, ranging from safety and security, to perks and time saving attributes.

Here are some of the reasons to have and use a credit card while traveling:

You can cancel/replace it when lost or stolen - This is of course true when you are home as well, but especially important within the confines of limited time in a new place. With only so many days or weeks in another country, you don't have time to spare. Cash comes with no guarantee, and if you lose it or are the victim of theft, you can be completely out of luck. If however you are traveling with credit, you can quickly report your lost card and cancel it to avoid any fraudulent expenses. Don't let lost money derail your vacation. Use a credit card, and keep a backup, second credit card (from a separate account) locked up in your hotel safe or another secure location.

The perks of membership - Many credit cards, especially those marketed to travelers, will come with additional benefits. The first one to look for is "no foreign transaction fees" because these small surcharges can add up. Most credit cards charge 1-3% on foreign purchases. Some cards will also offer things like free checked bags with certain airlines, pre-boarding passes for easier airport experiences, and other perks like rental car upgrades, free hotel meals, and more. Be sure to look into what your card or cards offer before you go, and take advantage of all you are entitled to. If you plan on making travel a priority moving forward, you may consider adding a credit card to your repertoire that focuses on these benefits, including cards that help you accumulate airline miles.

- Quicker, more favorable transactions - Just as at home, credit cards can offer ease of purchase by getting you in and out quickly with a simple swipe. They will also help you to get a favorable foreign exchange rate without a middleman taking a cut for converting bills.

- Why credit is (usually) better than debit - Make sure you fully understand the difference between booking with credit and debit, and choose accordingly. When it comes to incidentals and actual room fees, hotels treat both differently with different types of cards. With credit cards, an "authorization" is made (essentially the hotel verifies the total amount with your credit card company and checks that you have the line of credit available) but typically no actual charge is made until you check out, though some hotels may charge you all or a portion of your stay ahead of time. Confirm the hotel's booking policy when you make your reservation. With debit cards, the hotel will often charge the full amount of the stay right off the bat. For a weeklong stay this could mean a significant sum deducted from your account at once. Even if some of it will eventually get refunded (from holds for incidental charges), it may affect your spending ability during the trip. Credit is the better option if you have it available, and if you aren't carrying a balance on your account that is being charged interest.

Some things to note about using cards safely while traveling

- <u>Notify your card issuer before you go</u> - This is one of the most common mistakes people make when traveling. If you live in the United States and all of the sudden you try to make a of purchase in Norway, this will set off red flags with your issuing bank or credit card company. In this age of identity theft, the modus operandi of card issuers is to immediately suspend an account with "suspicious" activity to keep them from holding the bag on a bunch of unauthorized charges. Even if you used the same card to book your overseas flight, don't assume your issuer knows where you are and that you want to be making the purchases. Give them a call in advance of your trip, and alert them that for certain specific days you will be traveling, and tell them where you will be. This is supposed to prevent your card from getting frozen, which could do the same for your travel plans. If you don't let them know and do get shut down, it can take time to sort it all out. This isn't a perfect system, and on a recent trip one of our cards kept getting denied even though we had notified the company ahead of time. Each call to "unblock" the card took 20-30 minutes away from our vacation. These calls involved speaking to an operator overseas, then needing to be transferred back to a manager. We had to jump through the same hoops over and over again just to be allowed to use our card. It is rare to have this sort of notice ignored by a company, but the net result was the same as if we hadn't called ahead, and just goes to show that we know firsthand how frustrating it can be to have your card frozen.
- <u>Don't take a cash advance on a credit card</u> - Unless it is an absolute emergency, this is never a good idea. You'll be charged a fee on top of a foreign-transaction charge, as well as astronomical interest rates (sometimes twice what you pay for your credit card normally).
- <u>Verify any website you submit credit information to</u> - These days, you may book directly with a hotel or go through a third party booking site. There are the big

names, as well as many smaller outfits, some just as good and others not to be trusted. Before typing in your credit card information, make sure the site uses an encrypted server and if you don't trust the name, get out of there.

- <u>Do not send credit card information over email</u> - Some smaller excursions or in-country guides may ask you to, but it is a bad idea. Notoriously easy to hack, and even easier to forward to the wrong person, email is not a secure way to transmit data as valuable as your credit card number. You also want to make sure you get a confirmation number for all transactions, in case your reservation goes missing or you need to dispute a charge.

- <u>Double check the amounts</u> - When booking hotels you have to remember that taxes and fees may raise the originally quoted price, but you still need to make sure you are being charged the correct amount. This is especially important when booking with a third party and not the hotel directly. Were you promised a great deal and then charged the regular rate? You'll never know to dispute it if you simply assume they got it right.

- <u>Keep track of your payment method </u>- Carry multiple cards? Keep track of which you used. If you booked with one card and plan on paying with another, you want to double check that the hotel charges the right amount to the right card, that way you don't hit a limit or get hit with a fee by your bank for a charge you didn't actually intend to make.

- <u>Don't forget about incidentals</u> - If you use a debit card to book a hotel room, they may place a hold for incidental charges. Whether you use credit or debit, certain activities (namely those that rent something) may also place a hold in case of loss or damage. Keep this in mind, especially if you have a tight credit limit or limited cash on hand. Even a hold that is eventually removed may take days, and if that money was a part of your budget for the trip, it may affect your ability to make purchases while away.

Converting currency, and why not to use the airport ATM

Once upon a time, getting money upon arriving in a foreign country was a simple affair. The globalization of major banks meant that your bank likely had ATMs in other countries and you could simply use your card to get cash on arrival. Low or no ATM fees were in effect, and fair exchange rates promised you almost never lost more than 3% in the transaction. These times have *ended*.

Today, retail foreign exchange companies have struck deals with most of the major airports in Europe (for now) to establish a monopoly over airport ATMs. These new cash machines advertise "Free Withdrawal" and that is the case, but what they don't charge in fees, they make up for in poor exchange rates. You may lose 10 or 11 percent on a transaction as opposed to the three percent of days past - when you withdraw a few hundred dollars this can really add up fast.

These "free" ATMs may use Visa and MasterCard symbols and do in fact take your card, but because they are tied to retail foreign currency exchangers (who make their money off of exchange rates) they will put a sting in your wallet.

The best solution for getting cash abroad

If you're lucky, you have some local currency on you to get to your hotel. In fact, this is a good time to mention that most US banks will order you foreign currency in advance of your trip with enough notice. A few weeks before you go, visit your branch with specific amounts and denominations, and they should be able to order a mix of large and small bills in another currency for you. This will give you some or all of your "walking around money" for the trip without having to worry about it upon arrival.

If you don't have cash on arrival, many foreign metro and bus stations, even cabs, will take credit cards. Once away from the airport and in a city center, you should be able to find major bank ATMs that function like those of the good old days. You may only have to travel a few blocks from the airport, or you may have to travel a mile or two, but most foreign cities will have options that allow you to exchange at a fair rate. Once you get to you hotel, a friendly concierge should be able to help, or you can get online and find a bank ATM. If you have the time, do a little research before landing so you can get cash on hand early in your trip.

- Use your bank's ATM locator prior to your trip to plan a good spot to get cash, or provided your card is affiliated with Visa or MasterCard, you can use theirs as well.
- You can, through most banks, arrange arrival currency to pick up at your local branch before you leave home. That way you don't show up empty handed in a foreign country.
- If you didn't get to do either of these and you *need* cash to get to your hotel, only take out a little at the airport ATM. You'll feel the exchange rate, but can put off making a bigger withdrawal until you find a cash machine with a more favorable exchange rate.
- Try to avoid changing money at your hotel - they often have unfavorable exchange rates and the convenience comes at a cost.

Bottom line - the airport is quickly becoming the worst place to get your cash. This is currently true in Europe, but if the model works it will likely spread to other parts of the world as the new standard.

Another place to avoid getting cash abroad

Stay away from the so-called "no fee" bureau de change. The name is extremely misleading; these so-called "no-fee" currency exchanges are usually the most expensive ways to change your money. The conversion rates are almost always much worse than they would be at an ATM.

Thoughts about "dynamic currency conversion"

This is something new we have observed on recent trips to Europe and it bears an explanation. Many foreign ATMs and merchants are offering the option for so-called "dynamic currency conversion." What this means is that the cash machine or vendor will convert the amount of your withdrawal or transaction on the spot - as opposed to your bank doing it later on. The appeal is knowing exactly how much your transaction will cost as opposed to a vague idea. It can be especially appealing if the exchange rate is particularly low on a given day, and you want to jump on the chance to lock in this lower rate.

If only it were that simple...

The catch, or at least the potential catch here, is the risk of overpaying because of extra (and often undisclosed) fees. These "dynamic currency conversions" can charge in the neighborhood of 7% for their use, and end up negating any potential savings, or ultimately costing even more.

The solution?

Your best bet is to choose to be charged in the local currency, if possible using a credit card with no foreign transaction fee. Read your own bank's policy before you go, to make sure you understand any and all potential fees that could be charged while traveling abroad. Being well informed is your best asset.

A note about children and converting money

One of the most exciting parts of travel with children is the opportunity to teach them things. It may be exposure to a different culture or way of living, a new language, or perhaps facts about history or science picked up in a museum. When you vacation with your children you have the opportunity to expose them to new ideas and information. Some of these will excite their imagination and others will be very practical in their day to day lives. Yes, even converting your money while abroad can open new opportunities for education.

In this day and age our world is smaller and the notion of trading with other countries is far from limited to major transactions or obscure conditions. With a few clicks of a mouse, anyone in the world can order almost anything from the far corners of the world. Learning about foreign currency exchange helps children to respect the value of money, exercise math skills, learn basic economics and even history, as the reasons for different currencies in different regions provides a lens through which to view the development of a given region.

While the concepts are simple enough: X dollars are equivalent to Y euros, pounds, or other currency; in actuality, it requires research and discipline to manage money while traveling abroad. It is an important lesson to explain to children that a pound is the British "version" of a dollar; however their 5 dollars will not go as far as 5 pounds will. By the same token they may be amazed at simple items costing thousands of yen, but a little conversion will help them to see that the same concept is in place but with different parameters.

For some assistance understanding currency exchange and making real time calculations we recommend Oanda Currency Converter (www.oanda.com/currency/converter/). Their website has simple, accurate and easy to use tools for converting money in real time, as well as historical rates and other great features. For ease of use while on the go, they also offer mobile apps for all popular device operating systems.

When traveling in a foreign country, children are provided with a great opportunity to learn about the value of money. By giving them a small allowance or letting them bring their own money, and teaching them how far it can go, they can really learn "the value of a dollar" while learning the value of a euro, peso, or ruble. Let them use a currency converter or otherwise "do the math" themselves and see how practical the information they learn in school is.

If you want to raise the discussion up a notch, you can discuss fees and commissions one will encounter when exchanging funds overseas. Additionally, for teens it may be valuable to educate them on the various (and most cost effective!) means of exchanging currencies while traveling.

On a side note, collecting foreign currency can be a fun hobby for adults and children alike, and a few coins or small bills may make great souvenirs for children on top of helping them to solidify the notion of differing currencies.

Let the concept of different world currencies be an exciting and educational experience for children when traveling abroad. As you mix the extraordinary with the practical, even the economic responsibilities of your trip can become moments for bonding and growth.

Make the System Work For You

The world of travel means a new set of rules to learn and abide by.

The more you know about these rules, the more you are able to work within the system to find yourself better deals, and prevent unforeseen hiccups. The very same situation can be a setback or an opportunity, depending on how well informed you are and how you are prepared to adjust. Travel is part planning, and another part improvisation. Both can be improved and used to your advantage when you know the rules of the game and are equipped with some information to help avoid pitfalls and jump at chances to make smart choices.

Years of travel have educated us on a number of ways to travel smarter and better. This chapter is about pointing out things to look for, giving solutions for common problems, and learning how to best situate yourself for better travel through knowledge and preparation.

Recent changes in hotel cancellation policies

If you are one of the many people who use travel-related mobile apps, you will want to pay attention to some important changes that may affect your ability to score those awesome last-minute deals. Several of the world's largest hotel chains have recently made some hefty changes to their reservation cancellation policies.

Until now, most major hotel chains have allowed guests to cancel reservations even as late as the evening of their scheduled check-in date, without penalty. For some major hotel chains, this is no longer the case. Following these changes, guests must cancel their reservations by midnight the night before they are scheduled to stay. Late cancellations will result in a fee equal to the cost of one night's stay. More major hotel chains are also expected to follow suit.

These changes have been prompted by an emerging trend that sees folks booking hotel rooms online, then cancelling their reservations at the last minute when they find a better deal via popular hospitality-based mobile apps and websites.

Last-minute deal seekers have saved big bucks from the fine-free cancellation policies which, as you can imagine, has been felt by hotel chains. The resulting changes in cancellation policies are an attempt to thwart profit losses prompted by consumers finding creative ways to spare expenses wherever possible.

Be sure to double check the cancellation policy of any room you book, and be aware that while in some cases it pays to lock in a rate by booking something and then continuing to shop, other times it may cost you.

Which leads us to our next, and even more important, point...

The importance of reading the fine print

When it comes to so many things in the travel world, the times are changing and the rules can be hard to keep track of. Sometimes they change so subtly and quietly that you wouldn't even know.

Besides the aforementioned move towards altering cancellation policies, other trends in the travel world mean that it is all the more important not to assume anything these days. There is a growing movement in the travel industry. With the advent of online booking and the growth of new ways to travel, stay, plan and reserve, the industry is finding new ways to monetize the same products. This results in breaking down travel to the smallest possible pieces and offering fully customizable experiences. Nowadays less comes standard, but everything can be added, including something like the right to a last minute cancellation.

You need to read the fine print because otherwise you run the risk of assuming something is included, or that there is wiggle room to re-book or change your ticket, only to find out that you will be hit with another fee, or be totally unable to cancel. Sometimes the best deals come with strings attached; meaning that the reason you got such a good price is that you can't really change *anything* about your booking without a fee.

Knowing this before you book ensures you don't get caught off-guard, and understand what your options are (or aren't).

While it may seem like a tedious and boring task, reading the fine print is important and may save you valuable money on your vacation; this way you can make the best possible plans.

The Bottom Line: Don't assume it is included, if you have a specific concern about something like cancelling last minute, upgrading, using reward points or anything of the sort, check first. All reputable travel service providers will disclose the rules, hopefully in an obvious way. However, it is important to read over the fine print and be sure you know what you can expect and what you can't expect so that you don't get caught with an extra charge after the fact. Nothing sours great vacation memories like an extra-large bill on your way out the door.

How to clear a common travel hurdle: getting through airport security faster

Whether you travel frequently or only for an occasional vacation, getting from the airport door to your seat on the plane can be an exhausting experience. Between the physical ground to cover and the regulatory hoops to jump through, there is a lot to sweat. When traveling as a family, simply multiply everything by the number of children. Some new options are available so we have broken them down for you to help streamline your process.

Two new options are available that help US citizens clear immigration and security faster by skipping the lines and going through less invasive procedures. They are Global Entry and TSA Pre-Check.

Global Entry is run by the U.S. Customs and Border Protection and is the program that allows for quicker clearing of immigration when reentering the country. Travelers are allowed to use special kiosks that scan passports, check fingerprints and read declaration forms without the need to wait in line or deal with a human agent. This program is available for "pre-approved, low risk" travelers, meaning that you must be enrolled in the program prior to your trip. While a full list of requirements for the program are available online (www.cbp.gov/global-entry/about/eligibility), the basics are that you must have a record free of criminal offenses or customs violations and be either a US citizen, lawful permanent resident, Dutch citizen, South Korean citizen, or Mexican national. While Canadian citizens are not eligible for this specific program, there is a similar one available to them known as NEXUS.

To enroll in the program you must first submit an online application. A $100 application fee is also required and is non-refundable, even if you are denied. After your application is reviewed and a thorough background check performed, if still eligible you will be invited for an interview. These are conducted by border patrol agents at enrollment centers, which will most likely be an airport near you. Bring two forms of identification, and after a successful interview your photo and fingerprints will be taken and your Global Entry ID card will be mailed to you. The program lasts for 5 years, after which point you may renew.

NOTE: Some levels of certain credit cards may reimburse you for the $100 fee (though not necessarily for your whole family). Check with your credit card company and see.

TSA Pre-Check is a similar "trusted traveler" program that applies to airport security as opposed to immigration. With an active enrollment you can get on a shorter line and expedite the security screening process. This program is open to U.S. citizens and lawful permanent residents, who are not on any watch lists, have not been convicted of a criminal offense, and are not currently under indictment.

NOTE: Global entry automatically qualifies you to use TSA Pre-Check, however the reverse is not true.

Enrollment is very similar. First comes an online application, and an $85 application fee. An interview follows a successful application, after which you will be enrolled in the program and issued a Trusted Traveler Number. Membership also lasts for 5 years.

How to Use

Global Entry is as simple as bringing your ID card with you. You do not need to fill out the blue form on the plane for customs, but simply proceed to the Global Entry area and use one of the designated kiosks. Not all airports have these areas, check for a full list online. You should also have your passport with you. The kiosk will print a form for you (with your photo). Once you have completed the customs declaration at the kiosk, you will need to keep the completed form with you to hand to the customs agent as you leave the airport.

TSA Pre-Check requires that you use your Trusted Traveler Number when booking tickets (this will be your Global Entry number if you have Global Entry). This ensures you receive a special stamp on your boarding pass which denotes you as a member of the program. Then you proceed to the designated lines when entering security. You will have to show your boarding pass and ID. You likely will not have to remove belts, shoes or electronic devices, and while you may still only carry a quart sized bag of liquids, you will not have to remove them from your bag for inspection. To be sure your preferred airport participates, check online.

For Families

Global Entry officially DOES NOT allow members to fast track others. You cannot expect a spouse and/or children to be able to skip the regular lines as a part of your program status.

TSA Pre-Check DOES have specific guidelines and allowances for families. Children under 12 traveling with a parent or guardian who has a Pre-Check stamped boarding card should be able to use the expedited lines. Children 13 and older will have to use regular lines or apply themselves. Essentially, all family members 13 and older must be enrolled in the program if you wish for the whole family to skip security lines.

The bottom line is that either of these programs can save you time. You don't need both, since Global Entry includes TSA Pre-Check if you add your Global Entry number into your online reservation. Spend the extra $15 to enroll unless you only travel domestically. You can get children under 12 through security but not through immigration. If all adults in your group are enrolled, you will proceed through the lines much faster and have more time to think about your first activity.

Think smarter about a common hiccup: look beyond the airport hotel when your flight is canceled

We've all been there - flight cancelled, late at night, kids are tired and you're not going anywhere right now. It's a vacation nightmare, but it's also beyond your control. Sometimes you're just stuck.

Unless you're at the beginning of your journey, going home isn't an option. Even then, if the next flight is early enough the next morning it might make sense to stay as close as possible. So whether you're in your own city or a foreign one, you need to find a place for the night.

It used to be that the only option was the airport hotel. While this is just fine under some circumstances, today you have a choice. You can keep your family vacation rolling on a fun and exciting tone by looking beyond the airport hotel.

Make use of last minute booking apps to stay smarter

You can find something more comfortable, more fun, and often more affordable for your family by using one of today's "book now" travel apps.

Turn to HotelTonight, Roomlia, Priceline, or one of the apps mentioned in our earlier chapter about booking technology. You may just find something cheaper, better, and more conveniently located than the "standard" option available through the airport. By using these last minute deals apps you have a chance to put your family up somewhere great for the night, while still keeping costs low. All of these options are constantly expanding their cities and reach, and chances are there is a great deal near whatever airport you're stranded at.

When nothing goes wrong, but can still improve: our top tips for getting a room upgrade

The only thing better than VIP treatment is getting it for entry-level prices. Everyone loves an upgrade when traveling - whether it be an unexpected bump to first class or free access to an exclusive area. As a traveling family, hotel room upgrades are especially welcome as they mean more room to spread out, and can mean a better night's sleep for the entire clan.

While there is no way to guarantee an upgrade, you can position yourself to make it a possibility, with a little bit of insider information and advice.

- Building loyalty, booking through the hotel, and simply *asking* for the upgrade might work.

- We have come to find that hotels will often overbook the lower tier rooms in anticipation of last minute cancellations. The other bit of logic to this is that while they can easily bump up a customer with a basic room, they can't very well overbook their suites and inform a guest checking in that they will have to downgrade. What happens is, if they don't get the expected number of cancellations and the lower tier rooms fill up, they often move up guests to nicer rooms, one tier at a time.

- If you have your fingers crossed for an upgrade to a suite, do some research and find out what type of room at that particular property is directly below a suite on their scale of price and quality. As rooms fill up, you may get lucky and be bumped from your "premier" room to a suite, whereas the economy option may be too far down the scale for consideration.

It may seem like a bit of a gamble, but really it is just positioning yourself as the most attractive candidate for an upgrade. Combine this with being polite, loyal and open to negotiation, and you might just find yourself in a swanky upgraded room for a lot less than the hotel normally charges.

Having the Right Gear

Your brain and the careful work you put into planning will be your greatest assets while traveling, but a few key pieces of equipment certainly won't hurt. Certain things are simply essentials of travel, like luggage. Other things have become all but essential in this modern age, like things to entertain kids, electronics, and mobile power sources.

Here are a few of our suggestions for what gear is worth investing in, as well as some helpful information on one of our greatest modern necessities: cell phones.

Cell phones and international travel

Let's face it, in our modern technological society, we are used to having our cell phones on us at all times. Say what you like about our dependence on them, they really do come in quite handy. When traveling, they can be an even greater asset as we traverse unfamiliar territory and require guidance or references. Additionally, there is the security of knowing that if you get lost or separated you have a way of getting in touch.

Unfortunately, just as a phone can be your most useful tool when traveling internationally, deciphering a reasonable and affordable plan can be among the most difficult parts of planning. So what is the best plan of attack?

First up, using a phone on vacation

When carrying your own phone be sure to keep "airplane mode" activated. This will prevent your phone from trying to acquire a signal at all times (which it is programmed to do) and incurring unexpected roaming charges. With smartphones, even *trying* to connect to a data network can cost you money despite the fact that you may not check a single web page.

Instead, stick to free, secure WiFi connections. Plan ahead and try to do your research using your hotel's WiFi (if it is free or you are already paying for it) before setting out for the day.

Looking up information and storing it to your phone will save you having to log back onto a website while you are out. Saving information to a "notepad" app or taking screen shots are great ways to have relevant facts stored offline. This way you only use your phone data while out and about in emergencies. When it comes to calls you can save a ton by using free services like Skype or MagicApp.

To cover those times when you just can't help but use data on-the-go, consider a short term international package from your carrier. While they are by no means cheap (for reference, approximate prices at the time of this publication were $30 for 125 MB with AT&T or $25 for 100 MB with Verizon) they will be vastly less expensive than roaming data on your domestic plan, which can run upwards of $20 per MB. Think it out and plan ahead.

If you are staying longer, or know you will be using your phone extensively

There are more serious options you can look into. Prepaid international SIM cards are a great choice for those with compatible, unlocked phones. This option allows you to keep your current handset and essentially turn it into a local phone for the length of your stay. On the upside, you will be able to use your phone like a resident and for a fraction of the cost; on the downside it will change your number for as long as the card is in, and those calling you from home will incur international rates when doing so.

You may also consult your carrier for more robust international plans, or consider renting an international device for the length of your stay from a company that provides international phones.

Some quick notes on cell phone safety and efficiency while on the road

Plan ahead and program important numbers like your hotel and some destinations into your phone, as well as any guides you may be using or other important local information. Have as much as possible stored "offline" in case you don't have internet access or service at a particular stop along your day.

Assume that you will not have service and store things in notes or by taking pictures of them.

Do not leave anything too personal on your phone in case it is lost or stolen, and be sure to protect it with a passcode. Finally, make sure children have a list of important numbers in case of an emergency.

Keeping phones and other devices charged with travel tech

A family on the go is still a family is still a family in need of their devices. Whether it is a camera for taking great vacation pictures, a tablet or an eReader to entertain kids in transit, a phone for emergencies, or any other electronic device - keeping them charged while away from home is essential.

A few major categories of products can service your family's needs while traveling. Think about how many devices you plan on using, what categories they fall into, and how you will be using them. Depending on your needs, one or a combination of several of these choices will make the most sense for your family.

- Combination chargers - With two or more ports (we like ones with around five) allow you to charge most devices that use USB for power, all at the same time. Look for ones with "Intelligent Technology" that detects what each device needs and provides high speed charging without needing to find the "right" port.

- Tablet docking stations - Allow you to charge your device while still using it. This is perfect for quick stops in the room, or for letting kids wind down at the end of the day while still making sure the device is charged for use on the go the following morning. The best ones will also protect a device while adding functionality. Look for models that include a rechargeable battery that works with multiple USB devices and adds battery life. Also handy are features like wireless speakers, a wireless keyboard with shortcut keys, and horizontal or vertical positioning while docked for standing a device to read or watch video. This can also be a useful tool for watching videos in a hotel room that doesn't have a TV (or when extra charges apply and you want to cut costs) to let kids relax or to watch videos to prepare for your next day of travel.

- Phone cases with integrated chargers - Allow you to shed one unnecessary thing from your already full bag while traveling. They also have the benefit of protecting you from forgetting or losing a charger while on the go. The best options have prongs that fold out of the body, integrating the charger with your phone. Look for options that also offer a USB pass-through, should you choose to charge by cord or plug in an accessory.

- External battery packs - Like the ones offered by Mophie help provide you with extra juice on the go. This is great for extended periods in between outlets, which can happen both during long flights or drives, as well as within foreign countries with limited access to electricity. Standard sizes of around 4,000 mAh will allow you to charge a standard phone 2-3 times (or 2-3 phones for families) with a single charge of the battery pack. Larger sizes of around 12,000 mAh allow for 8-9 full charges, with the best also adding the ability to charge multiple devices at once.

- Small, cables for charging and syncing - You're still going to need a cable with you while traveling to use most chargers and batteries, as well as if you want to sync a device to backup photos or load data for tomorrow's excursion. Look for small cables that can fit in your pocket easily, or "flex" options you can twist to hang off a backpack or wrap around anything, including your wrist. While long cables that reach from the wall to a table may be best at home, on the road micro cables in the two to six inch range make it easier to carry a cable with you, and harder to forget on the go.

- Car Charger - If you are going to be renting a car (or driving your own) a car charger will come in handy. It lets you take advantage of travel time to charge your devices (rather than having to stop and wait at a hotel or other source of outlets) and also lets you keep a phone or other device used for GPS charged while providing driving directions. Try to buy one with two or more ports so you can charge multiple devices at once.

Know the difference between adapters and converters for travel charging

If you are traveling internationally, you will need to do a little research as to what type of plugs a country uses and their voltage requirements. Based on this information you may simply need an *adapter* (changes the plug layouts) or you may need a *converter* (aka transformer) that also adjusts the current.

Without the right plug you'll get no juice, and if you don't use a converter when needed you run the risk of shorting out certain devices. Great all in one options make it as simple as buying a single item.

Research ahead of your trip and be sure you know what you need. Being forced to buy something at the airport or in-country may see you spending twice as much for the same thing, so it pays to do the legwork up front.

One thing worth investing in: Headphones

Travel can involve a lot of downtime, between waiting at airports, long flights and/or drives, and that time spent waiting for everyone to get ready in the morning. A good pair of headphones can be very helpful for keeping kids happy and occupied, so you all get the most out of your real time together.

A good pair of headphones is worth the investment for traveling families who want to keep children appeased as well as enjoy audio tours.

Look for pairs that are tough and durable, able to stand up to a variety of types of abuse from both the rigors of travel and handling by children. Noise cancelling features will provide the best sound for loud destinations, and have the added benefit of functioning as "white noise" devices for long flights or rides. Also look for comfortable ear buds or clips that help when worn for long periods of time.

Some solid headphones will be of great use to kids while traveling. Consider them as a gift for an upcoming birthday or holiday, as a way to get kids excited for an upcoming vacation by giving them something they can use alongside their family.

Some thoughts about luggage

One of your most important pieces of travel equipment will be the luggage you choose. If you buy smartly and take care of it, your luggage may see you through years of future trips. Whether you are a seasoned traveler or an occasional one, having the perfect suitcase and carryon for your journey can make a world of difference. Yet with so many options to choose from, it can be a little challenging to select the right one for you.

First, consider the size and weight of the bag without your belongings inside it. Whether you plan to do strictly carry-on or checked baggage, the empty weight of the bag is of utmost importance. Almost all travelers will agree that the lighter the bag, the better. This way you can carry as much stuff as you need to - and have room to bring back souvenirs

If you tend to travel light or mainly just for weekends, you can get away with a larger carry-on suitcase. You will just need to ensure that it does not exceed your airline's size and weight restrictions. Airlines include the wheels when measuring dimensions, so be sure that you do this too.

For longer stays or for those who travel with more belongings than others, checked baggage is the way to go. Not only do most airlines have size restrictions for checked luggage, they also have weight restrictions. The lighter your empty bag weighs, the more you can fit and the less likely you are to incur expensive overweight baggage fees.

In your browsing, you will notice that some bags have only two wheels, while others have four. Those with two are less likely to sustain damage to the wheels and do better on uneven surfaces. However, they must be dragged behind you, which can cause strain on wrists and shoulders. Suitcases with four wheels allow for movement in all directions and can be pushed in front of you, towed beside you, or dragged behind you. Their main drawback is that the wheels are not recessed within the bag, making them more prone to being damaged (and remember, the wheels are included in the maximum size as measured by airlines). It is best to go to a store and try these two variations in person, to see which you are more comfortable with.

You should also consider the construction of the bag. There are two main options in this area: hard-sided or soft-sided. While the former offers more protection, they do tend to weigh more, which can be a problem for travelers who pack more on the heavy side. Soft-sided bags are usually lighter in weight and offer more flexibility (which is particularly important when you are dealing with cramming them into overhead bins).

Other things to keep in mind while shopping for a new suitcase include handle construction and length (for your towing comfort), zippers (the bigger they are, the longer they last), TSA-approved locks (for extra security), and pockets (soft-sided bags have more pockets than hard-sided ones, which is great for super-organized travelers). You will also want to pay close attention to the warranty on the suitcase. Obviously, lifetime warranties are ideal.

Finally, price is always an important consideration. When it comes to luggage, you definitely get what you pay for. You may want to consider investing a little more in your suitcase, especially if you travel a lot, or are looking to turn over a new travel leaf and commit to vacationing better.

A final note about luggage and airport restrictions

Find out what you are allowed to bring as far as the number and size of bags, and make sure you abide by the rules. There may be additional charges for sports equipment, like skis and golf bags. Always be sure to ask so you can plan for these charges.

Also remember that if you are connecting, or flying a different airline home than the one you flew out with, you will need to conform to the *more restrictive airline's policy*. This is also true of taking a bus to a plane, or a flight to a cruise ship, etc. Check the rules of all carriers you will be traveling with and find out all of their baggage restrictions. For some international carriers you may want (or need) to make a phone call if their website is less revealing.

Whatever carrier you'll be traveling on has the smallest size restriction and lowest number of bags, that's who you'll have to pack for (unless you are willing to pay additional fees). It may seem annoying to make these calls or spend time looking online before you go, but it is better than enjoying a great European vacation only to find out you can't fly home the bag you flew out with unless you pay a surprise, and often hefty, fee.

What the Experts Say About Family Travel

In our effort to provide the most comprehensive information possible to traveling families, sometimes we have to look past ourselves. If it is the wise man who admits what he does not know, then this chapter is us saying that while we know a great deal about family travel, we won't pretend to know it all.

In an attempt to make sure that things which might have passed us by are still a part of this book, we reached out to professional sources to help fill in any gaps. Some of the information may overlap with things that we cover elsewhere in this book, but is presented in a slightly different way, and any repetition merely goes to show that a number of people believe that a particular idea is important.

This chapter features advice from experts actively involved in family travel. They represent a cross section of travel writers, agents, tour guides, operators, and a number of other relevant fields. We put out the call for their best pieces of advice for traveling families. This chapter covers what experts in the field of family travel really think is important, and what they believe should be conveyed to traveling families above all other advice.

For each tip we offer a quick description of the nature of the advice, the expert's travel tip, and some information about who provided it. While we have not booked or worked with any of these professionals ourselves, we are most appreciative of them answering our call and contributing to this section. By all means, feel free to use their biographical information to research whether they are a company you might want to use, and track down more of their writing, or information about the services they provide.

The Headline: Tips for Smarter Family Cruising

The Tips:

- Arrive on the ship first! If the ship advertises boarding at 1:00PM, be there at 1:00PM. You can enjoy an extra lunch, an extra afternoon at the pool, and the best spa and restaurant reservations. Even if you have to come into the city a night prior, the rewards will be worth the effort. Besides, you are getting an extra day on your cruise!

- Hire a private local guide or even hire a local taxi for a day of touring, instead of the huge bus tours. You will be able to see 50% more and get the local flavor of the island or city. If you register for one of the standard tours, over half your time is spent standing in a line or sitting on a bus.

The Expert:

Rhonda Sand, founder of Living Passages Cruises and Tours (livingpassages.com). Living Passages specializes in Christian cruises and tours. Having brought many large and small groups on cruise lines, one of their goals is to create a wonderful experience for all ages.

The Headline: Phones, Flexibility, and Planning - Tips From a Year-Long Family Adventure

The Tips:

- Be prepared for chaos, especially on travel days. Having a strong mindset helps because you are sure to experience a hurdle or two.

- Seize the moment. When you're thinking about doing something, do it. Many times in the beginning of the trip, a family is prone to pass a sight or something else interesting and say to themselves 'let's come back here later.' Invariably, you just end up doing something else - another path leads to another adventure. A few days later you leave that destination realizing that you should have gone into that shop, museum, or whatever it was, when you had the chance. Bottom line - live in the present when you're traveling with kids. Because everyday life will interrupt your travels!

- Leave free time. Don't plan it all out.
- Get a SIM card. I have bought SIM cards in 13 different countries. They allow you to use maps on your cell phone, make skype calls, and a lot of other practical things. On top of this, they can be really cheap (most of the time around $25 for 30 days and plenty of data).
- Plan the big legs. If you use frequent flier miles this is an absolute necessity.

The Expert:

Adam Dailey ran Ludus Tours, a tour operator that was on the Inc. 500. During his time there, the company took more than 15,000 guests on their excursions. Last year, Adam decided to take a one year sabbatical with his family (including four small children age 6 and under).

The Headline: The Importance of Seeking Local Expertise

The Tip:

Engage the services of a tour operator who has experience in selling family tours. They have unparalleled access to local destination information, and many of their employees on the ground in the destinations have families of their own, so they are very aware of what is and is not suitable for children. They also know the ins and outs of unique family activities that are off the beaten tourist path, where families can have a totally original and unique experience.

The Expert:

David Capaldi, president of specialist travel agency Discover Latin America, a company that sells a large number of family tours. They creates custom, specialized, and luxury travel experiences in Latin America, with personalized consultations.

The Headline: Start the Fun Before You Start the Trip

The Tip:

For travel, especially with children and to places of historical significance, it helps to get them excited and interested before you actually take off. For example, if you're planning a family trip to Japan: find some age-appropriate literature about Japanese history and culture and read it together as a family. Look at maps of Japan and have the kids visually see where you will be moving in the country and what cities you will be visiting. Also, don't forget the food - introduce them to ramen, sushi, yakitori at some restaurants that are in your hometown to start exposing them to the cuisine of your destination. These little details will prepare you as a family for the trip you're about to go on together, get everyone excited, and prepare the kids for the most enriching cultural and educational experience.

The Expert:

Irina Vishnevskaya, founder of allé, a custom travel planning service for families who are seeking to go off the beaten path to really experience their destinations. They focus on planning unique, one of a kind trips that are custom made for each traveler/group of travelers - focusing primarily on multi-generational travel. Allé is designed to be a good fit for all budgets and works on the flat-fee model (http://alletravel.co/).

The Headline: Your Vacation Should Be About YOUR Interests

The Tip:

Although you may be traveling with kids, choosing what to do and where to go should start with what your kid's interests are. That is the same way the best tour companies plan all their excursions for clients. Personal interests should be the deciding factor - most everything else can be adjusted to suit you. Doing an online search for a given destination by simply typing in "the name of the city/country for kids" will yield the typical and most popular results. Consider tailoring your search to your interests. If your children are interested in chocolate, archaeology, farming - whatever it may be, consider searching by these interests and your destination to find unique opportunities for your vacation that include their hobbies. Don't assume anything is too far out there; you never know until you search. Also, don't assume that a stop you find is "too adult" without doing your due diligence and making an inquiry. Once you find places that match your children's interests, <u>then</u> you can find out if they accommodate children - many do! Don't just search for the basics and don't rule things out too early. Your vacation can be much more interesting if you go out of your way to really make it "yours."

The Expert:

Abigail Ekue, CEO and operator of Native Creative Concierge and NYC Travel Specialist. Native Creative curates and leads private excursions around New York City (www.nativecreativeconcierge.com/).

The Headline: Sometimes Multigenerational Travel Means Separate Time for Each Generation

The Tip:

From a company who deals with multi-generational family wildlife safaris to Africa, the best advice for all family clients is to make sure they plan at least one child-friendly activity (just for children) PER DAY. This includes kids going on their own separate trek with guides, Junior Ranger program activities, cooking lessons etc. For any vacation that features a "kid's club" or child/teen groups and activities, taking advantage of them will go a long way to helping both children and parents get the most out of their time. This comes into play not only on safari, but on cruise ships, all-inclusive resorts, and any place with staffed amenities for kids. The key is to allow some time for your kids to be with other kids. At the same time, this allows adults to be adults and do their thing while children are away. The time apart may just help you appreciate your time together that much more.

The Expert:

Rumit Mehta of tour company Immersion Journeys - 2012, 2013 & 2015 National Geographic Traveler - '50 Tours of a Lifetime' winners and safari/adventure travel experts (www.immersionjourneys.com/).

The Headline: Don't Be Afraid to Go Local...Or Adventurous!

The Tip:

When planning your family vacation, don't be afraid to go off the beaten track and maybe take a 4x4 Tour rather than staying in one place. The opportunities for new experiences and education for all the family are so much richer than sitting by the pool for a week! In many countries, such as Sri Lanka and Morocco, where family is so important and children almost revered, your driver or guides will often be excellent companions; spending time playing football, sand-boarding and Jumbe drumming. Together with the experience of a diverse range of locations and activities, this type of vacation gives your children the chance to meet local people and really connect with a culture. On your travels, it is also worth checking out the more adventurous activities which are usually reserved for adults. You may find child-friendly versions or other options which leave you time to chill out or take part yourself. Kitesurfing in Dakhla (Morocco), Camel Trekking in the Sahara, or Elephant Riding in Kandy (Sri Lanka) spring to mind!

When planning a trip like this, it can really be beneficial to find a smaller tour operator who has experience with families, who really knows the country, and who has traveled every road you will take. People like this tend to go that extra mile to make sure your vacation is well planned to suit your needs and the ages of your children, because their reputation depends upon all of you having an excellent time!

The Expert:

Rebecca Hutley is the Founder of, and a travel consultant for, Moroccan Journeys (www.moroccanjourneys.com). This UK

Tour Company specializes in private tours throughout Morocco. She is also the mother of a 12 year old daughter who always needs a lot to keep her occupied when away! She has traveled extensively with her daughter from when she was 10 weeks old.

The Headline: Snacks, Jetlag, and Helping Hands - Two Moms Who Know Travel

The Tips:

- If you'll be traveling with younger children - especially if you'll be going far enough away that jet lag will become an issue - try to create a bedtime routine a few weeks prior to your trip that will signal to your kids that it's time to go to sleep. Then, continue to stick to the same routine while on the trip for a smoother bedtime experience for all involved. If your kids' routine involves putting on pajamas and brushing teeth, then a familiar bedtime story followed by quiet time (potentially cuddling with a special blanket or stuffed animal brought from home), then do that all on vacation as well. If you are on a red-eye flight, start this routine with your kids as soon as you get on the plane so they will be asleep through most of the flight (with a little luck). -April Cole

- Before your trip, tell your kids where you're going, why, and what the schedule is for while you're there. If you give your kids the itineraries, and have them help you pack for your trip, they have a chance to relax and look forward to the experience more. As adults, we forget what a mystery a lot of life is when you're young. And traveling - at any age - is a lot more fun when you feel in control. -April Cole

- Pack a lot of snacks, including a "meal" for the plane. Some kids inevitably hate the food served on the airplane, so to help them get through the very long flights, it is a good idea to keep them well fed. -Andrea Ross

The Experts:

Andrea Ross is the founder and CEO of Journeys Within Tour Company, and has raised her two children (ages 8 and 10) on the road and in Southeast Asia for much of their lives.

April Cole is a Vice President of Sales for Journeys Within Tour Company, and has two children of her own (ages 5 and 9) who have accompanied her and her husband on many of their trips to Southeast Asia and around the world. Journeys Within is a boutique Southeast Asia tour company dedicated to delivering its guests unforgettable, customized trips through Cambodia, Thailand, Laos, Myanmar and Vietnam. For more information visit www.Journeys-Within.com.

The Headline: Stay in the Moment and Avoid Distractions

The Tip:

Put the smartphone away. Be sure to limit the use of tablets, smartphones, etc, to ensure you are present and engaged in the destination. Of course, smart phones double as cameras, but we actively discourage their use for playing games, texting friends, and using them for other purposes that are distractions. Some of the great joys of family travel are the bonds (or "bridges") that are formed when different generations share new and enriching experiences together, and it's simply harder for that to happen when kids or parents have their noses pressed up against their iPhone.

The Expert:

Tom Armstrong is a father of two and the corporate communications manager for Tauck's collection of Tauck Bridges guided land tours and cruises. Tauck is a 90-year fixture in guided travel, with over 100 journeys to more than 70 countries and all seven continents. "Bridges" family trips launched in 2003, and today operates 19 itineraries in Europe, North America, Africa, South America and Central America.

The Headline: Tips for Gluten Free Travel

The Tip:

Planning a gluten-free vacation can be daunting to some people. Celiac and gluten-intolerant travelers are afraid of getting sick from accidental gluten so far from home. With a little preparation and some research about your destination, you can travel worry-free this year.

1. Do your research. Search for gluten-free friendly restaurants, local support groups, and even bloggers to help you plan your meals away before your leave for your vacation.

2. Use an app. There are many "on-the-go" apps like AllergyEats and FindMeGlutenFree which help you find local gluten-free friendly restaurants based on your GPS location.

3. Pack a bag. Better safe than hungry! Always pack gluten-free food in your carry-on bag. Have a good mix of protein and snacks with food such as gluten-free jerky, sunbutter, pretzels, fruit, and nuts. Use frozen grapes to keep your food cold on the go.

The Expert:

Erin Smith is the founder of Gluten-Free Globetrotter®, a website that focuses on gluten-free travel. As someone personally living with celiac disease for more than thirty years, Erin requires a completely gluten-free lifestyle to remain healthy. Erin's goal is to help you navigate the gluten-free globe with top tips, travel maps, and even gluten-free itineraries. Learn more about Erin Smith and Gluten-Free Globetrotter at www.glutenfreeglobetrotter.com.

The Headline: Planning, Booking, and Making the Most of Your Time

The Tips:

Getting the most out of shared time while away:

- Allow for downtime. Downtime leads to creativity and spur of the moment activities that may end up being the highlight of your trip.
- Minimize social media time. You need to be in the moment with those around you.
- Keep it simple. Especially when younger children are involved.
- Be active… a vacation should be time to both see and DO. Everyone should do something that is a bit out of their comfort zone.
- Be flexible and encourage the trying of new things, such as new foods, activities, etc.
- Don't make every activity a group activity. Divide and conquer according to interests and share your stories at dinner time.
- Keep expectations reasonable.
- Take plenty of family photos along the way!
- How to plan and book a trip:
- Talk as a family about the wants and needs of each person, as well as the difference between wants and needs. Needs come first and include such considerations as when, how long, budget, and special requirements. Wants typically revolve around where to go, where to stay, how to travel, and available activities.
- Gather everyone's input and spend time discussing where to go as a group.
- After these discussions, involve a travel professional. They can weigh the wants, needs, and opinions of everyone involved. They may suggest options you might not have considered or even known about.

The Expert:

Connie Miller is a Business Development Manager for Travel Leaders. Travel Leaders (www.travelleaders.com/) describes itself as the largest travel agency franchisor in North America with more than 1,000 full-service locations. Travel Leaders Franchise Group has been named the top travel business franchisor in *Entrepreneur*'s Franchise 500 for the past 19 consecutive years.

When several experts agree on the same point, it gives us a strong indication that this is a great idea for you to consider. Here are a few common threads of advice and the experts who shared them.

IT PAYS TO INVOLVE KIDS IN PLANNING

It seems several top players in the field agree with us when we say that involving kids in the creation of your trip pays off big when it comes time to actually take it.

The Headline: Building Excitement Requires Action

The Tip:

Many parents have the experience of "dragging" their kids to a particular activity, whether on vacation or at home. If you are traveling, the stakes are higher and you want to get the best experience and value for your time. Create a sense of anticipation. Talk about the things you're going to do. Don't spring the activities on them while you are there. Look at it this way: you wouldn't want to go somewhere you know nothing about, or where you didn't know what to expect. Why would your children be any different? They don't know what's going on (unless you tell them), but they do know what is comfortable. Make them comfortable and excite them, not just about a theme park, but about the things you want to do.

The Expert:

Chris Oler, president and lead writer of Color Marketing & Design. He and his wife created a children's book series (Molly and the Magic Suitcase Book Series) based around travel. There is a destination immersion aspect to the books, though the focus is introducing children to cultures around the world (www.colormktg.com/).

The Headline: Experience Something New Together

The Tips:

Vacations are all about creating memories with your children...memories that you'll talk about over dinner and bring up at family reunions for years to come. What better way to create a memory than by picking one "new" activity to do with your family each time you travel? It's easy to get locked into our comfort zones and do the same old thing every time you travel. But the same old thing done on every vacation isn't going to be what the kids latch onto for years to come. They're going to remember the new, the exciting, the thrilling, the adrenaline-inducing, the unique, the different. These "new" activities can be anything you or your kids dream up and oftentimes can be the jumping off point for planning a vacation. Figure out your budget and decide just how simple or extravagant you want to go. Sometimes it can be just as much fun to research the activities with your kids beforehand! New experiences can be as simple and inexpensive as waking up in the middle of the night to look for shooting stars (bring a blanket and hot cocoa!) Or you can budget a more expensive activity (or multiple if you can afford to), like zip lining or whitewater rafting for the first time. Whatever you choose, make the kids a part of the planning process and have fun with it!

Involve the entire family in the process and make the selection and planning a big part of the fun. Bring the family together and ask a few simple questions to get started.

- If you could go anywhere in the world, where would you go and why?
- What are the top 3 things you look forward to doing on vacation?
- What sort of adventure - soft or challenging?
- What level of comfort? Camping, hotels, eco-lodges?

Look through lots of brochures and websites together, and note who reacts to what. Example: if everyone lights up at the shot of white water rafting, that will help you plan where and what. Then ask others around you what they did, what they liked and what they didn't. That is just a start. With all this insight, you need to keep copious notes and files. Make it a fun event and combine it with a pizza night, so all look forward to it. Get everyone involved during the planning process, and it will make the actual vacation that much more enjoyable for all.

The Expert:

Kasey Austin, Vice President of Operations & Senior Family Tour Guide at Austin Adventures (austinadventures.com/). 2012 & 2013: Named one of the "Top Young Travel Industry Professionals 35 and Under" by Travalliance Media. 2014: Named The World's Top Family Guide by the editors of Outside Magazine.

The Headline: Let Children's Involvement Grow Along With Them

The Tip:

When traveling with kids it pays to get them involved with the planning process. This task can vary from asking them simple A and B questions when they're little, to encouraging them to research a destination or plan a budget when they're older. This process gets them involved emotionally and builds excitement for the trip plus, if the trip doesn't go as well as planned, the blame doesn't rest entirely on mom's or dad's shoulders (as the ones who typically plan family vacations). Encouraging your kids to assist in travel planning also builds confidence when the time comes for them to plan their own trips in the future.

The Expert:

Tonya Prater is a travel writer for her own site, The Traveling Praters, as well as Ohio TravelingMom for Traveling-Mom.com. Her family has traveled extensively, having spent time in hotel rooms, as an RV family, and as avid roadtrippers. Her kids are now college age and plan their own getaways, while she and her husband adjust to the empty nest years and travel as a couple instead of a family of five.

THINK OUTSIDE THE HOTEL BOX

Multiple experts agree that it is worth thinking about looking past hotels and resorts for your lodging needs.

The Headline: Thinking More Locally About Lodging

The Tip:

When traveling as a family, especially on a budget, it is a good idea to consider renting an apartment through a vacation rental website or a local agent. Renting an apartment can often be cheaper, more centrally-located, and better for the family's routine than staying in a hotel. In a rental apartment with a kitchen, you can provide your kids with the breakfast they like, make sandwiches to take with you for lunch, and even make dinner for picky children (or adults) who may not want to try the local cuisine. Find a place with a washing machine, since we all know children are physically incapable of keeping clothes clean for a day. Read all of the reviews of a place before renting, because everyone has different ideas of what is acceptable and what is not, and you want to really understand all the dynamics of a place before renting. 20 people might say it's fantastic, and the 21st might mention that the 4 story walk-up is a little tough on the knees, or the pop up nightclub next door kept them awake all night, or the smelly dishwasher that the first 20 people didn't use. Do your research, and you can find some wonderfully charming places that let you feel like a local when you are far from home.

The Expert:

Paige Conner Totaro of "All Over The Map," a family vacation specialty consultancy based in Alexandria, Virginia, USA. In 2012 she took a year-long trip around the world with her husband and twin 12-year-old daughters, and knows a thing or two about traveling as a family (www.alloverthemap.net/).

The Headline: Serviced Apartments Bridge the Gap Between Rentals and Hotels

The Tip:

While hotels may be seen as the default choice to some when traveling abroad, many people haven't yet discovered that serviced apartments are a family-friendly accommodation and a spacious yet affordable alternative to hotels. Here is how serviced apartments can offer far greater value for your money in a family vacation:

- Spacious home-like environment - Although they may be priced similarly, serviced apartments often offer much more space than hotel rooms. With separate living space and bedrooms, parents can enjoy some space to relax after a busy day out without disturbing their children.

- Kitchen facilities and appliances - serviced apartments eliminate parents' concerns to store and use equipment such as sterilizers and food blenders.

- Serviced in line with hotels - Some serviced apartments even have 24-hour concierge in place where parents can inquire about babysitting services and lifestyle services such as ticket ordering and airport transfers.

The Expert:

Monique Fok is a representative of Marlin Apartments (www.marlinapartments.com/). Marlin is the biggest owner-operator of serviced apartments in the UK, with over 700 apartments located in six key leisure destinations in London including London Bridge, Canary Wharf, Aldgate, Stratford, Limehouse, and Queen Street.

The Headline: More Room Space Means More Personal Space

The Tip:

As wonderful as spending time together can be, it can also be stressful. Accommodations that offer the opportunity for personal space are a great way to help alleviate this stress. An apartment or house can provide not only private space for mom and dad but also for the kids who might need to have a little privacy of their own. It also provides common area space so that when one person wants to stay up later, they have a place to go other than the bathroom. While this sounds expensive, it could prove to be a cost saver. If you are traveling outside of the US, many rooms accommodate only two people thereby requiring two rooms for a family. This can be quite expensive. Also, apartments have kitchens! Having the ability to cook meals or even just to serve a continental breakfast can be a huge cost savings; eating out is expensive! Another bonus to renting is that it enables you to feel more like a "local," which is always a bonus when it comes to traveling.

The Expert:

In June, 2008, Lisa Shusterman, her husband, and two nine year old daughters set off for a one year trip around the world. They left behind the security of the lives they built for themselves in Cincinnati, Ohio, for a life of the unknown. Lisa is author of "Around the World in Easy Ways, A Guide to Planning Long-Term Travel With or Without Your Kids." Check out her blog at www.oneworldonetrip.blogspot.com.

SLOWING THINGS DOWN

It may be difficult to fight the urge to pack as much as possible into your trip, but experienced travelers and professionals agree that it is worth the effort.

The Headline: Letting Yourselves Breathe

The Tip:

Have a day, or several days ideally, where there are no reservations, no trains or planes to catch. Families tend to be over-scheduled at home and keeping children on a demanding schedule is a common source of tension and frustration between parents and children. How often do you say, "Hurray, we are going to be late!" in a typical week? If you find yourself saying it at the beach to be on time for some sandcastle-building class, you have just transported you and your children back home.

The Expert:

Robin Hutson, publisher of Luxe Recess (http://luxerecess.com/). This family travel magazine was created for parents who like nice hotels, and seek a luxury hotel directory and parenting magazine in one.

The Headline: Sometimes Less is More

The Tips:

Consider slow travel. Not that you have to drive really slow or avoid airplanes, just don't try to cram everything in. Travel with kids can be exhausting, or exhilarating. To achieve the latter you must leave room to play at the playground, to admire the grasshoppers, and to pick up stones and throw them in the stream. This is how kids experience and enjoy travel. This also helps you avoid the "I need a vacation after my vacation" feeling. Do not simply fill every day with activities, but take it easy, slow down and skip "must see" activities in order to allow kids to make memories at the local playground, on the soccer field with kids who don't speak English, or in the grocery store.

The Expert:

Paul Kortman, of nomadtogether.com - a community of location independent families. The Kortmans are a full time traveling family. They sold their house and stuff to travel the world with four kids ages 7 and under. Two years later they are still doing it and loving it.

Packing Lists and Checklists for You to Use

Packing is a key component of planning, and forgetting something can throw a wrench in your travel plans. Not having everything you need can throw off both your schedule and your budget, forcing you to spend time and money replacing something you already have at home.

Anticipating your every possible need, while also packing light enough to avoid heavy bag fees is more art than science. With more experience you will learn what works best for your family and master this important skill. The first step is to invest in some good gear, as discussed in a previous chapter. Lighter suitcases give you more room to work with, and devices that combine multiple benefits into one small package free up additional room by combining functionality.

Here we share with you some basic packing lists for a few common types of vacation. Use them as a starting point for your family, and customize them to suit your needs. The general list applies to all vacations. Add to it either the beach or winter checklists if your vacation falls into either of these types. We have also included a handy supplemental checklist for those traveling with infants and toddlers.

Additionally, we have provided a "last day" checklist, which can serve as a valuable tool before you leave your hotel room, rental home, or other accommodations for the last time. Use this list to help make sure you didn't forget anything, either that you need to bring or to do before heading home.

Our "booking checklist" covers information from the next section of the book, but makes sense to have here with our comprehensive collection of lists. Use it to make sure you are taking all the necessary steps to find the best deals and cover all your bases when planning your trip.

Finally, our "Pre-Trip Checklist" compiles much of the information from this third section of the book, and condenses all you need to remember about logistics before stepping out the door.

All the lists are presented on their own page (or pages) for easy reference. Make copies of them, pack them with you or use them at home and make physical marks to check off things as you do them, in order to avoid forgetting anything important.

RealFamilyTrips.com's General Vacation Packing List

Travel Related Essentials:

- Confirmations from Airline, Hotel, Activities, Etc.
- Pre-Boarding Passes, Club Passes, Etc.
- Any Tickets, Passes, or Other Admission You Have Purchased in Advance
- Passport/Visa (in carry-on or in your pocket)
- Driver's License, Foreign Endorsements, and Auto Insurance Information (if driving)
- Credit Cards (store separately when carrying several)
- Itinerary
- Maps/Directions
- Cash (preferably in home currency and that of your destination)
- Guidebook (or any research materials that can help you choose and alternate activities in case of a cancellation)
- Membership Cards (AAA, loyalty clubs, etc.)
- Phrasebook or Translator App
- Medical Insurance Card
- Travel Insurance Documents
- Emergency Contact Information (for you)

- Contact Information for Airline, Hotel, Activities, Guides, Restaurants, Etc. (anyone you have booked with or plan on visiting)
- Contact Information for Credit Card Company
- Copies of Passport/Visa and Other Travel Documents
- *Electronics, Entertainment, and Related:*
- Cell Phone
- Camera (still and video - unless you use your phone or other device for this)
- Chargers for Electronic Devices, Battery Packs, and Other Accessories
- Cables For Devices, and a Backup (store in separate places)
- Voltage Adapters and/or Converters
- Batteries for Devices that Use Them
- Film/Memory Cards
- Something to Read
- Material to Entertain Children (tablets, MP3 Players, eReaders, video games, books, toys, etc.)
- Headphones
- Notepads, Pens, Pencils, Art Supplies
- *Toiletries:*
- List Of Medications/Doctor's Letter
- Prescriptions in Original Packaging (pack in your carry-on)
- A Small First Aid Kit
- Over the Counter Remedies for Common Ailments (cold, upset stomach, etc.)
- Toothbrushes
- Toothpaste

- Floss
- Soap
- Deodorant
- Shampoo
- Conditioner
- Vitamins
- Brush/Comb
- Moisturizer
- Glasses/Contacts (if applicable, pack in your carry-on) and Backups (pack separately)
- Contact Solution and Case (if applicable)
- Shaving Supplies
- Personal Hygiene Products
- Makeup (and makeup remover)
- Nail File/Clippers
- Cotton Swabs
- *Clothing:*
- Underwear
- Socks
- Undershirts
- Sleepwear
- Casual Shirts
- Formal Shirts
- Pants/Skirts/Dresses
- Shorts
- Sweaters/Sweatshirts
- Lightweight, Packable Jacket

- Formal Shoes
- Casual Shoes
- Belt
- Jewelry

RealFamilyTrips.com's Beach Vacation Packing List

- **[Everything From the General Vacation Packing List]**
- Plastic Bags or Other Waterproof Solutions for Electronics and Valuables
- Sunscreen
- Facial Sunscreen (if you use a special one for your face, recommended)
- Lip Balm with SPF
- Towels (may not be necessary, depends on your hotel or rental)
- Bathing Suits (at least 2 per family member)
- Beach Cover-ups
- Changes of Clothes for After Beach/Pool Days
- Sandals or Other Easy-To-Remove Footwear
- Water Shoes for Walking/Wading (we like Keen's)
- Beach Bag or Tote for Day Trips
- Sunglasses
- Hats
- Cooler Bag for Snacks and Drinks
- Beach Toys
- Water
- Goggles

- Aloe Vera Gel for Sunburns
- Any Safety/Flotation Devices
- Insect Repellant
- Disposable Wipes for Quick Cleaning
- Books and Reading Material for Downtime
- Beach Badges, Passes, or Any Tickets You Have Purchased in Advance

RealFamilyTrips.com's Ski, Snow and Winter Vacation Packing List

- [Everything From the General Vacation Packing List]
- Hats
- Gloves (heavy for the slopes, lighter for walking around)
- Scarves
- Boots (ski and hiking)
- Slippers or Other Warm Footwear (for around the house)
- Sunglasses
- Goggles
- Long Underwear
- Heavy Sweaters/Sweatshirts
- Ski Mask
- Waterproof Ski Jacket
- Waterproof Ski Pants
- Heavy Wool and/or Waterproof Socks
- Hair Dryer (unless sure hotel/lodging will provide one)
- Hand Warmers

- Ski Lock
- Skis/Snowboards
- Poles
- Helmets
- Put Ski Carrier on Car if Driving
- Sunscreen
- Extra Lip Balm, Moisturizer, and Vaseline
- Hydration Pack (like Camelbak or other water delivery systems)
- Lift Passes and Any Other Tickets You Have Purchased In Advance

RealFamilyTrips.com's Infant/Toddler Vacation Packing List

- **[Everything From the General Vacation Packing List]**
- Stroller
- Pack and Play
- Waterproof Sheets
- Car (or booster) Seat
- Portable High Chair/Booster
- Children's Toilet Seat
- Baby Carrier
- Bottles/Sippy Cups (with extra caps and tops)
- Formula
- Wipes
- Diapers
- Changing Pad
- Diaper Bag

- Bibs
- Extra Clothes
- Baby Food
- Spoon
- Pacifiers
- Ointment
- Blankets
- Juice (remember to buy <u>after</u> security if flying)
- Baby Toiletries (shampoo, soap, lotion)
- Baby Pain Medication (and mini first aid kit)
- Baby Sunblock, Insect Repellant
- Toothbrush and Toothpaste
- Baby Monitor

NOTE: Consider shipping some of these items (for example, diapers, wipes, baby food) ahead of time, or making arrangements with your hotel or a local store to have them delivered to you upon arrival.

RealFamilyTrips.com's "Last Day of Vacation" Checklist

- Stop to pick up any last minute souvenirs you have been on the fence about, or to retrieve any gifts you may have ordered or placed on hold.
- Ship home any large items or things you aren't allowed to travel with.
- Don't forget to take extra pictures of your last day, and fill in any gaps you might have missed in terms of city photos, pictures of the kids, or group shots.
- Pack layers in an easily accessible place, in an outside pocket or the top of the clothes in your suitcase, so you can grab them before your flight (if flying home).

- Be sure to double check room to not leave anything behind.
- Double check outlets to make sure you haven't left chargers plugged in and forgotten.
- Pack reading material, small games, and other entertainment to keep children happy during the return trip.
- Fully charge devices for the flight/drive/ride back.
- Be sure to download music, movies, eBooks and other digital materials before leaving.
- If you rented a home or apartment, make sure you did not leave appliances on, shut off all the lights, closed the BBQ, locked all doors and windows, and followed their rules regarding garbage removal (as well as any other check-out procedures).

RealFamilyTrips.com's Vacation Booking and Planning Checklist

- Select Vacation Dates
- Explore Possible Destinations and Research Prices
- Select a Destination
- Quick Browse to Narrow Down Possibilities
- Consider Holidays and Events at Your Destination
- Choose Cities/Locations
- Browse Activities
- Browse Flights, Cruises, and Other Transportation
- Browse Hotels and Accommodations
- Browse Package Deals
- Check Blackout Dates for Bookings and Sales
- Make Sure to Check Both Aggregator Sites and Airline/Hotel/Cruise Line Websites

- Be Sure to Compare Package Deals to Booking Individual Elements, Do This On Both Aggregator Sites and Airline/Hotel/Cruise Line Websites
- Check for Available Discounts from Your Credit Cards, Bank, Membership in Organizations like AAA, Loyalty Clubs, and the Like
- Book Transportation and Accommodations
- Discuss Activities With Family
- Research Guides
- Look Into Getting Around At Destination - Rental Car vs. Public Transit or Driver
- Does Anything Require Certifications, Permissions, Permits?
- Begin Playing Around With Choices to Create Days that "Fit" Together and Have A Linear Path
- Book Activities, Meals, and Excursions
- Create a Clean Copy of Your Itinerary Broken Down By Day To Pack and Bring on Your Trip
- Import All Information into Any Travel Apps You Choose to Use

RealFamilyTrips.com's Pre-Trip Checklist (Some Not Applicable for Domestic Travel)

- Check Passports, Renew if Needed
- Research Vaccinations and Other Medical Requirements
- Get Any Necessary Inoculations
- While At Doctor, Get Letter to Confirm Your Inoculations and to Clarify Any Medications You Are Taking
- Secure Necessary Visas
- Research Your Medical Insurance (confirm it will cover you abroad)

- Purchase Travel Insurance
- Make Arrangements for International Cell Phone Use
- Reserve a Car and Double Check Requirements for Driving at Your Destination (including that your auto insurance covers you abroad)
- Alert Credit Cards to Upcoming Trip
- If Possible, Secure Foreign Cash Before Leaving (or have a plan on arrival)
- Begin Adjusting Your Schedule a Few Days In Advance of Trip to Avoid Jetlag
- Make Any Requests of In-Flight Meals for Special Dietary Needs
- Request Non-Smoking Accommodations For Your Lodging
- Make Copies of Travel Documents
- Pack
- Make Sure Home is Secure, Arrangements Are Made
- Have a Plan for Care of Any Pets
- Stop Mail and Newspapers (or make arrangements with a neighbor/friend to pick up and check on house)
- Pay Upcoming Bills (for duration of your time away, and a few days after to be safe)
- Leave Emergency Contact Information and Itinerary (with a friend or relative)
- Get and Set Randomized Light Timers for Extra Security
- Double Check Tickets and Reservation Information
- Update Email Auto-Reply Message (helps fight temptation to check in while away)
- Arrange Transportation to Airport/Train Station (and transport home at the end)

- Throw Away Perishable Items in Refrigerator
- Empty Trash
- Adjust Thermostat
- Power Off Home Electronics, Unplug If Possible
- Check That Flights Are On-Schedule (and that you have/can get seats together)
- Online Flight Check In (note that some airlines will allow you to pay a lesser fee for luggage if you do this online instead of at the airport)
- Have Appropriate Denominations to Tip Airport Porters and Hotel Bellmen
- Lock all Luggage (and make sure ID tags have current information)
- Load Luggage Into The Car (or place by door if being picked up, you don't want to leave a full suitcase behind)
- Lock All Doors and Windows
- Set The Alarm

Part IV

Guide to Online Resources and Booking

You Can't Go Unless You Book. As we have tried to stress throughout this book, thoughtful preparation will make every aspect of your vacation better. It will help you to clear as many questions and concerns as possible beforehand, and enable you to remain present once you arrive.

Knowing your options will also allow you to find the best possible vacation for you and your family.

Careful planning means knowing your resources and how to use them. Today's traveler has a wealth of information that was previously beyond the reach of anyone but an expert. Today a wealth of books, websites, videos, and other resources literally put a world of travel resources at your fingertips.

At the same time, not every source can be trusted. At the very least, some are better than others, and considering your time at home is valuable as well, knowing where to look will help you enjoy your family more and help you spend less time on your computer researching.

In this section of the book we break down some of our favorite resources for planning and booking vacations. These are our best bets for making your vacation happen.

Additionally, we have laid out some general guidelines for booking, as well as some helpful tips and tricks.

Knowing what resources are available to you, what their assets and limitations are, as well as how to use them, will empower you to research any vacation you want to. Some will also help you to discover ideas and inspire trips that you might not have thought of in the first place.

Knowing the best booking resources and how to use them is also a major component of enabling bigger and better vacations. Through our discussion of the value of travel, as well as some examples of great destinations, we have tried to stress that amazing trips can be achieved, often within your family's budget. Knowing and using online resources for planning and booking represent your ticket to fun and excitement.

The Websites We Use (And You Should Too)

The following resources represent a "best of the web" in terms of sites that help to plan, book, and improve family travel. Here you will find sites that compile deals, and help you to find great airfare, accommodations, guides, cruises, and more.

Some sites also help to nail down the more minor details, like getting seats together on an airplane, or providing helpful travel hints.

Some of these should become constant companions, sites you browse on a recurring basis to stay in the loop and to be informed of new trends in pricing, and available destinations. Others will be go-to resources when you are in the process of actively planning a trip and locking down reservations.

These are all sites we use or have used ourselves, and we wouldn't recommend any that we didn't see value in for our own family vacations.

That being said, no site is perfect (not even our own!) and so we have noted some key information about each. Here you will find a brief overview of what the site has to offer, what we like about it, and anything important to note (or that we think could use some work) in order to help you make the most out of your time with it.

Resources change constantly, and unfortunately, as a result of the fast pace of changing technology, some of this list may become outdated soon after this book is published. Sadly, there is no way around this fact. As of the late summer of 2015, these are the resources we use to plan our own trips. As new things emerge over time, you will find other resources to suit your family needs. Once you get in the habit of making some degree of travel reading a part of your regular life, you will inevitably hear about some new sites and experiment with others. We will also continue to share our own information and opinions at RealFamilyTrips.com.

Talk to your friends and family about what they use to to plan your vacations and share resources with them. After all, that is what we hope this book and RealFamilyTrips.com can be for you, our readers. We are here to share what has enabled such great travel for us, so that you can enjoy the same.

TripAdvisor

What Do They Do?

TripAdvisor is primarily an engine for reviews of vacation related services - and it covers just about all of them. Here you will find information about lodging, rental properties, restaurants, activities (called "things to do"), and flights. You will also find location and interest based forums, a nod to the site's reliance on user generated content. This open-sourced way of gathering information relies on user generated reviews and reviewer-submitted locations. The site does retain some oversight and discourages "paid-for" endorsements, but as with any public forum there is a lot of grey area. Use it to research activities and places to stay, both for the reviews themselves and as a tool for discovery.

What We Like Best:

- The sheer *volume* of information is incredible, you can find just about anything here.
- The interface is smooth and easy to use.
- The ratings are very useful…but there is a catch (see below).

Things to Note:

While it seems that many people use TripAdvisor primarily for reviews, you can book some flights, accommodations, and activities directly through the site. TripAdvisor is quickly becoming a travel empire, and they own several other sites, some of which we will discuss further in this chapter. It is worth looking at their prices while you are already on their site, to see if it makes sense to book through them.

The ratings need to be taken with a grain of salt. Some are more thoughtful than others, some people have axes to grind, and you have no way of knowing if a reviewing person or family has similar taste/values to your own. It is hard to know who to trust, and would be nice if they were sorted by usefulness.

Their list of top attractions is very helpful, but for many destinations may seem like a hodgepodge of activities, hotels, restaurants, theater, activities and more. It is a good place to start, but tough to wade through.

Orbitz

What Do They Do?

A true giant of the booking world, Orbitz compiles listings on everything from flights, hotels, cars, and activities, to vacation packages in one place. You can browse for inspiration or search for specific activities and destinations. Regular deals can equal big savings, and they let you search a number of vendors at once.

What We Like Best:

- Their interface is great and makes it easy to find what you are looking for.

- A good choice for larger families with tools that help bigger and more complicated bookings simpler. They are one of the few sites that allow us to search for 8 tickets at once (though their system for this is not perfect).

- Airline courtesy cancellation from Orbitz means you can cancel your flight within 24 hours (by 10PM CST) for a full refund to your credit card, with no airline penalties. This is great for the early booking phase, and lets you quickly pull the trigger on a good looking deal, then circle back and confirm dates and schedules with the family. Check the fine print here before pulling the trigger to confirm that your booking qualifies for this free cancellation policy. Also, some service charges may still apply, and the time window varies with some "budget" airlines.

Things to Note:

Customer service can be lacking, even at the supervisor level. It can be hard to get a real person who can solve your problems when complications arise. Package deals do not allow you the option to fly into one airport and out of another, which makes it a less useful tool for regional tours. When the number of discounted tickets are limited their interface may see you lose out on a deal. If there are only a couple cheaper seats left, and you try to book a larger party, it will tell you that there aren't discounted seats available for your party, as opposed to telling you that you can purchase two at the cheaper rate and the rest at full price.

TravelZoo

What Do They Do?

TravelZoo compiles deals from across the travel world. Think of it as a "best of" digest for where in the world you can go and where on the web you can save. Their newsletter is one of the better ones around, and can be great for deals as well as inspiration. Their staff of "deal experts" represents former journalists and researchers who aggregate, negotiate, and highlight deals for lodging, flights, cruises, restaurants, spas, cars, activities, and entertainment.

What We Like Best:

- <u>Weekly deals</u> not only provide fantastic savings, but keep you in the loop and can inspire destinations you hadn't thought of.
- <u>Organization</u> is wonderful here, and makes finding what you are looking for simple.

Things to Note:

Their email flashes are geo-targeted, and can be tailored to both where you live and where you want to go. Their local deals resemble Groupon or LivingSocial, and allow you to purchase vouchers to later redeem at a local merchant. Note that companies pay to advertise their deals here, though TravelZoo does exercise oversight over which ones they choose to list.

Changing your mind is harder than we would like it to be. Prepaying for deals means you have to lock into a specific promotion and pay for the privilege of using it, so you can't book and then change your mind without a penalty. A lack of family oriented deals here means that you have to wade through a lot of things that won't apply to you, and won't be able to enjoy all the savings they have to offer.

Jetsetter

What Do They Do?

Another major booking site, Jetsetter compiles deals for all major categories of travel, and arranges them in a beautiful site that makes browsing easy. Here you can browse by destination, or see a list of their current hot picks and top destinations. They have a great magazine and blog section that is a wonderful place to look for inspiration and explore possibilities. They organize information by a variety of qualifiers, helping you to find a particular "feel" for your vacation. Choose from "posh" or "brilliant" hotels, as well as browse vacation "collections" like the best all-inclusives, or editor's picks. Frequent sales offer great savings, while editorial content rises above what most aggregators provide to their users.

What We Like Best:

- The interface is one of the cleanest around, with sleek and intuitive styling that makes finding deals easy.
- Many of the deals are great. When you find a relevant sale for your family, chances are it will be one of the best prices out there. They also offer a wide array of deals at any given time.

Things to Note:

Cancellation options are limited. When you book here, you need to plan on actually going. For this reason it is much better for definite and/or short term travel planning and booking, as opposed to playing around to research and explore possibilities. JetSetter is a TripAdvisor company, and offers many of the bookings on that site - information flows back and forth between the two.

Kayak

What Do They Do?

Kayak is one of the biggest sites for aggregating travel deals, pulling information from an incredible number of resources to offer prices and openings for hotels, flights, cars, and package deals. The sheer number of deals compiled makes it a solid starting point for getting the lay of the land, and determining whether a certain trip is possible or not before leaning into locking down the very best price. Useful tools help you to browse by location and see minimum prices, giving you a solid idea of what is within your price range after taking their discounts into consideration.

What We Like Best:

- Interface here is a strong suit, with easy searchability and good organization.
- The flexible dates option is a great tool to help find a way to make a trip work for your family. When you have more wiggle room on when you leave or return, you can save a lot and Kayak's interface makes it easy to see the difference between certain dates and times.

Things to Note:

You do not book directly through them which can lead to a delay in information. The deal you see and like may be gone by the time you move over to actually book it, which can be frustrating. They also have one of the most popular mobile apps for a travel booking company, which can be great for idly browsing deals during downtime and discovering your next trip while out and about.

Airbnb

What Do They Do?

A leader in the world of peer to peer vacation rentals and presenting almost anything as a lodging option while away. People rent everything from entire apartments and homes, to rooms, tents, treehouses, and truly unique properties. This is a great place to find something with a special flavor to it, and you can opt to travel more like a local by avoiding touristy hotels or areas. Booking like this can be a good way to save money; you can find a property tailored to your exact size and location requirements, and sacrifice some amenities for savings.

What We Like Best:

- <u>Interface</u> is a big plus here and very easy to use, with simple navigation.

- <u>Favorites</u> let you easily save multiple properties as you browse an often impressive number of listings, and gradually narrow down without having to repeat your search.

- <u>Ratings</u> are both useful and simple to follow, which is a great help in narrowing your search.

Things to Note:

The rating system also goes both ways, so you may have some trouble booking until you build up your score and prove yourself reliable. You can only contact the owner through Airbnb and their interface, at least until you commit to rent. After locking in, you can get direct phone and/or email for them. We understand that this protects the site's commission and avoids circumventing them to book directly, but this can get in the way of smooth communication when you have detailed questions to ask before making a commitment. Also note that there are fees on top of the rental price that get paid by both the person renting and the guest. It is their business, but can be frustrating to pay for the right to rent.

HomeAway

What Do They Do?

Similar to Airbnb, HomeAway connects you with vacation rental properties varying from rooms and apartments to whole homes and unique spaces. While Airbnb keeps everything internal, HomeAway is essentially an online classified ad, in which owners pay to be listed and negotiate with potential renters directly. This can be a great resource to find different and affordable options for lodging, potentially enhancing your vacation by saving money or opening up different opportunities.

What We Like Best:

- Good selection means a lot of quality options to choose from.
- No commission to be paid by the tenant can help save money over similar services.
- Useful rating system helps narrow down the possibilities quickly and efficiently.
- Direct communication with property owners makes the process easier, and you can ask as many questions as you like with quicker responses.

Things to Note:

Their favorites interface is lacking over competitors in the same category.

VRBO

What Do They Do?

Like Airbnb and HomeAway, this is a place to go to find vacation rentals. More like HomeAway than Airbnb, this online classified section puts you in direct contact with the owners of rental properties and empowers you to search, negotiate, and book yourself. Hosts here tend more often to be professionals who list for a living, as opposed to casual users who are "just trying out" posting something for the fun of it or some extra cash.

What We Like Best:

- Good selection means a lot of quality options to choose from.
- No commission to be paid by the tenant can help save money over similar services.
- Useful rating system helps narrow down the possibilities quickly and efficiently.
- Direct communication with property owners makes the process easier, and you can ask as many questions as you like with quicker responses.

Things to Note:

Their favorites interface is lacking over competitors in the same category. The site is owned by HomeAway, which may lead to some repetition in listings and similar offerings. At the same time, do not assume that everything is cross listed and do yourself the favor of searching both, in case the ideal listing for you is only on one or the other.

AirfareWatchdog

What Do They Do?

This aggregator compiles deals on flights from most major (and many more obscure) airlines in one place. It is a great tool to search once and see just what sorts of prices are available. Its greatest feature, however, is the ability to set up customized alerts for a particular route to track prices over time. This is the place you go to program your dream vacations and watch as fares develop and new sales arise. When you know where you want to go and want to wait for the best price, their alerts will keep you in the know with less effort on your part. Aside from alerts on your chosen destinations, regular email digests also highlight the places you can fly with the most money saved at any given time.

What We Like Best:

- Alerts make for incredible opportunities to save. Just sit back and watch deals come to you and pounce on the one that makes your dream trip possible. We have gotten New York City to Hawaii tickets for under $200 (round trip) using alerts.

Things to Note:

Interface here is less intuitive and makes booking more complicated than it needs to be. The fast paced nature of deals and alerts here makes preparation key. Discuss where you want to go and an acceptable budget so you are ready to jump quickly when the right fare comes along. Waiting could cost you a fantastic opportunity.

Fare Compare

What Do They Do?

Another airline aggregator, this site helps you find great prices on tickets from a variety of airlines. They distinguish themselves from the competition with unique tools that help you browse available fares in new and exciting ways. While AirfareWatchdog is the go-to when you know exactly where you want to go, this site is better for browsing with a more open mind. If you know *when* you want to travel but not necessarily *where*, the browsing tools here will help you find the best deals and track current trends in the airline world. They also provide planning services and travel advice, further positioning them as a great tool for those looking to expand their knowledge of travel and explore with an open mind.

What We Like Best:

- The interactive map is perhaps their best feature. Simply plug in the month you want to travel and watch the map change to show you trends in worldwide prices and see where low fares are at a given time. This helps discover areas that are more affordable than you may think, and help you realize that a vacation imagined as a distant dream may actually be possible today.

Things to Note:

Interface here is less intuitive and makes booking more complicated than it needs to be. Besides which areas of the world are more affordable at a given time, watching the trends here can help teach you which times of year you can book travel to avoid higher pricing.

AirlineQuality.com

What Do They Do?

Here airlines themselves are put in the spotlight, as opposed to their fares. User reviews are compiled and indexed to provide comprehensive ratings on airline quality and safety. You will also find reviews on seats, airport lounges, and actual airports. When you have a lot of options, or are dealing with smaller or lesser known airlines with whom you are unfamiliar, it pays to be informed before you book so that you don't end up in a nightmare situation.

What We Like Best:

- A great tool to research information on airlines themselves. This is especially useful for more obscure carriers, when looking to book through a regional carrier for a foreign nation you have no experience with.

Things to Note:

This is not a site to book on, just a tool for research. You can also contribute your own reviews to highlight a great experience or voice a concern about a bad trip. Please note that peer reviews open up all the usual concerns: not knowing who is writing and how much to believe. You may have to spend some time browsing a lot of reviews to get a good feel for things.

CruiseCompete

What Do They Do?

As the name indicates, this site puts cruise agents in direct competition with one another, in order to offer the best deals on cruises and to help you to get the best price for your family. With cruises from a wide range of lines and most routes covered here, it is a fantastic tool for both research and booking. You can find significant discounts that make cruising a more affordable option. You can browse current deals, search for specific cruises or routes, request a quote, or contact an agent. The ability to talk to agents puts you in touch with experts who know cruising, and allows you to learn a lot as you look to save.

What We Like Best:

- Deals on cruises here are hard to beat, and you can get some of the best prices available.
- Interface is a strong suit and makes the site easy to use.
- Quick responses to questions make research a breeze and help you book more confidently.

Things to Note:

Agents here *can* be more sales oriented than concerned with customer service. This varies from agent to agent and shouldn't be assumed, but something to watch for when you get someone on the phone. You *do* get the benefit of seeing numerous quotes all in one place.

The service is free to consumers and agents don't have your contact information until you decide to contact them. While cruises are the main event here, you can also book shore excursions through their competitive pricing model. Consider using this tool to see what the options are during an upcoming trip, and find discounted admission for popular on-shore activities.

SeatGuru

What Do They Do?

This is the place to go to browse available seats and to find out not just what flights are available, but where exactly you might sit. This is a great tool for families who prefer not to be surprised, and for whom where they sit is an important factor. The longer the flight, the more useful the site can be. Seat-

Guru allows for some shopping for flights here, as well as reviews of seat comfort, but the main feature is information on the available seating for upcoming flights.

What We Like Best:

- <u>A great tool</u> for finding the best seats on the plane.
- <u>Ideal for families</u> who like to sit together, or who are willing to split up but only in specific configurations.

Things to Note:

Sometimes their seat configurations will not match with a given flight because of slight variations in aircraft. It would be helpful if they could point out exactly which aircraft a flight will be using, rather than have the passenger try to match the two up. This is a TripAdvisor company, owned by the travel giant and sharing some information across sites.

Vacations To Go

What Do They Do?

Looking to take a cruise? This cruise price aggregator specializes in last minute bookings and deals for upcoming sailings. They compile a massive amount of data and present one of the broadest pictures of what is available in the world of seabound vacations. You can browse available cruises and current deals by cruise line, region, or current savings. This is a great tool for discovery and can help you to book, as well as learn about available cruises for your family.

What We Like Best:

- <u>A great place to start</u> your research and get the lay of the land before you start diving in for more details and specifics.
- <u>List of cruises</u> here is the single most comprehensive tool available. Find out all available cruises in a given time period.

Things to Note:

Pricing here is not as competitive as many similar sites. This of course varies, and they may well have the best deal at times, but by and large we find them to lag behind other sites in this department. They also have a comprehensive list of discounts, allowing you to find cruises that offer special pricing for seniors, teachers, firefighters, police, military, and other specialized categories.

ToursByLocals.com

What Do They Do?

A local guide is a great way to get the most out of an exotic destination, a new country, or a place you are unfamiliar with. Guides can also offer unique opportunities based on their specialized skills or connections, which help you and your family connect with exciting possibilities not found through "regular" channels. ToursByLocals creates a marketplace for local guides, drivers, and experts to sell their services to the traveling public. Once you have a location in mind, even if you don't think you *need* a guide, we recommend browsing the site to see what is available. You may find something you didn't know existed, or a better deal than you expected.

What We Like Best:

- A ton of locations are available here.

- Organization makes it easy to find what you are looking for quickly.

- Ratings are a helpful tool for identifying the best times and learning from the experiences of others. They are well done and easy to follow.

Things to Note:

We have had mixed success due to the open nature of the service, but recognize that it is part of the game. At the same time, guides we have hired in the past have mostly varied from good to great.

The tour guides available through the site are freelancers. This site is all about compiling listings, more like a classified section. However...

According to Them:

ToursByLocals does not list just anyone: we only accept about 1 in every 10 applicants. We curate the guides on our site *very* carefully. They are all hand-picked by our recruitment team, and then coached by a full staff of guide support managers. As you note, customer reviews are a great way to read feedback on any specific guide, but prior to becoming a ToursByLocals guide-partner, each guide undergoes a series of Skype interviews, reference checks, and then one on one online and phone coaching with their designated support manager. If issues arise with any specific guide, they are removed from the site. We do all this in the hopes that people *don't* have to roll the dice when they book a TBL guide.

Additionally, TBL states that they feel hiring a local guide for a private tour is a great option for families, who benefit from the flexibility and spontaneity that kids crave and that you won't find on standard bus tours. Some of their guides are particularly good with children and have even designed tours that incorporate features like scavenger hunts to help make learning history (or whatever the subject) more engaging.

Afar

What Do They Do?

Afar is a travel magazine, which also boasts a robust website (Afar.com), and handy mobile app. Afar makes planning great trips simple, assisting you with each step of the process. They can help you narrow down destinations based on location or interests, and locate a variety of essentials like the best activities and hotels. You can quickly and easily browse their lists of favorite cities, countries, states, and regions for ideas and inspiration. Their online and mobile tools can help you add elements to your trip much like an online shopping site, and export your selected activities and hotels to the mobile app to carry with you. Stunning photos, well-written articles, and very original content are the hallmarks here. Afar is one of our favorite places to browse for the latest and greatest - there is always something new to enjoy.

What We Like Best:

- Beauty is the first word that comes to mind when you look at their website (or magazine). Stunning pictures and an attractive layout make browsing a pleasure, and it is easy to be inspired by the wonderful things they share.

- Layout is simple and intuitive. Quickly browsable lists, and organization based on what you want to find now make searches easy.

- Variety is a big part of what they offer. You can find individual hotels, locations, or interests, as well as fully packaged journeys. Their offerings also cover the "usual suspects" of destinations, as well as a number of far-flung and exotic locales to meet most any needs.

Things to Note:

The site and website are not specifically for families. While a very good resource, Afar caters to the general travel audience and that amazing thing you find here might not end up being kid-friendly. Afar is still a solid resource to browse, but keep this fact in mind while you look.

The magazine is published 7 times per year. You can subscribe in print, or if you have a tablet or eReader, digitally as well (you can also request a free trial issue if you have never subscribed before). Their online newsletter is free, as is their mobile app. It is also worth noting that Afar operates a non-profit foundation which provides scholarships for educational journeys for students.

RealFamilyTrips.com

So we'll have to admit to a little bit of bias here. We love the site because we founded it, and the resource that was the idea behind this book wouldn't exist if we didn't believe in the mission.

RealFamilyTrips.com is a dynamic resource for families who love to travel. We recognize that vacationing with children presents a unique set of requirements, while at the same time opens up a unique set of possibilities for growth, fun, excitement and becoming closer to one another. We know there are a wealth of travel planning resources available, but none that cater to families like we do. This is because we recognize:

- **Families need realistic itineraries**, which take into consideration what children of a given age can handle, as well as what it takes to keep them engaged.

- **Every family is different**. While some like to take in every possible sight, others may prefer more relaxing, fun or exciting experiences. Still others yearn for local culture or want travel to be educational as well as fun.

- **Time and money are precious** commodities when raising a family. Time spent researching destinations and savings is time not spent enjoying family life. There are a wealth of opportunities to save if you know where to look, which we do. We bring the plans and the deals to you.

- **Our goal** is to combine the shared knowledge of real families and travel experts so that users can benefit from their experiences and maximize their potential through the use of helpful shortcuts and secrets.

What Do We Offer?

Our pride and joy lies in an expansive collection of itineraries that cover so many places a family could dream of going; and it is always expanding. All of them are written with families in mind and strive to keep a variety of ages entertained and engaged. They are well organized and can be browsed by region, country or city. If *where* you are going isn't as important as *what* you are doing we also organize them by the type of day/activity. Families can seek out a city vacation, beach day, educational experience, cultural excursion, active venture or a totally unique experience.

We are always sensitive to family needs and try to make note of activities that may be restricted by age or other criteria. Our robust search feature makes finding the perfect day simple.

We also offer Travel Tips which cover a wide range of topics. Some are specific to families and children, while others offer more general travel advice. All of them are meant to make the experience simpler and to answer questions you didn't even know you had. This is our collection of advice, shortcuts and inside scoops; all meant to empower users to save time and energy.

Why RealFamilyTrips.com? "Travel technology industry leaders agree that consumers are looking for online expertise when planning their trips," according to author Harvey Chipkin.

We are that expertise when it comes to family travel.

According to the New York Times, with regards to online travel sites: "It's not that one site is necessarily better than another; it's that one is better for you." There are a thousand places online to find opinions, not all are well written or reliable, but more importantly, not all relate to a given user. Families want and need advice from other families, as well as travel experts who specialize in family vacations. Enter RealFamilyTrips.com.

Among the myriad travel sites available, our goals and our tastes are the ones best suited for families:

- Our experts consider families first and "travel industry" second. Our reviews and suggestions are based on what is best for parents and their children, not industry standards or personal biases.

- We curate and cultivate our itineraries, tips and deals. There aren't the extraneous reviews of aggregator sites, or the hundreds of paragraphs to wade through. We get to the point quickly and efficiently.

- No one organizes their information like we do so that your family can find the exact destination or activity that they want.

At RealFamilyTrips.com, we believe the world becomes more real and more understandable to your children when you travel together. Stay in your comfort zone, or step out of it. Whatever suits you, we can help. Hopefully we can move you to consider places you might not have otherwise. Ultimately, our goal is to inspire parents to travel with their children; to expose them to the world around us so that they can learn and experience it together as a family. We hope we can inspire you to travel - whether near or far - to ordinary and extraordinary destinations, and build lifelong memories as a family!

How to Book Better and Smarter

Armed with these great new resources to identify great locations and research fares and rates, now comes the time to actually pull the trigger on something and set about booking a vacation.

While we have tried our best to highlight both the benefits and shortcomings of a number of popular resources, the important information does not end there.

For many who are new to travel, or at least to booking more elaborate vacations, the process can be a bit daunting. You have probably heard a lot of conflicting information about how to get the best rates. Once you go about browsing booking sites and signing up for a few newsletters (a good idea and great way to stay in the loop) the process is further muddied by the bright lights of flashy ads that promise a lot but don't always actually have the best deals.

When booking a vacation there are a lot of moving pieces. The big elements are transportation to and from your destination, as well as where you stay. Then there are the activities. Depending on the trip, you might also have to arrange transportation within your destination, book a guide, or make other arrangements. If your planned trip will see you hopping around a country or even a continent, all these questions are multiplied as you research multiple airfares, hotels and more.

Do you book everything as part of one package? Select individual items ala carte? Should you book with the hotel directly, or go through a major travel aggregator?

All these questions and more confront the family busy planning their vacation. Here we will break down a few solid rules of thumb, as well as lay out some good strategies for booking that will help streamline the process and allow you to book with confidence.

We will also lay out a few options that are available to you, and strategies to help aid you in your process of learning to book better.

Remember - travel is an ongoing process. Not only will you get better at it as you go, but global trends will shift, making new areas affordable and opening new doors for you and your family. The deal that isn't there today may be tomorrow, or next week, or next year. Remain flexible and take your time. You and your children have many great trips ahead of you.

Go With Reputable Sites

By all means, in your quest for bigger and better family vacations, you should widen the scope of your search and avail yourself of the best prices you can find. At the same time, it is important to stick with websites with a good reputation, a history of reliability, and an acceptable level of customer service. Saving a few (or a ton of) dollars means nothing if you end up losing your money on a scam.

Similarly, if you are spending large chunks of time dealing with poor customer service, the savings may not have been worth it in the end. There is a lot to be said for the value of your time, and the importance of being able to make changes or get answers in a reasonable manner.

This will be tricky, especially those newer to family vacationing or who are beginning to widen their net when it comes to where they look and where they book. Chances are, that to accomplish some of the types of vacations we have been talking about throughout this book, you are going to be expanding your resources to new websites and vendors with which you are not familiar. This is a good thing, and we encourage you to search high and low.

At the same time, expanding your notion of where to look will also require some common sense, an inquisitive nature, and a willingness to research your own research.

According to recent statistics from the American Hotel & Lodging Association (AH&LA), fraudulent websites in the travel sector take over 2.5 million North American residents for a whopping $220 million every year. We don't share this information to scare you, but to make you aware that not everyone out there is on the up and up.

The more unfortunate news is that these dummy sites and scam artists often appear by advertising appealing packages that rank high in search results. We should all know well enough not to submit our credit cards to the neon green website with the smiley face clip art on it that looks like it was created in 1993, but modern scammers are savvy and dedicate great resources to separating consumers from their money.

The worst offenders of the false-booking universe are the proverbial lion in sheep's clothing. They make use of deceptive URLs and website names, and will often appear in the "sponsored results" section of popular search engines. Attractive stock and pirated photos from legitimate websites further allow these fraudulent sites to present themselves much in the same way as legitimate ones.

These fraudulent websites will take your money, but instead of delivering on lofty promises, their bookings result in unfulfilled requests and bogus amenities. In some cases, even the reservations themselves are a lie, and they take money without ever contacting a hotel, airline, or otherwise doing anything to deliver on your promised vacation.

This is a growing problem, with such websites numbering in the thousands according to recent estimations. The Senate Judiciary Committee has recently called for an investigation by the Federal Trade Commission, but sadly, sites like this will likely always exist. Just as spam emailers, hackers, and other Internet scam artists will always be hunted, they will continually reinvent themselves to find ways around the rules and their enforcement.

Again, this is not to say that booking travel should be a scary proposition. Yes, we have heard some horror stories from people we know, as well as people on travel forums, but there is no reason to fear being ripped off if you follow some reasonable guidelines.

Tips for not getting taken when making a reservation

- Stick to major sites, at least for your bookings. It can't hurt to cast a very wide net with your searches. By all means, if you have the time and energy, you should check prices on a good number of websites. Take note of who is offering what deal, and see what is available. Check both the vendor directly (whether it is an airline, hotel, or other source) as well as price aggregators and deal sites (more on this to come). *However*, when it comes to actually pulling the trigger and giving someone your credit card number, stick with the bigger names. See what is out there in your research phase, but only book with the ones you know you can trust.

- <u>Who can you trust?</u> This is a constantly evolving world, and new sites emerge while others fold frequently. The easiest places to trust will always be the vendors themselves. You can typically feel confident booking directly with a reputable, financially sound airline, hotel, cruise line, rental car agency, or other company that actually holds the responsibility for providing the promised service themselves. Other safe bets are the major travel aggregator sites that almost everyone has heard of. Booking through Travelocity, Priceline, Kayak, TripAdvisor, Orbitz, Expedia, and the like, generally represent a safe bet. There are many others, as well as many smaller outfits that are just as reputable. So seeing as we could never provide a timeless and comprehensive list here, what are you to do? This is where researching your own research comes into play. Take the time to search not only a purported travel deals site for their prices, but research the site itself for its business practices. Check Consumer Reports, the Better Business Bureau, and other organizations that compile information on businesses. Read travel forums and search out information from other people that have tried booking through a particular service. You should be able to find information to help you see which side of the law a particular site falls on. If you can't find anything about them, that is a red flag as well and it may be better to walk away and be safe, rather than sorry.

- <u>But what if the best deal is only on a questionable site?</u> Don't let your thirst for a great deal cause you to do something impulsive and chase the great price over your common sense. Gather all the information you can about a particular offering, including as many details as you can find on the unknown site you have stumbled upon, and take it to one of the "big guys." Go to the vendor directly, or to one of the booking sites you know to be reputable, and float the price by them. Say that you found this great deal, but that you would rather book through their trusted system. In some cases, they may honor the deal, or meet you halfway to get your business. On the other hand, if this so-called deal never really existed outside of some scam artist's head, you may be out of luck. Either way you come out ahead. You may save money and still get to book with one of the "good guys," or you may simply get confirmation that the deal which smelled a little funny, actually was.

- Ask questions and get confirmations. Open a dialogue and ask specific questions as part of your booking process. This not only helps you get informed about what you may be walking into, but gives you a chance to "test the waters." If the site you are looking at can't give you detailed information, or answer your questions in a satisfactory manner, this should be another red flag. If their basic M.O. is "I'm not sure, but give me your money and we will figure it out," they probably aren't the real deal. Also make sure that you get detailed confirmation information following any booking you make. This is another good sign that an organization is legitimate. If you get confirmation numbers (for reservations, not just credit card transactions) then you can feel better about the choice you made. If you made your booking through a major travel aggregator, follow up with the hotel or airline using your name and confirmation number to make sure they have you on record as well. Do this as soon as possible, rather than waiting until a week before you leave only to find out your reservation never existed in the first place.

- <u>Use your credit card if possible.</u> We can't guarantee that it will always get you out of a scrape, but if you have a major credit card, backed by a big bank or other powerful institution, you may have an ally in recouping money from a fraudulent source.

- <u>Travel agents can be your friends as well.</u> Once again, not everyone who calls themselves a "travel agent" necessarily is one, at least in the world of the Internet. We mean reputable agents with solid references. For the traveler particularly concerned about booking online and being taken by a scam artist, dealing with an actual human being may be a good bet for you. Sometimes they have the best prices, oftentimes they charge a little more. Keep in mind the other advice about doing your research, and bringing deals you find to see if they can match them. An agent may end up costing you more, but it may be worth it.

- In the end, most of this advice is geared towards the "biggest" components of your trip. Flights, trains, cars, cruises, accommodations, and other major bookings are more likely to be backed by similarly large resources that allow you to book them. When it comes to activities, meals, and excursions - you may have less choice in the matter.

- Especially when looking at a more exotic destination, or a developing country, activities may be limited to small, independent vendors with their own websites. In many cases these may be ramshackle by our standards, and throw up red flags when you look to book on one. In many cases this simply can't be avoided.

- For major activities and/or major destinations, you may be able to book all to most of your activities through major websites. At the same time, in both developed and developing areas, the thing that appeals to you most may end up being the fantastic snorkel guide who runs his business out of a van, or the mom and pop art workshop that barely knows how to use email.

- You will need to be a bit more open minded when it comes to the security of booking your activities, but exercise the same common sense. Fortunately, the stakes tend to be lower for these anyway. You may spend thousands on airfare while you spend less than a hundred dollars on a single activity on the ground. There is some comfort in this, but caution still needs to be exercised.
- <u>Don't give out your credit card information by email</u> or other insecure channels.
- <u>Negotiate not only prices, but payment methods</u>. When possible, agree to pay a deposit up front on arrival at a venue, and the balance at the end of your tour (as opposed to credit card information before even arriving in the country). Most companies (even the smaller ones) will likely want a deposit up front when you book.
- <u>Do the same amount of research *about* the vendor</u> as you do about the booking site. Make sure they have delivered on promises in the past. You may even be able to find information about how others have arranged payment. Search for them on well-known research and review sites to find past experiences of other travelers with their service. If they have been in business for a while, you should be able to find some information about them. If not, then that is a red flag in itself.
- <u>Get confirmations, as well as contact information</u>. Make sure there is an official record of any payment made, in case you need to dispute it later. Also, get a phone number and email address for them when possible. Test this out after you get it. A call or an email to ask a question, or just to thank them and tell them how much you look forward to your visit, can help make sure that you actually have a means of getting in touch and following up on services promised to you.
- <u>Double check the charges</u>. Do this both with the vendor before booking, and on your own statement (or app if your card has one) as soon as the charge goes

through. This will not only keep everyone honest, but can protect you from unforeseen charges. Some vendors that rent materials may put a hold on your card for a certain amount to protect their bikes, dive gear, or other materials. Ask about these charges beforehand, and work them into your budget.

Stretch your comfort zone a little when it comes to activities, but not so much that you recklessly give out financial information. Even if the stakes are lower, your credit card number in the wrong hands can do plenty of damage.

Above all else, common sense will be your greatest guide. If a deal looks too good to be true, there is a good chance that it is. Make sure you know who you are giving your money to before you sign off, and avail yourself of resources to be as informed as possible. Travel often requires leaps of faith, but save them for that exotic experience or the diving board at the hotel pool, not with your wallet before you even leave.

An Overview of Basic Good Booking Practices

With a solid understanding of what *not* to do and potential problems that could result from booking irresponsibly, it is time to talk about what does work. There are a number of great strategies for booking a vacation, and new technology continues to reshape the landscape of how we travel as well as plan.

Your ability to find deals will grow with time. As with all aspects of the planning process, the more you practice these principles, the more easily they will come to you. Eventually, browsing travel sites and staying informed will be a part of your regular routine. Booking a big trip every year or every few months will be second nature, and you will discover which sites tend to have deals that appeal to you, as well as which vendors your family prefers.

To start out this new way of booking, and thinking, about travel, we recommend a few simple strategies to help guide you on the road to bigger and more exciting vacations.

The best times to book

A large number of variables affect prices for a given destination at any time. Airfare costs are affected by everything from fuel prices and government regulation, to standard influencers like supply and demand. General trends emerge for certain places over time, as popular seasons for travel and patterns in where people go will dictate what airlines can and do charge. Prices for things like hotels and activities can also vary based on a number of factors: holidays, busy tourist seasons, the local economy, and expanding businesses, just to name a few.

Through your research you will find better and worse times for a particular destination that you are looking at. Unfortunately you will also find that winter and summer tend to be the busiest season for most locations, partly because everyone with children has a similar window for travel based on school schedules.

What really matters as far as you are concerned is the timetable of **when you book** as opposed to when you travel. With the latter largely dictated by when you all have available time to go, the idea of thinking closely about when you buy your tickets is the single biggest factor you can influence.

Generally speaking, there are two particularly auspicious times in which you can book your trip, and they are either very early in the game, or very late. That is to say booking either six months to a year out, or within the last month before you leave, as very broad and general guidelines.

Simple logic can explain why the "middle range" sees the highest prices for the exact same seats, rooms, and activities. Very far out, once an airline or hotel (for example) first opens up a new block of time for reservations, they have nothing on the books. They need a certain number of bodies occupying their space to make sure that they get to the point where they can breathe a sigh of relief and know that they have their minimum number of bookings.

Then comes the middle period where costs rise because, at this point, the vendor can test the waters with higher prices. It pays for vendors to push the limits and see just what people are willing to pay for the privilege of getting somewhere or enjoying something. This is also when most people are booking, so the competition is strong, and supply and demand comes into full effect. When, on a daily basis, entire flights, floors, and excursions can be snapped up, this frenzy of bookings results in a mentality that pushes consumers to spend more and vendors jump on this.

Finally, in the "end game" phase of booking, there are likely only a few spots left in a given hotel, flight, or trip. At this point, vendors once again lower their prices, often adopting a "something is better than nothing" attitude towards their product. While hotels and cruise ships often reserve a couple rooms and cabins, and flights may purposely leave a few seats for special purposes, they want to be as full as possible.

They receive zero dollars for an empty room or cabin, or unfilled seats on a flight, so they once again lower prices to try and get something out of those empty rooms, cabins, and seats.

This explains the general trends in pricing related to any given point in time. It is also important to note that these cycles may exist on an even smaller scale for a given window of travel. Once again, there are a lot of variables. A particular flight may be selling so well that an airline decides to put another plane on that route for a similar day and time to capitalize on interest. One airline in particular may have too many seats available and run a sale, causing other airlines to scramble to lower prices in order to match. This means that halfway through the cycle, there may be another dip in prices, followed by another surge, and another dip. A hotel may add a booking for a major event, or lose a block of reservations from a large group. In either event, a large collection of rooms that was open may no longer be, and vice versa. This can affect their pricing and cause them to change up the rules in the middle of the process to account for changes on their end.

This is why it pays to keep watching, and stay informed. Don't make assumptions, but do follow the general trends. Sometimes it can feel a bit like playing the stock market.

For most families, the idea of waiting until the last minute will be unappealing, if not impossible. It may also work for part of your trip, but not another. Most feel more comfortable locking in at least the airfare as early as possible, while they may wait to book accommodations or activities to see if prices ease up.

For this reason, the idea of booking early seems like the safest bet for most. It is a good way to get a fair price, though not necessarily the very best. Dream vacations may take a lot of time to put together, but the sooner you start watching trends and keeping an eye on things, the better informed you will be when you actually want, and are ready to, jump on them.

Check airline and hotel sites as well as major booking services

We have touched on and made mention of this practice before, but this is where we really want to hit home with the importance of this process.

Travel aggregator sites, and major deal/sale purveyors are fantastic. They put incredible amounts of information in one place, and simplify the process of searching for things. As time has gone on, they have also amassed a substantial amount of "juice" within the industry, allowing them to not just compile deals offered by vendors, but push for their own as well. They are an industry force to be reckoned with, and for many people, a great place to start.

Especially as you set out to get a feel for pricing regarding a new destination that you know little about, by all means, start with the people who give you the most information at once. Time is precious and this is a smart way to browse a lot of offers in one sitting.

The "big sites" will often have some of the best deals as well, yet another reason it pays to start looking there.

Just **don't** limit your search to deal and savings sites.

As you begin to zero in on exact dates, times, and flights it really pays - often literally - to check with the vendor directly. Do not assume that the price on one of the aggregator sites is the best... or the worst.

When you have details in hand, you can look at an exact flight, an exact room type, or a particular cruise cabin from the source. In some cases, you will find that the vendor actually has a better price than the deal website. In others, the flight that seemed to be very high on the deal website may actually be even higher on the airline's website. It helps you see how far your money actually goes.

Collect information and narrow your search. Find a number of different flights on a number of different airlines (a couple on each) ignoring the prices for a minute and focusing on the window of time in which you want to travel. With these options in hand, check the prices on a couple of travel deal sites, as well as each airline. You may be surprised by the results, and how wide the price range is for essentially (or exactly) the same offering. In the end, the one that wins out may have been the best one from the beginning, or it may have been something outrageously overpriced on your first source, but ultimately cheapest from another.

Consider alternate accommodations

While alternate ways of booking and staying may not be for everyone, it is worth considering just how badly you want to go somewhere, and what aspects of your budget you are willing to stretch. Airfare is one of the most difficult things to alter, as there are so many places in the world you simply *need* to fly to in order to enjoy. Activities are something that you can compromise on, but don't want to because they bring the most joy to your trip. So it naturally falls to accommodations as a possible area for compromise and the exploration of possibilities.

Consider last minute booking services, home and apartment rentals, and even camping if it is something that appeals to your family. These days there are more and more ways to stay, as well as to book accommodations. Explore them and see if they might just help make a dream vacation a real possibility.

Consider playing around with this part of your planning, and seeing what is out there in terms of pricing and options for a particular place you want to go. The possibilities may surprise you, and may be well worth the trade-off.

Package deals can save you money…or not

The advent of big booking sites has also expanded the notion of packaging services and vacations into "all in one" deals. It isn't a new idea; travel agencies have been doing it for years. The most modern iteration is simply bigger and more complex than ever.

A recent trip to Vienna had us playing around with flights and hotels for what was ultimately a fairly last-minute trip. After looking at possible flights and hotels alone, we found that by bundling the flight with the hotel, we could ultimately book both for literally a few dollars more than the flight alone. This is a rather extreme case, but if we hadn't been open to even considering a package, we would have missed out on big savings.

At the same time, that old fallback of convenience can often lay a trap for prices that look good (and probably are) while still not being the *best*. The more pieces to the puzzle, the easier it can be to mask the prices. Beware of deals that put too many services into one, as you may well be saving on one or two of them, only to make up the difference by being overcharged for a third and fourth, essentially creating a wash.

Also, packaging deals brings other questions and concerns to the table that you need to be aware of:

- <u>Lack of flexibility</u> doesn't always need to be the case with packages, but can come with the territory. The way package deals are marketed means that they will sell you a complicated deal with a simplified wording. "Flight and hotel for $500" may sound great for a European vacation. Then, when you find out that it is only one particular redeye flight and a mediocre hotel in an inferior location, the deal may become less appealing. Be sure to find out exactly what they are selling before committing.

- <u>Flexibility is in the details</u> as well. While the flight, hotel, and other services included in the package may work fine for you, you may also run into problems as you look to plan the trip you actually want to take. Many package deals will place restrictions on things like flying out of a different airport than you fly into, or booking a hotel for less than the entire period between flights. If you want to move around within a country, spend a few days visiting relatives, or otherwise "tinker with" the plan once you have arrived, make sure that the deal you have found will allow it.

- You may have to lock *everything* in. Again, it pays to be sure before you pull the trigger. If you haven't thoroughly researched your destination yet, you may have no idea what part of the city you want to stay in, whether or not you will need a car, or how long you want to stay. Packages often come with very specific qualifiers, and if you get a car as part of it that you ultimately decide you don't want, locking in the deal may mean that you are left holding the bag for that expense.

Package deals are not a trap set for unsuspecting travelers. We have saved a lot of money booking things together in the past. We simply recommend that you become informed and understand the rules and the fine print of any package deal before you commit to it.

Package deals can lump together everything from airfare, hotel accommodations, rental cars, activities, meals, and more. See what all the possibilities are before booking anything. Adding or removing a service may save you money. Don't assume that a package will be the same from one site to the next, or one trip to the next. Always take the time to move around all the pieces, as the number of variables can mean a wide variety of possibilities.

Also, research each individual component on its own. The only way to know if a package deal is cheaper is to see what all the moving parts cost by themselves. This may seem like an obvious statement, but with so many vendors, the possibilities are too numerous to predict. Also, different flights and hotels may be cheaper when coupled together, but ultimately not as cheap as other standalone options.

You need to compare prices on individual components and different configurations of deals to be sure. You also need to carefully read the fine print on any bookings you make to ensure that a good price does not come at the expense of restrictions that prohibit the best possible experience.

With package deals you *may* have to lock in a rate and sacrifice some flexibility, but you may also save a ton. Just be sure to put in the paces and stay informed. It may seem like a major headache, but this is all for a good cause.

Social media is a new front for travel deals

On this notion of alerts, it is worth mentioning that social media is an emerging market for the sharing of great prices and alerting consumers to deals.

Every company wants to build their social following. Those "likes" and "followers" help lend clout to a business, and nowadays it seems that every brand wants you to interact with them on social media. They are also catching on to the fact that you don't necessarily *need* to be "friends" with a faceless corporate entity, so they need to bring something to the table as an incentive.

The new quid pro quo of gaining social media followers for travel companies comes in the form of sharing early access to deals, and highlighting their best prices and offerings. Take a few of your favorite airlines, hotel chains, and deal websites and follow them on Facebook, twitter, and the like. Information they put out on their news feeds may contain great prices and deals, as part of something you likely check on a regular basis anyway.

This is a win-win. It is a way to consolidate a lot of brand information in one place, and quickly gain access to anything that interests you. Some brands even share other content, like articles about destinations or travel advice that may also interest you.

While this cannot be relied on as a beginning *and* an end to your research on prices and booking, it is a great supplemental activity that can alert you to prices and keep your foot in the door of the travel world. It is free, often helpful, and certainly can't hurt.

One last thought, and technique, to save

While we have just finished saying that airfare is one thing that is hard to do much to alter the price of, and that careful eyes (and potentially package deals) are your best bets to possibly shave money off a flight, there is one more option to consider: flying *in*direct.

This can be a pain, and for many families, will result in discomfort that may not be worth your while. It is a particularly difficult proposition for larger families, and as we previously discussed in the section on seasonal travel concerns, it is a poor idea for winter travel.

So just what does "flying indirect mean?"

Direct flights are in the highest demand and typically command the highest prices. For these reasons they will book up quickly and may not get the best discounts. If you are willing to connect somewhere, and slightly reroute your flight, you can save lots of money, even more if you are willing to layover.

And how do I use this to save?

One of the best techniques for this is to figure out which cities act as "hubs" for each airline. A hub serves as a home base for the company, with greater numbers of flights departing from that city. This increase in volume means more options, and a greater chance of an undersold flight with discounted seats. Find hub cities for your preferred airlines and/or along your path on a given trip and take connecting flights through them in order to save more money.

This technique of purposely finding flights that take you out of your way and add travel time to your vacation may be less than ideal, but they can lead to big savings.

Once again, it is all about your family and your priorities. If getting to your dream destination is worth it, and the only way to swing things is by compromising on the way, then by all means look into more creative ways to get there. If you can walk in with both eyes open and say the inconvenience is worth it to you, then enjoy making your dream vacation possible today.

Part V

Making a Trip Work for You

Choosing the type of vacation that is right for your family, and making the most of it, is really the name of the game. If you can feel confident that you have selected the best options for you and your children, then great things await you.

Over the first sections of this book we have described the "why" of great family travel, as well as the "where" to go, "what" to do, and "how" to book better. We have covered the basics, and hopefully have given you ideas about vacation and thoughts on how to implement them.

In this section we kick things up, and discuss some ideas that really help you capitalize on every opportunity.

Consider this final section of the book our master's course in family travel. That is not to say that the ideas contained here are particularly difficult, or complicated. Quite the contrary. We believe that anything discussed in this book is within reach of any family at any time. From the way you plan your time, to the memories you bring home and the things you do - this section is about mastering the smaller components to help you travel your best.

We will also explore alternate means of transportation and travel, as well as different ideas about planning that change up the pace and offer something new. For the family that feels they have gotten a good hold on the essentials and wants to change things up, we present some additional thoughts for you to consider.

As you expand your vision of travel to encompass years of trips and a lifetime of vacations, use the tools here to make sure that things never get boring. We hope that over the course of your future trips, and the coming years of your lives, that this reference will help you to expand your vision of what is possible, and push you to enjoy the very best during your time together.

Family vacation time is precious. Make the most of every moment, and lend thoughtfulness to every step you take. These are the times you will remember always - it is worth availing yourself of every possible consideration.

Cruising: The Good, The Bad, and the Exciting

For much of this book we have focused on more generalized notions about travel, and a lot of advice involved the more general practice of flying/driving/riding somewhere, arriving, and touring at your own pace. For families serious about travel, there are a number of other great options to these more "traditional" modes of travel, and it is time to talk about one of our favorites: cruising.

Cruise vacations are a great option for most families. Cruises can simplify travel while also opening up doors to new opportunities and fantastic destinations. As a very specific type of all-inclusive travel option, cruises allow you to spend less time planning logistics and more time enjoying your trip.

We have had immense fun on many cruises over the years. While there are many different cruise lines, and many different types of experiences, there are a few amazing benefits that hold true to just about all of them.

Some of our favorite things about cruising:

- Exploring the world with ease. Cruises allow you to tour from a centralized location while still experiencing much of the world. While you have to get yourself to the point that the ship departs from, and home after, in between almost all of the logistics are taken care of. You can experience several countries in a week, without having to worry about making multiple flights, trains, or driving yourself. A cruise ship is like a sailing all-inclusive resort, allowing you to enjoy great amenities while your destination comes to you. The relative ease with which you can see a lot of different places in one vacation is hard to match, and the style and comfort that go along with this are a big plus.

- Set your own pace. We have talked about the importance of finding a solid balance for your family, and catering to your personal needs. Cruises make this process even simpler, by providing a bevy of options for you. Modern cruise ships are like floating cities replete with all sorts of options for everything from dining to activities. You can get active on a rock climbing wall on some ships, or lounge lazily by the pool. You can eat a 4-star gourmet meal, or grab a quick burger on the deck. You can change your mind on the fly, and easily adapt each day to your family's mood, often without much advance preparation. Cruising represents an opportunity to really cater to everyone's needs on any given day. All this is yours on a more standard cruise, and looking at specialty cruises and options can do even more to suit your particular family's needs.

- <u>Excursions</u> represent another level of opportunity to both explore and really customize your experience. For most days in port, you will want to get off the ship and explore the new surroundings. While you may choose to just wander and see what happens, most families will want to book activities to make the most out of your time off the ship. You have a whole new world of options here, as you can book through your cruise line or work outside of it, to find something that works best for you. Find a local guide to take you around, visit popular destinations, or see what sorts of fun activities the ship recommends and sponsors trips to. You can plan as much or as little as you want, and really find what speaks to your family. We recommend booking most excursions yourself. This will open you up to more possibilities and save you money, though there is some element of risk (and a little more work involved). Cruise ships will always recommend that you book their "sponsored" excursions because they see a cut of the profits. We never do this ourselves, and always try to think outside the box. We advise that you do as well.

- <u>Amenities</u> on modern cruise ships are great. You will find wonderful things to do, great shopping, and much more. There are also family-oriented specifics that can really enhance your trip. Kid's Clubs are of particular note, and will be discussed in further detail below. Specialty programs for kids and teens allow your children and teens to enjoy themselves on their own level, and meet new friends. Far from ever feeling trapped on a cruise ship during even a longer trip, instead we usually leave feeling we wish we had time to do more.

- Freedom is an important aspect to cruising that is almost unique, especially when it comes to international vacations. By freedom, we mean the ability to enjoy activities as a family, as well as apart, with relative ease and comfort. The self-enclosed nature of a cruise ship means that no one is going to "wander off" and get lost (though children do need to be properly supervised, and ground rules should be put in place - a ship, after all, is like a floating city, and should be treated as such). Some ships even offer services like phones with shipboard text messaging to let parents communicate with kids when they are apart. With designated (and supervised) kid and teen activities, cruising represents an opportunity for you to give your kids a little space and a little trust to strike out on their own, within reason. This ability to let everyone find what they like best can lead to an enhanced appreciation of your time all together, and helps ensure healthy growth. The idea that you can enjoy this type of freedom at night and on shipboard days, while exploring faraway cities and islands during other days, is hard to beat.

- Entertainment can be another big draw on bigger-name cruise ships. Many modern cruises feature top-notch performers, brand-name entertainment, Broadway touring companies, and much, much more. There are also big name chefs lending their cuisine to cruise ships, as well as a number of other lesser known (but equally great) names in entertainment and food that make cruise ships not just a chance to enjoy something, but something spectacular and hard to rival on land.

These opportunities to enjoy a variety of different locations from a central base camp, packed with features and amenities, make cruising a great option for many families.

A note about cruise pricing

Many families may have an interest in cruising, but have shied away from it due to a preconceived notion about the expense. While cruising is not a dirt-cheap way to travel, there are a variety of options in this sphere, as well as ways to book that can save money.

Do your best to shed any misconceptions that cruising is *only* for the elite and wealthy. Just like airlines and hotels, there are a variety of lines that vary greatly in their pricing. There are also a variety of ships within a given line, and a number of cabin choices within a given ship. All of this means that there are a wide variety of price points, and cruising may be more affordable than you think. Also, when you consider what is included in your fare, it can represent a great value.

The newest ships will typically be the most expensive, as high demand to experience the latest and greatest drives prices higher. These newer ships also tend to be very large, however, so a wide variety of cabin choices and a higher number of cabins to fill can also lead to opportunities for savings.

Many cruise ships have designated areas that are a little more luxurious or exclusive than others. This is worth noting if you have the means and desire to look for the very best, as they can be a way to ensure a little additional privacy and comfort. Having enjoyed these exclusive enclaves ourselves, we can tell you that they are worth considering, depending on the type of ship you are on.

The most affordable rooms will lack balconies, or even ocean views, but you don't want to be spending your vacation in the cabin anyway. Look to book inside cabins if you want to enjoy the greatest savings.

Also keep in mind that cruising includes some hidden costs beyond just the cabin fare you book. These can include things like tips (for waiters, maids, and others depending on the type of trip you enjoy), certain activities, and specialty food options. Be sure to read the fine print and research the ship you are staying on. Find out what food and beverage options are included and what may be extra. Read about activities with an extra cost, and find out how many staff members you will be interacting with on a regular basis. If you make use of the spa or kids club during your stay, that adds a few more people you will want to tip.

Cruises are another area of travel where it pays to look at both provider and travel deal websites. There are a number of deal aggregators (several mentioned in Part IV) that deal either specifically in cruises, or include them in their wider variety of deals. It pays to check these places often, as a cruise booked at peak time and full price may be out of reach for you, while the same cruise on sale may be much, much less.

Like any other part of travel, cruises also vary a lot by season and with current demand. Just like a hotel or an airplane, a cruise ship makes nothing off an empty cabin, and they will do their best to sail at capacity every time. As upcoming sails get closer and closer, prices will often drop on unsold rooms to try and fill the ship up before departure. If you track current deals and are willing to book closer to the date, you may enjoy great savings and an opportunity otherwise out of reach.

Keep in mind that connecting cabins, quad cabins, and cabins close together will be harder to reserve as you get closer to your travel date. You may save some money waiting for a discount, but you may also need to be open-minded about how close (or far) you and your children may be from each other in terms of accommodations.

Some of the most popular cruise destinations

While this will in no way constitute a comprehensive list of the places cruise ships sail, these are some of the most popular routes sailed by major cruise lines. Smaller lines and specialty companies may expand even further, into very exotic and exciting destinations. For the beginning cruisers, here are some itineraries worth considering:

- <u>Alaska</u> - One of the USA's most overlooked states for travel, the archipelago and mainland of Alaska lend themselves to amazing cruises. In addition to enjoying some of the major cities, you can spend cruise days swimming in a heated pool while overlooking frozen tundra.

- Caribbean - Many of the islands of the Caribbean are available to you on cruises. Most popular lines divide them into western and eastern regions, with the western Caribbean featuring getaways like Jamaica, the Cayman Islands, the Bahamas, and more, as well as points in Mexico, Central America and Florida. Eastern Caribbean cruises include places like the US and British Virgin Islands, Puerto Rico, the Bahamas, St. Maarten, as well as Florida. Some will restrict themselves to US territories and forgo the need for a passport, and leave from multiple points in the southern, as well as eastern, United States.

- Europe - There are cruises of the Greek Isles, as well as Adriatic cruises that tour Greece, Turkey, and more. Mediterranean cruises explore places like Spain, France, Italy, Morocco, the Canary Islands, and other popular places. Baltic Cruises take you to the north, with destinations in Russia, Germany, Norway, Sweden, Estonia, Finland and Denmark. These are just some of the possibilities, but these cruises allow you to see incredible combinations of great cities and countries.

- Asia - China, Vietnam, Cambodia, Thailand, Singapore, India, Malaysia, Sri Lanka, Oman, the United Arab Emirates, Japan, and many more destinations open up with tours that run in places like the South China Sea, and the Pacific and Indian Oceans. Some even combine with trips to Australia for epic journeys if you are able to be away for an extended period.

- Hawaii - While getting around these islands on your own isn't too hard, forgoing an all-inclusive resort on land and experiencing more of Hawaii from an all-inclusive at sea can be a winning option for many families.

- Australia and New Zealand - Hopping around to multiple points in these far-flung countries, or within one, takes you to some amazing beaches, and exposes you to unique culture.

- Pacific Coast - While we have suggested the northern California road trip, experiencing the north of this state, as well as the beauty of Washington and Oregon is a chance to experience some of the United States' greatest natural beauty, and an area growing in popularity.

- Canada and New England - Chances to dart up and down the northern Atlantic coast and experience the best of New England, as well as the pristine Canadian water and wilderness to the north, can be a great introduction to cruising.

- South America - See how the "other half" of the Americas live in places like Chile, Argentina, Uruguay, the Falkland Islands, and more. Exciting excursions here can take you to places like Easter Island, as well as stunning waterfalls and ancient ruins.

- Central America - Beautiful places like Honduras, Costa Rica, Mexico, and more are great for cruises. See dense jungles and beautiful beaches, with destinations that lend themselves to active families. Cruises of the "Mexican Riviera" can also be very relaxing, with one resort town after the next.

Some thoughts about specialty cruises

As we have mentioned, beyond the joys of "normal" cruising (if there is such a thing), specialty cruises open up even more possibilities. As the cruising world expands, smaller lines, and the smaller ships of big companies, have created niche and custom offerings that further expand the world of cruising as a place where everyone can find something they love.

Some of the first specialty cruises catered towards two very different dynamics: singles and families. The idea that both groups had very different wants and needs led lines to start developing special itineraries and planning specific activities with different groups of people on board. Today you can find specialty cruises for just about anything.

Since we could never find space to list everything that is available, and new offerings open up all the time, we will offer a small cross section to give you an idea. Just as the destinations in Part II of this book were meant to get your creative juices flowing, consider this another list of ideas that is not meant to be an end, but a beginning. Take this list and the ideas contained in it to see if it sparks an idea in you for a potential cruise opportunity.

Just some popular specialty cruises

For Artistic Kids and Families

The Cruise: Cunard's Queen Mary II

Who is it for? Families with children who have an interest in the arts, especially teenagers.

What Do They Offer? A weeklong arts camp at sea, while on a route from New England to Quebec, Canada. Events include theater workshops, dance classes, and even astronomy presentations in a shipboard planetarium.

For Curious Kids and Junior Explorers

The Cruise: Un-Cruise's Safari Endeavor

Who is it for? Perfect for all ages, and for families who prefer or don't mind a small ship (84 passengers).

What Do They Offer? Choose a focus for your family cruise, from options including photography, marine biology or ornithology (bird watching). You'll spend the week expanding your knowledge of this subject as you explore the Baja Peninsula of Mexico, throughout the stunning Sea of Cortez.

Take an Alaskan Adventure

The Cruise: Lindblad's National Geographic Sea Bird

Who is it for? Perfect for older kids and active families. While it is still vacation, this is *not* for those just looking to relax. Prepare for activity and reap the rewards.

What Do They Offer? Pass by glaciers, wind through Fjords, and make stops in national parks. This cruise sets sail from Juneau, spends a week winding south to explore the Alaskan coastline, and drops you off for wilderness excursions. The ship is small (62 guests) and the excursions rigorous, but if this is up your alley you will find unforgettable experiences along the way.

A Unique and Luxurious Experience, Going Where Few Families Ever Go

The Cruise: Jacada's private 12 person yacht charters

Who is it for? The most discerning families who are looking for adventure and who appreciate the finest details. This trip is a travel investment, where your family of up to 12 people, are served by a large, dedicated crew.

What Do They Offer? This is a very unique experience, as you and your family have a chance to experience premium travel and top notch amenities while being the only guests on the boat. On top of the incredible feeling of having your run of the ship, Jacada offers premium charters to Antarctica, a destination few others have ever seen and a sure way to guarantee your family will come home with memories to last a lifetime. Stop in a bay with over 100,000 penguins, dine with off-duty scientists, and swim in volcanically heated waters. More impressively, you can choose the itinerary, and change it at a moment's notice. This is the ultimate custom vacation, for those with a large travel budget.

A note about on-board kid's clubs

As we have mentioned before, one of the greatest features of many cruise ships has to be the activities they offer for kids (and teens). The ability to place your children in the care of professionals allows you each to have some freedom, and allows kids to interact socially with contemporaries. The activities can also be a great way for kids to operate at their own level of energy, without parents or siblings needing to slow down or speed up to match. In short, they can help ensure that vacation remains vacation for the entire family.

The time apart may just make you appreciate each other more.

There are a few more things to love about them (though note that these are general guidelines, and may not apply to *all* cruise lines and ships):

- Kid's clubs are generally complimentary from age 3 (depends on the cruise line), and included in your cruise price up front. While you may want to tip counsellors on your last day for a job well done, you don't have to shell out extra money for "daycare." This can be a welcome addition, especially if you end up using it much more or less than you planned on.

- Activities tend to start every half hour, or hour, depending on the cruise and their plan. This frequency means that you have a lot more freedom. You can do something together and drop kids off later, or join in when you like. Not having to commit to a whole or even half day means that you don't have to spend vacation working around the same strict schedules at home, and can enjoy more freedom. Keep in mind that the kid's clubs may not be open all day or evening. Check the hours ahead of time to coordinate their hours with your plans.

- They aren't *just* for "kids." These days, most major cruise lines will run a variety of programs spanning ages 0-18. With infant and toddler care, there typically will be an additional cost, and it is much more about providing basic health and safety, with a little fun mixed in. Activities then evolve as kids get older, meeting them on their own level. You'll find things like arts and crafts, pool time and other standbys for younger kids. Older kids and teens get pushed a bit more with active ventures, while the oldest "kids" (just don't call them that!) can enjoy teen activities in places equipped with things like video games, lounge areas, and computers. Teens may even have dances or club nights of their very own, ensuring that their personal space feels safe, and everything can be as "cool" as they need it to be.

To get the most out of your kid's club experience with your family, don't expect everything to just happen on its own. There are a few simple steps you can take to make sure your kids get the full benefit of their time:

- On embarkation day, after depositing your bags and possibly grabbing a quick bite, make it a priority to head right over to the kid's club as soon as possible. They will have counselors on hand, greeting families, giving tours and signing kids up in their respective, age-tiered programs. If you can get there before eating, you will likely have a shorter line to register your kids.

- Bring the whole family, not just those that plan on attending. The first reason for this is so you all know where it is, in case you need a sibling to pick up a younger child (some clubs allow this, others do not), or use it as a family meeting place later. The other is so that all your kids can see what the facility has to offer. A teen who might have thought it was too "lame" for them before, may get excited about something they see and change their minds. This allows everyone to be informed and make their own choices.

- Take the time, as a family, to get a feel for the space, meet the counselors, find out about upcoming activities, and learn the rules.

- Take the opportunity to introduce yourselves to other families with children of similar ages so that your child will know someone when they return, possibly by themselves, if they are old enough to do this (each cruise line has their own rules for this). This can help instill a sense of comfort, and encourage independence.

- On the first day you make use of the facilities, resist the urge to drop your kid off for a half-day. Start with a couple of hours, maybe even just an hour or so. Let them get their feet wet with the program, maybe connect with other kids, then pick them up and get their unfiltered review. See what they thought, and if it is a good fit for them. Not every kid's club is created equal.

Sometimes it takes your child connecting with another kid or a counsellor, and this is hard to predict. Variations in the particular vacation, and where your child is on a given day may have them hating the same kid's club they loved on another cruise. Feel it out and play things by ear, rather than leaving them for a whole day only to find out they were miserable and are now down on the whole trip.

- If they did have fun, you can consider gradually increasing the time spent there each day. As you leave them for longer stretches, you may want to check in with them in between pool time and a snack, to make sure everything is going well.

Some final thoughts on family cruising

We hope we have provided you with a lot of information, food for thought, and a few ideas to love about cruising. We have enjoyed this as a way of vacationing in the past, and find it to be a great option for many families.

Just as doing any one thing too many times will get repetitive, making every vacation a cruise will get old at some point. At the same time, doing very similar touring on your own year after year may leave you feeling like you need to change things up. Mixing even the occasional cruise into your travel repertoire is a great way to keep things fresh, and may be your best option for a dream destination that is simply made much easier by having your accommodations do the work of taking you from place to place.

Some final tips to aid you in future cruises:

- Stay informed while on the ship. Read the daily digest from the cruise to be informed about the day's activities and opportunities onboard. Many cruise lines will also put this information on the shipboard TV system, and several also offer apps you can download to stay apprised of what is going on. If you don't stay in the loop, you may miss something that really appeals to you.

- Make reservations in advance. It pays to have your excursions planned before you board. This not only helps to guarantee you get to do what you really want, but also ensures you spend your time enjoying vacation ra-rather than booking things while in paradise. On some cruises you may also have to book certain meals and tickets to shows. Whenever possible, do this online before you leave for the very same reasons.

- Pay attention to age recommendations on shows and entertainment. While many cruises consist of a substantial number of families, they also have singles and young adults, and they also provide activities for parents who split up from their kids. Don't assume everything is appropriate for all ages, and ask before you go.

- Go easy on the food. One of the most exciting things for many cruisers is the seemingly unlimited supply of food. With multiple buffets a day, and food around almost every corner, it can be tempting to overdo it. Take your time and pace yourselves, lest you end up losing valuable vacation time to upset stomachs from overindulgence.

- At the same time, remember the food is included (with the possible exception of certain restaurants, specialty food, and alcohol/coffee bars). While this may run somewhat contrary to the last tip, remember that there is a ton of already-paid-for food included in your cruise price. When you compare a land-based trip to a cruise, consider this in your budget. Families looking to cut costs and save money may do well to eat up in the morning on port days, and come back to the ship for dinner. While it may be tempting to indulge in local favorites, they will often tailor the ship's menu to local cuisine, and offer similar food that you have already paid for if you just eat before and after your excursion, as opposed to during.

- Internet service can be spotty at best. While this varies from ship to ship, and line to line, it seems to be an almost universal truth that cruise lines have not solved the problem of reliable Internet service. Connecting can also tend to be prohibitively expensive. Chances are you don't want to spend your whole trip doing something you could be doing at home anyway, but it is important to note when planning. Have as much information about your destinations printed or saved offline as possible. Don't count on being able to do much online while you are away.

We also encourage you to follow up with the information on RealFamilyTrips.com regarding cruising. We have a number of Travel Tips and other Spotlights, including advice from trusted professionals. These pieces about specific cruises, and specific aspects of cruising will help you to further develop your image of cruise vacations, and may just aid you in finding a line or an itinerary that appeals to you.

Flying Solo, or Joining Another Family?

A question that faces many families during the course of their travel careers is whether or not to allow others to join in their journey. Your children may have friends that they wish to bring along, or another family that you enjoy spending time with who might make good vacation partners. You might be considering a family vacation of another sort, in which extended family joins your immediate clan, allowing cousins and other children to enter the fold along with your own. Yet another option would be to bring your own parents or other family members along to create an intergenerational family adventure. There are numerous possibilities, both for different configurations and opportunities for enrichment.

Like so many concepts related to travel, there is no "right" or "wrong" answer to whether or not it makes sense for you to share your vacation time with others. It is a personal choice, related to a number of specific questions in your own lives, and carries a number of considerations.

The idea of sharing your vacation with another family, or a few additional individuals, can add a lot to your experience. When you are talking about a family that shares children of similar ages to your own, whether they are cousins or close friends, this allows your children to have "partners in crime" to share the sights and sounds of a new location with. An additional set of parents can also provide you with friends to share the joy, as well as the responsibility, with.

Traveling with another family allows you to have days where you split the itinerary. One group may take off to a more active excursion, opting to go hiking or to try something else to get the blood pumping. Another group may want to take it slower and relax, or take in something educational like a museum. When you have more adults in your party, you can have different configurations "leading" these excursions, while kids can opt to go to whatever suits them best that day. This flexibility can be a great boon, allowing different combinations of people to enjoy what they most want to.

This can take many forms, and may be as simple as one of your children running off to join the other family on something more their speed. It could involve age-based considerations, in which one set of parents (or one from each family) take older children to something on their level, while another set of parents take younger children to a more appropriate activity.

The fringe benefits of having another family can also mean things like an additional car. This can further enable you to go in different directions, or simply allow some people to pack it in early when tired, as opposed to forcing someone to stay longer, or leave sooner, than they would like at a given destination.

Traveling with another family or some additional individuals may also be a boon when it comes to the financial aspects of your trip, and the logistics of booking. More people may mean that you can qualify for a group rate, rent a bigger home, or otherwise upgrade your situation by pooling resources. You may also qualify for activities that you wouldn't have been able to on your own. In some cases you may need 10 people to qualify for a group rate, while in others, you may need that same 10 people to even qualify for a booking.

Traveling with another family or with additional company may not work for your family. Among the concerns for some families is the fact that your shared time will be somewhat "diluted" by adding more people to the mix. We have spoken at length about the bonding potential of family travel, and the opportunities to enrich the relationships that make up your family by sharing in exciting adventures together. While adding another family or some more people to the mix will not totally negate these effects, they *may* diminish them somewhat.

As much as it is great to have other children for your kids to spend time with, and/or other adults for you to talk to; there is a risk that any and all of you may spend more time bonding with contemporaries rather than your family unit. While there may be some comfort in having people very similar in ages and interests along for the ride, the art of great travel is in pushing yourselves to be just uncomfortable enough to grow. Your children may find that say, a rock climbing adventure is more fun and comfortable when enjoyed with their friends or cousins. At the same time, the surprise of how much fun it is with their mother and father is one of the unique experiences offered by vacation, and not one to sacrifice too readily.

Besides the risk of interfering with opportunities for family bonding, sharing your journey with others can also lead to logistical concerns, just as easily as it can benefit them. Traveling with a very large group may help make certain activities more affordable, or new ones possible, but it will have quite the opposite effect on others. Some activities catered towards smaller groups may not be able to accommodate you. Traveling to a large location like a museum or a marketplace with so many people may become more difficult. Certain activities may force you to go in smaller groups, leading to twice as much time, and half your party waiting for the other to finish so they can start or catch up.

Adding additional people to your party can also help or hurt the planning and booking process. While stretching the number of people involved is often easier and even cheaper when it comes to accommodations, this may not always be the case with travel. Trying to book 10 seats on an airplane may be difficult. One obvious solution is to arrive separately, though the timing of arriving separately may interfere with your ability to stay together or may force one family to carry the cost of a villa for a day.

The planning process can be complicated enough when trying to take into consideration the opinions of both parents and all children. When you increase the number of participants, the number of different tastes and concerns that other non-family members add to the mix may rise to the point of being too complicated. As one party almost inevitably "takes the lead" in the planning process, there is also the consideration of whether one family will feel slighted in a trip that they are more or less "tacked onto." At the same time, sharing in the planning process may allow additional levels of fun, and may help children get even more excited about the trip by having friends to daydream with as they contemplate the coming adventure.

You will need a "plan for how to plan" your trip if you opt to share it with others. Either let someone take the lead, or let each family do research and pool it together, making the choices as a team. While the latter will bring more ideas to the table, it will also add a lot of time to the already lengthy process of planning a vacation. You need to walk in with both eyes open, and establish guidelines so that no one gets hurt as you make choices. You will also need to be firm about things like dates and desires, so that you are all ready to pull the trigger at the same time when the moment is right to book things. There are so many moving pieces in a vacation that you will need to be on the same page at all times.

If you do plan a trip with another family, there will need to be excellent communication and a lot of openness about things like budget, likes and dislikes, as well as how to go about making final decisions. If one family or party feels pushed to do things beyond their means, or feels forced to pass on things they want to do for the sake of the other people involved, the vacation may morph into a less than ideal experience. If you decide to travel with others, you need to be very close, very open, and committed to the idea of truly sharing a vacation. All the ins and outs of travel force you to open your minds and wallets quite a bit. This is not something to be shared with casual acquaintances or people you have an issue being totally forthright with.

Some vacation types will lend themselves better to sharing than others. Any trip where you stay in one place will be the easiest, as well as the most logical to share. This means that renting that summer beach house for a week or the ski chalet with another family may make sense. Not only is there the fact that you only have to book a couple of things (accommodations and possibly airfare, and/or a car, depending on location), but it is easy to see that pooling resources can get you access to an upgraded situation. When you stay in one place and move about on your own, families will have more room to come together, or spread out, depending on their needs at a given time.

This type of "single accommodations" trip also includes resort getaways and cruises. In either case, you may be able to get away and enjoy an exotic locale (or several, on a cruise) and have your own room or rooms for your family, while having another family nearby to join up with or strike out on your own. On these types of trips you have a lot of freedom to make choices about how much time you spend together, and the self-enclosed nature makes it easier for kids to make their own choices. Cruises also afford you opportunities to book land excursions on your own or separately. You may just meet your companions for dinner and share about very different days. This can be an opportunity to allow your family to see a foreign country or city the way you want to, while another family sees the city the way they want to, and still have the benefits of children enjoying time with friends before and after.

More difficult types of trips to team up for include anything where you will be touring around, especially in a foreign country. If you plan on hopping around to multiple locations, staying in a number of hotels or other accommodations, and booking your own activities - more bodies will make for a more complicated experience. The logistics of both planning and taking a fully customized trip will raise the greatest number of questions and concerns.

The single most important thing to consider is your family dynamic. Think about what your family wants and needs from vacation. Your own family's needs should come first. You can then consider whether having another family along would add to or detract from certain elements of a trip. There are a host of issues to mull over, and all need to be taken into careful consideration.

Besides the concerns already raised, an important thing to consider is your family's compatibility with another, on many levels. While there is some room for flexibility (as you may split up for some or all activities) you need to ask yourself if the family in question travels enough like you do for it to make sense. If you are early risers and they like to sleep in, concerns will likely arise. If you don't even know the answers to questions like this, you need to either ask, or simply say that it isn't worth rolling the dice until you can say for sure.

Compatibility among the children will also be important. The children should be close, or at least get along very well and show a potential for closeness. You also need to take age and sex into consideration. If kids are of similar ages, it should ideally be across the board. If you have three children and two have "counterparts" in the other family, but one does not, that one child may feel left out. If you have a boy and a girl, teaming up with a family of all boys or all girls may leave a child feeling uncomfortable, depending on how close the children are. Things that are great for one child, or even most children, may not be worth it if others are made to sacrifice for their benefit.

Before getting too excited about the prospects of traveling with another family, or bringing friends/extended family along for the ride, consider the needs of everyone involved. Family travel time is precious. Travel should be about fun and togetherness. Things that meaningfully detract from the overall experience for even one person may make vacation less valuable.

For much of this chapter we have focused on the idea of traveling with another family, or adding additional children to your itinerary. It is important to speak briefly about intergenerational travel.

Intergenerational travel typically means adding another relative or relatives along for the ride. This often means bringing along grandma and grandpa, or a great aunt, uncle, or other older family member. It may also mean that, if you have older children with families of their own, bringing them along with your school aged children as well.

Intergenerational travel can have amazing benefits, both to the logistics of your trip and the shared time. This can be especially true when traveling to a place of significance to your elder family members. Let your children see "the homeland" through the eyes of relatives who lived there, or a favorite vacation spot of their grandparents. This can allow children to view the destination through the experiences of their elders, and for those elders to feel the joy of watching their youngest family members take in something they have cherished.

It can also mean the benefits that come with bringing along more adults, including opportunities to vary activities and split up if need be. At the same time, it is important to not simply bring along grandma and grandpa as travel babysitters, but to think about their wants and needs as you craft a trip that works for everyone. Traveling with extended family should be about creating a shared experience that benefits all involved. If this appeals to you and your family, strive to find destinations and activities that lend themselves to your intergenerational gang. Try not to simply plan a vacation around you and your children and "add on" grandparents or others at the last minute, resulting in the feeling that they have to adapt to you, or you to them.

With some of the potential benefits, and concerns, of traveling with others laid out, it comes time to make decisions for your family. The experience can open up unique opportunities, as well as hold you back in certain areas. The choice is yours and will need to be made with your specific family and the intended vacation in mind. Weigh the pros and cons and see what works for you.

While traveling with others will work better for certain families than others, it will also work better for certain vacations than others. Keep this in mind, and once again, we encourage you to look at your family's shared travels as a lifetime of experiences.

There is always another trip, and while your next one might not be the right one to share with others, another down the road may make more sense. At the same time, just because you have had a good experience traveling with others doesn't mean that you should push to try every vacation that way. Take things on a case by case basis, and always consider all the options before committing.

It is likely that over the course of your family's travel career, it will make sense to share your travels at some point and not others. Mixing things up can allow you to enjoy the best of both worlds. In the end, it is merely something to consider. As with all aspects of vacationing, make the choice for *your* family. Don't force yourselves to be something that you are not, but do set out to have the fun that you want to have, together.

How Active Are You?

This is one of the most important questions any traveling family will need to ask itself. Ask it during the process of selecting a destination, planning a trip, and enjoying your time on the ground. A family that can answer this question both thoroughly and honestly has already won half the battle of creating a great vacation experience.

Level of activity helps you to zero in on the things that matter to you, as well as dictate the pace of your trip. Getting to and staying at the right level of activity will help you to appreciate everything you do, and ensure that vacation never gets boring or overwhelming.

While we have talked a lot about concepts like pacing your trip, varying the activities, and creating captivating experiences - there is also a general arc of activity that each family needs to arrive at for themselves.

If you are a particularly active bunch, you will need to seek out new and exciting things to continue pushing the limits. Even a particularly educational or cultural vacation will need to be augmented with things that get your pulse up. These could be hands-on experiences, like swinging from a rope or climbing something, or could be more passive, like a speedboat ride or a really immersive children's museum.

If you are a bunch who likes to take things slower, you should embrace this. While you will want to push your boundaries a little, don't force a zip lining adventure on yourselves if you would rather be in a museum. Active may mean *activity* more than it means *action*. Get hands on and crafty, rather than athletic, if this suits your family's needs.

While this is not a simple question of "yes or no" and involves some nuance, finding where you lie on the active scale will keep you generally happier while you travel. You may also prefer brief spurts of activity in between bigger lulls, or quick lulls in between days of adventure.

This will first come into play when choosing a destination. While you will want and need to vary your activities, and there are always unexpected things lurking in even the most homogenous of destinations, use common sense and careful research in identifying locations that work for your general level of activity. Beaches, parks, rainforests and warm-weather locales typically lend themselves to a lot of activity. Similarly, the very cold and mountainous locales will allow you to get out and get active to your heart's content. Cities tend to have a mix of both, though this can vary a lot with the age, type, and tenor of a given city. Old European cultural institutions tend to slow things down a little bit. A bustling metropolis may have a lot of active ventures. The biggest cities will often have a healthy mix of both.

Don't make assumptions about destinations before doing your research, but make sure that a destination has activity to meet your family's needs. As much as it may seem worthwhile to travel to a certain location, it may not be the right fit for your family right now if your vacation needs are above or below the pulse of that location.

Your family's needs and desires regarding levels of activity may ebb and flow with time. When your children are very young, you will need to slow things down to suit their shorter levels of active time. Once they hit school age, they tend to have far more energy, and will need to be kept engaged through constant fun and adventure. The teenage years can vary a lot, and children may slow down and want to engage their minds more than their bodies, or may swing the opposite way and really require high levels of action to maintain focus.

The fact is that you need to evolve your patterns over time, and constantly reassess what your family needs.

While you want to make sure that you choose destinations that cater to your general level of preferred activity, you will also select individual activities that suit your needs. You may even choose your accommodations based on how active you choose to get. You may want to situate yourselves closer to, or further from, the heart of it all so that where you lay your heads can either help get you amped for the coming day, or be a relaxing retreat from it all.

You will still need to vary things so that you enjoy the many benefits of cultural, educational, bonding, and other types of experiences - but make sure that your level of activity helps dictate most of your choices in some way. If you need to keep moving to really be having fun, find the more immersive experiences that combine activity with learning and culture so that you get more out of it. Remember, if you choose things that are "important" but also boring to you, ultimately their benefits will be lost. Keeping the right pace for your family will ensure that you get the most out of each experience.

You may also want or need to vary your level of activity based on the time of year, and your particular schedule or needs at a given point in your lives. The winter may be a time for more relaxing vacations, as the school year is in full swing and puts extra demands on your time. Maybe summer works best for the most active trips, as everyone has more time to focus on the trip at hand. Your work schedule may or may not reflect this, and the specifics of your workload, children's activities, and the time in your lives may swing the pendulum further in one direction than the other. Take stock of what everyone has going on and choose a level of activity that suits your family at that time.

While the many other concepts that we have discussed in this book all come into play, level of activity is a good baseline and starting point as you choose both your destination, and the activities you enjoy while away. It will help dictate pace, and ensure that your vacation isn't something you are forcing on your family, but a welcome change of pace from the realities of your lives at that point.

You may be very active, or not at all. Neither is a right or wrong way to travel. The only potential pitfall is not being honest with yourself about what your family needs. Listen and learn from your experiences - better vacations will await you as a result.

Planes, Trains, and Automobiles

Transportation is an essential component of any vacation. Depending on the trip, it may only come into play when getting to and coming back from your destination. On others, it may be about many small trips within your larger one, and may mean a number of flights, rides, and drives to cover all the ground you want to.

Having already spoken some about cruising at the beginning of this section, it is important to talk about land and air-based means of transportation and the benefits and considerations that come with each. For you, this may mean learning a thing or two you didn't know. It may mean considering a means of transportation that you hadn't in the past. It may simply mean saving a couple bucks or booking a little smarter. In any event, we hope you can learn from our experiences regarding some of the most popular ways to get around.

Planes

Flying is one of the most popular ways of getting from point A to point B on vacation, and with good reason. It is quick, efficient, and in many cases, it is the only way to get to certain destinations. Whether you *need* to fly or choose to, there are a few things we can all consider to fly *better* and make the process smoother for your whole family.

We have already discussed booking in Part IV, and some tips for airport security and such in Section III. Beyond booking tickets, and making your airport experience better, what remains to be discussed is the experience on the actual plane.

Here are some of our top tips for flying with children

Flights, especially long ones, can be very difficult situations for children. Confined quarters, the need to be quiet, and unfamiliar surroundings can all throw off even the best behaved children. Add to this the excitement and possible anxiety of being on your way to an exciting new place (or on your way back from a week of fun) and you have a potential recipe for disaster. You need to find ways to keep both your children, and your neighboring passengers, happy. Here are our step by step guidelines for easing the process:

Before the Flight

- Allow extra time to get through security, especially when traveling with younger children.
- Strollers can typically be brought through airport security and gate-checked to make travel with small children easier.
- Make sure children wear layers, as well as shoes that are easy to remove for security checks (though children under 12 are no longer required to remove shoes).
- Prepare your children for the security process by talking with them. Explain that they will have to empty pockets, remove jackets, and place bags on a conveyer belt for x-ray screening. Discuss with them that it is important to avoid words like "bomb" and "explosion" because even when spoken by a child, jokingly or when referring to a movie or game, they can hold up the process for everyone.
- Talk to your children about flying itself. Reassure them that it's safe, especially if they have never been on a plane before.
- If possible, book your flight during times that coincide with your children's sleeping patterns, such as early morning, late at night, or afternoon naptime.
- Pack a healthy amount of your children's favorite snack. A hungry kid is not a happy kid.
- If your children have a favorite stuffed animal or blanket, then pack it and ensure that it's readily available to them during the flight. Simple comforts go a long way.

Takeoff and Landing

- Ears can pop painfully as a result of pressure changes during takeoff and landing. There are several ways to alleviate this:
- Drink lots of water.
- Chew on a pacifier (for infants and toddlers) or gum/chewy candy (for older children).
- Force yourself to yawn and/or swallow frequently.
- The takeoff and landing process can be especially unnerving for early flyers. Chances are that you won't be able to use electronic devices as a distraction either. Talk to your children throughout the process, give them the window seat so they have something to watch, or be sure to pack a book, magazine, or coloring materials for this electronics-free time. Keep them engaged to soothe nerves.

During Long Flights

- Give your children a special ticket for every half-hour that passes. Children can get impatient on long flights, but giving them a physical, tangible indicator of the passage of time that tells them exactly how much time has passed and how much time is left will make the flight go by faster.
- Have a secret stash of toys at the ready. In order to make sure they don't get bored, give them one toy at a time. Reward them for fifteen minute or half-hour blocks of being well-behaved with a new toy. That way, the novelty doesn't wear off by having all the toys at once, and good behaviors are reinforced.
- Some suggestions for plane friendly toys:
- Coloring books
- Play-Doh
- Etch-A-Sketch

- Have an iPad or other tablet? Sit your children down with a movie or their favorite TV show and they'll be entertained for hours on end.
- Plane games and creativity go a long way as well. Here are some suggestions for more original ways to entertain kids:
- Wear jewelry, especially jewelry that makes a little (non-intrusive) noise, such as beaded necklaces. The noise and stimulation is perfect for amusing babies.
- Bring post-its from home and let your children use them to decorate their tray table.
- Do each other's hair and/or makeup, especially if they like to play dress up.
- Pack some scrap paper or cardboard and a sticker book, and let them go to town!
- Finally, a car/travel seat may be your best friend. First, you have to make sure it is FAA approved by going to their website and checking for guidelines. For very young children, strapping them in can have the psychological effect of easing stress and feeling more secure. It can also alleviate the antsiness of staying still by eliminating the desire to get up and walk around. While you can stretch your legs from time to time on a plane, giving kids the option may ultimately make them more restless. Encourage them to stay seated unless they *really* need the bathroom, and remove one variable that can lead to restlessness.

Planes can be new and exciting, or big and scary. A lot of this has to do with the attitude about them before getting in. Make sure that children get a good night of sleep before any flight, and also discuss any concerns and prepare them for what is going to happen before they get on. The better rested they are, and the fewer surprises that come, the better they will feel and the smoother your flight will be.

Trains

While trains will not be an option for every destination, they should be a real consideration for you on trips where they are physically possible. Once the preferred mode of travel, trains have fallen out of favor to a large degree. With air travel becoming nearly ubiquitous, and flights and trains leveling out in price, it can be harder for some families to see the benefits of train travel.

Trains have evolved over time, from the trailblazing gateway to the west, to industrial powerhouse, to the romantic era of high class personal escape. Today the modern train has added a new identity: catering their offerings to family travel.

Traveling by train is a comfortable and enjoyable way to take yourself and your kids to destinations both near and far. There is no worrying about rest stops and long, tiring drives.

At the same time, you can avoid the stress of having to arrive early for security checks and the hassle of paying for checked luggage. Trains allow you and the family to sit back and relax on your way to the destination, while children enjoy watching the country fly by their window, the many things there are to see, and potentially a little extra room to spread out.

Train travel has the simplicity of getting on and kicking back, coupled with the reduction of many of the hassles associated with air travel. For many this is a "best of both worlds" scenario that is worth considering.

In an effort to win back traveling families who have fled to air travel, Amtrak and other train providers are also courting potential passengers with all sorts of discounts. Just some of the recent and ongoing promotions we have seen include kids under 2 ride free, kids 2-12 ride for half price, and buy one get one tickets for families that travel together.

Amtrak also provides discounts for students, seniors, veterans, AAA members and more. While some train tickets may be comparable in price to their airborne counterparts, the preponderance of discounts should be taken into account when considering your options. Just because the "sticker price" is the same or higher, does not mean that a train could not ultimately be more affordable.

When it comes to touring the United States, and other industrialized nations/areas, train travel is an option worth considering. It has many of the benefits of air travel, while freeing you up from the efforts of driving. If nothing else, it may be fun to mix things up and expose children to something they have never experienced. Even seasoned 12 year old fliers may be thrown for a loop getting on their first train, affording you an opportunity to expand their world and experience something different.

Cars

Renting a car, or bringing along your own, may be a terrific option to reduce costs, increase mobility, and avoid the hassles of lugging along bigger ticket items or more luggage for a nearby vacation opportunity.

Even if you fly, sail, or ride to your ultimate destination, renting a car while there may be an important part of your plan for getting around once you have arrived. You may rent for your entire trip, or just a day here and there.

Here are a few important things to note about car rentals and safety:

- Whether you drive or ride in a cab in a foreign country, roads can be hazardous, especially in developing areas. Take it slow and make sure everyone is buckled up. If someone else is driving, explain that you are not in a hurry, and request that they take their time and not be on a cell phone.

- You should follow the same rules and guidelines for car seats that you do at home (though check local regulations in case they are stricter than they are at home). If your child flew in their approved car seat, you have it with you. If you do not use it on the plane, it is still a good idea to bring your own. Airlines will typically allow families to bring a child's car safety seat as an extra luggage item with no additional expense.

- If you decide not to bring yours along or it gets lost in transit, most rental car companies can arrange a car seat for you if you ask. They may, however, have a very limited selection and there may be an extra charge. Make sure you double check that the seat you get is appropriate for your child's size, is in good condition, and comes with an instruction manual to ensure you can use it properly. Calling ahead of your trip can help with this.

No matter what the specifics are for you, if you do choose to rent a car, it is important to note that prices can vary quite a bit, even for the same car during the same trip.

Not long ago, we had occasion to reserve a car rental for a trip we were taking. By browsing several sites, we were able to find a wide range of prices for similar cars despite looking in the same city and for the same weekend. After making an initial booking, we revisited the same sites a few weeks later on a whim to find still more (and quite drastic) variations in price; including some much cheaper than our initial reservation.

Here are three quick, simple tips to help ensure you get the best possible price when renting a car.

Get Multiple Quotes (not too many, or too few)

It may seem like a no brainer, but you're unlikely to get the best price by just going with your first quote. We all know it pays to shop around, however we also recognize that time is a commodity…especially as a parent. You want to hit that sweet spot between looking at one price and rolling the dice with your money, and spending every free moment trying to scrape dollars off a quote. You may also find it interesting to know that while there are a seemingly endless number of options out there, not all of them will ultimately be all that different.

Many of these companies are owned by or have deals with one another, making their offers redundant. We find the magic number to be three, and that it is best to look at major travel booking sites and aggregators when looking for cars. While it does pay to check the actual company you plan to book with after finding something, browsing each and every one for car deals does not pay off in the same way it does when looking at hotels and flights.

Check Back Even After Your Initial Booking

It generally pays to book early, as there is a better chance of getting a great deal. Reserve early and lock in a good price, then check again closer to the date and see if something even better came along. If you follow our first tip, it won't take long, and could end up being more than worth your while.

Make Sure You Take Advantage of All Available Discounts

Do you also drive at home? If you are a member of AAA, Hertz will give you a discount of 10%-20% off your rental and/or other bonuses like free upgrades or double rewards points. Every little bit helps so if you hold a membership in a specific group (or certain credit cards), check to see if the benefits include a car rental discount, and don't forget to take advantage of all possible savings. Check all of your pertinent memberships and also check to see if you can get discounts by packaging your car rental with your flight, hotel, or both.

Car rentals are sometimes an afterthought for many travelers, who wait until arrival to grab whatever is at the airport. Just keep in mind that if you want to save, or need a specific vehicle for your family, this is not something to be left until the last minute.

On that note, it is important to consider what type of vehicle you wish to rent, and if *vehicles* might make more sense. If you are a large family, you may feel that you are locked into getting only the largest van or SUV available to rent. After all, it is the only thing that will fit your family, right?

You should also consider renting two, smaller vehicles for your trip. While it means you can't all be together in the same vehicle, and may have to pay double for things like parking and gas, it may ultimately make more sense. First there is the consideration of price, and if cars are in abundance at a particular destination while vans are in high demand, you may end up paying less for two cars than one large vehicle.

Second, having multiple cars adds flexibility to your trip. If you have two cars, you can split up and take kids to different activities if it seems fitting. You also have the option to head to the same place, but send one car back early if kids get tired out, while others still want to play.

This may not be for everyone, but is certainly worth considering depending on your destination, and the complexity of your itinerary. Think smarter about booking and using cars while away, and your vacation will be that much better for it.

Making Each Stop Work

When it comes to enjoying great places and new experiences for children, it will require some thought on your part to make sure that you maximize the potential of each step of the way. We don't like to think of it as "work" or "effort," as much as it is traveling smartly. Once you internalize a few key concepts, making the most of each stop will become almost second nature.

Making each stop work is about finding ways to "team up" with your location, allowing the city or area you are in to feel like an additional family member. Think of each destination and activity as an opportunity to meet someone new. Just as you apply different levels of influence with your children at home during playtime and study time, consider different activities while on vacation as individual entities, each requiring a special approach.

You cannot expect to simply show up and instantly find the best of everything, particularly in a very large, or very different location on your itinerary. A little research beforehand, some simple planning, and the right attitude will all go a long way to helping you gain as much as possible from the experience.

It is also worth noting that different stops will hold different expectations for children. This can work for or against you. In the end, any stop can be exciting if you frame it in the right way. Also consider your own attitude. Children (and even teenagers) take cues from their parents. If you enter with an attitude of excitement and wonder, your children are much more likely to follow suit.

Some activities will be inherently exciting to children. Kid-specific activities, workshops, beaches, games, and any number of activities that hold a lot of fun "on the surface" will always be an easy sell to kids. These types of things, and anything that children helped select when planning an itinerary, will be exciting from the get-go.

Other activities may require more in the way of smart traveling to take advantage of all their benefits. This can be especially true of certain educational activities and cultural experiences. While it certainly doesn't have to be true, and the old stereotypes will hopefully be eroded for your family over years of good traveling, at first you may have to get over the hump of "museums are boring" with your children. Let's take a minute to talk more about this idea.

Most families seeking to include some level of culture or education into a vacation find themselves doing so by way of museums. There are also some museums so unique, or so famous in their own right that they practically demand a pilgrimage when visiting their home city. Sites like the Louvre in Paris, or The Hermitage in Saint Petersburg come to mind as "must see" museums.

If those are the reasons *why* we visit museums, what about *how* to visit a museum? The first thing you need to consider? <u>Slow down</u> and enjoy a museum. Take a more relaxed pace, accept that you won't see it all, stop taking so many pictures and actually appreciate the art (or history, science, etc.) with your own eyes.

Travel experts and recent studies show that the average visitor will spend about 2 hours in a museum. Firsthand accounts show that these same visitors, despite crowds and distance to cover, will dart around the building trying to take in as much as possible. Statistically, travelers will spend 15-30 seconds observing a given piece before moving on, placing their emphasis on clearing a room and laying eyes on everything, rather than understanding anything.

Museum-going is not a contest! You don't "win" by seeing the most, or by trying to cram an entire building into an hour or so. We also know that unfortunately, many travelers can see museums as exhausting ordeals. This may more accurately be a product of the way visitors treat them, as opposed to an inherent problem of museums themselves. Covering a mile's worth of corridors and eyeballing 200 paintings is an ordeal, however, gently strolling a small wing and enjoying a handful of exhibits can be an inspiring and even rejuvenating process.

So how do you best enjoy a museum? However you want! This is a matter of personal preference. If you have had a "bad history" with museums or battle children who hate the idea of visiting them, it may be worth trying a different strategy to enhance your visits.

Here are 4 simple tips on how to tackle a museum with your family:

- Choose one or two wings, exhibits, or sections of a museum. Accept that you won't cover the whole place and take the chunk of time you had allotted and stretch it out to spend more time covering less distance. Spend minutes and not seconds with a given piece.

- Plan ahead. If the museum is large, and if your family has varied tastes, then be sure to plan that you spend your valuable time in an area that will appeal to all of you. Find a wing or area with a style you like, or if you are set on seeing a certain piece, find out where it is and make that display your destination. If everyone likes different things, let different family members choose where to focus. Some will be happier than others, but it may be better than all being miserable from running around too much.

- Consider avoiding the most famous works. Unless they are of particular significance to you or strike a special chord, you may have a more relaxed and positive experience in some of the less crowded areas. Let yourself become a connoisseur rather than a tourist. You may discover something you didn't even know you liked.

- Within the area you choose to spend your time, start by wandering a bit and take note of what speaks to you, then circle back and spend time with your favorite pieces. This will give you a better chance of finding one or two things you really connect with, which can be the difference between "seeing" a museum and *experiencing* it. Forming a connection with a few pieces will make the memory all the more rewarding, especially for children who will have a better chance of remembering a painting or exhibit, rather than an entire building.

Also consider the idea that using a guide to help you explore a museum can add to the experience by providing unique insight and personalized attention. Using a guide can especially help your children to appreciate a museum experience. Just be sure to employ these same guidelines. Whoever is planning the trip and coordinating with the guide should identify a few key works or areas that you wish to focus on, and explain that you would like to spend more time taking in these areas you think your family will appreciate.

Museums are places of culture and education; neither of those things can be rushed or boiled down and condensed into quick jaunts. They also shouldn't become stressful, tedious experiences to the point where they become dreaded ordeals. By simply slowing down the pace and adjusting your approach, you can change the game when it comes to the way your family experiences museums. They can (and should) be an important component to your vacations.

Moreover, these same simple principles and adjustments to your outlook can go far beyond just how you enjoy a museum. These same ideas can help reveal a better way to enjoy each of your stops, and your entire vacation.

Vacations come in many shapes and sizes. "City" vacations tend to be busier and less relaxing in nature than beach vacations and island getaways. There is nothing wrong with being the kind of person or family who tries to pack a lot into the time they have; some places you visit are once in a lifetime opportunities. We simply want to point out that just because you are willing to run around a city to see all it has to offer, that does not mean you have to run around each stop within that city in the same frenzied manner.

Slowing down, paying attention to what matters, and trying to really savor a few things as opposed to simply cruising by "everything" will lead to a much happier and more productive vacation.

Not only will this enhance the educational experiences of places like museums, it will enhance the fun factor of active stops, the cultural value of artistic ones, and allow you to appreciate the specialness of those truly unique stops. Taking the time to experience each stop the way it was meant to be, rather than just as quickly as possible, will allow your vacation to take on a greater meaning.

Some of the more elusive and difficult to quantify benefits of travel, namely family bonding and personal growth, will also benefit from traveling smarter rather than quicker. When you take the time to enjoy something, and form connections with each stop you make before rushing onto the next, you set yourselves up to bond over these shared experiences. Growing closer to one another is not a race, and if your pace is all about running around, you minimize your chances to stop and really enjoy moments together. Without this, your chances for great memories are fewer, and vacation can become an ordeal rather than a joy.

By looking at these suggestions for how to better enjoy one of the "harder sells" of vacationing with children, we hope we have arrived at some good direction and general thoughts on how to make each stop count. Each stop can and should be rewarding. Don't look at vacation as a series of things that are important but boring, sprinkled with things that are fun. Take the time and put in the paces to make each stop the very best it can be. In this way, you show your children the importance of the place you are visiting, and set your family up for that all-important chance to grow closer while enjoying it.

Rest Days

Just as it is important to make each stop on your journey count, it is also important to know when to slow down and catch your breath. In fact, these ideas are very closely tied together. When you don't take the time to rest, or if you stretch yourselves too thin, you can easily hit a wall and begin to lose your ability to take anything else in. Overdoing things on vacation may have you under the illusion that you are seeing and doing more. In actuality, once you and/or your children have hit your limit, you stop taking in anything, and all that running around ends up being for nothing.

In short, sometimes less is more. "Sacrificing" a few stops, or even an entire day, to relax and catch up, will actually help you get more out of your trip. Don't think of it as giving time up, but as making time count. You can't do it all, so set yourselves up for being able to get the most out of what you actually do.

You probably don't run around for 12-14 hours a day, 7 days a week when you are at home (If you do, then good for you, and maybe you need to take a *really* relaxing vacation!). Stop trying to live vacation like a race to the finish and allow yourselves to take a break here and there. Spending time in a very special place that you may only get to enjoy once can make taking any sort of break feel like a loss. This type of thinking will see you burning out quickly, losing many of the benefits of the trip you are on.

If you are the type who has had trouble "keeping up with the pace" of vacations in the past, this may be one of our most important pieces of advice for you. At the same time, this will be key for those looking to transition from the world of weeklong beach trips to active and engaging travel. Whether you have already pushed yourselves on past trips, or are just starting to now, it is important to give yourself license to take a break here and there.

The excitement of a new place will make taking a break harder to try and fit in once you arrive, so it is important to commit yourself to this notion before you get there. Even if you don't build a rest day into your itinerary, make sure you establish with your family that it is ok to take a day off from touring. Build in several breaks sprinkled throughout your schedule. Encourage anyone who needs time during the trip to speak up, and separate yourself from the idea that you are "losing out" if you stop moving at any point during your trip.

We talked at length about the idea of pacing yourself while away. This is very important, but also a particularly elusive and difficult concept to arrive at. It will take time, and many trips, to learn exactly where your family's boundaries lie. They will also change and evolve with time. Even the "best" traveling families require time to catch their breath and relax. Don't think of it as a shortcoming.

Think of these as "vacations within your vacation." You might end up taking an entire day off, or simply planning a "half day" that allows you to sleep in and start late, or come back early. Use this time to share a longer meal, rest by the pool, or do something low key. These rest times can also be valuable opportunities for your family to spread out and have some alone time.

For some families it can be a mistake to spend every waking second together on vacation. While growing closer to one another is a primary goal, just as too much time spent touring can max you out, too much time together can actually backfire.

Rest days should be chances for everyone to recharge their batteries on their own terms. For young children, this may mean the opposite of what it means for older siblings and parents. While rest for the teens and adults of your group may mean sleeping, reading, or lounging, little kids may still want to run around and play. It is the break from structure and plans that will help them to rejuvenate and approach the next day with new vigor. Again, let each person decide for themselves what resting is. The more you make an effort to allow everyone to have aspects of the vacation that are "theirs," the more this sense of ownership and personal space will pay off during the time spent together and exploring.

Know when enough is enough, and make sure you understand that sometimes it takes hours or even a day off, to really make the other ones count. Whether planned or simply taken "as needed," a rest day or portion of a day spent without plans can be just what your vacation needs to go the extra mile. Listen to your family and remember that above all else, you are there to have *fun*.

Preserving Memories

Vacation is all about enjoying yourselves and creating memories. While the time spent on the ground enjoying things together will be your greatest reward - it pays to bring home another reminder or two.

You will be investing time, money, and energy into making a great vacation possible. Your children also won't stay young forever, and this precious time is meant to be treasured. For all these reasons and more, it pays to put a little thought into how best to preserve these memories that you are making, and creating opportunities to relive your vacation after it happens.

Besides the stories you tell and the discussions you share, physical reminders will help to keep your vacation alive long after your return home. The two main ways you will do this are through photographs and souvenirs.

Photographs

During every family vacation, be sure to take plenty of photographs. You will want to ensure that you capture the beautiful places and important monuments that you visit. Also be sure to capture your children and your family at these places, ensuring a healthy mix of what you saw and did, as well as how you all looked enjoying it.

You should photograph at least every major place you visit on your trip, because photographs are memories frozen in time that can be remembered and relived for the rest of your life. While you certainly could pull out your itinerary down the road to remind yourself of each stop you made, a visual representation will provide a much better keepsake. This will also provide for opportunities to share the blow-by-blow of your vacation with others upon your return.

Given how easy it is nowadays, and the fact that it does not necessarily require specialized or even extra equipment, also be sure to include videos. These can make for a great way to relive vacation moments in a way pictures never could. They also open you and your children up to even greater creativity in what you capture and how. Allow yourselves to have fun and make something special to all of you. Reliving it later will be that much more fun.

Involve your kids with the vacation photography

You or your spouse may be the best shot when it comes to photographs, but once you've gotten the photos you've wanted to take for a particular site, allow your children to have a chance at taking a picture. Over time, you may very well find that your children and teens have gotten quite proficient at taking pictures during your travels. They may even turn out to be better at taking photographs than you are! Whatever their skill level, the idea that they have taken some of the pictures will have its own benefits. It will help children to take ownership of pictures they took, and they will be that much more excited when you share them upon return. It also helps kids from getting antsy. You want to preserve a great record of your trip, but when photography becomes the exclusive province of mommy or daddy, children can get frustrated by the lack of involvement, and may be thrown off track. Keeping them a part of the process lets it be a bonding experience, and one that they take joy in during, as well as after, the fact.

Organizing photos with your kids when you return home

When you return home, gather all of the photographs you have taken and invite your children and teens to go through them with you. You will find that it will motivate and inspire your children and teens to discuss their memories and opinions of the trip; quite possibly some you haven't heard before. Allow your children to help you organize the photos within a photo album and keep them in a safe place. We like Shutterfly for their photo books, though plenty of similar options exist.

Taking a lot of photos during your trip can sometimes feel like a hassle when you're trying to move through your itinerary and keeping your children and teens in order, so make every picture count and make it a memorable experience. Try to wait for a great moment when everyone is in good spirits when taking your next photograph. A picture is more than just a thousand words, it's a lifetime of memories for you and your family.

Pulling out the album after vacation

This is a very important thing to do that you should do on occasion. Pulling out your album of the photographs you have taken during your trip will allow your children and teens to recall the excitement they had during the trip and will help you and your family to relive the moments. Also, you will find that your younger children may not even remember being on the trip or when the picture was taken; having a photo album can aid your younger children in remembering their time, or at least appreciating and acknowledging the fact they have been there.

Consider keeping your albums in an accessible locations, for example, your family room coffee table. This way, your children can peruse them whenever they want. Don't hide them on your bookshelf in a spot where you and your kids may never look at them.

Souvenirs

While photographs are one of the best reminders of the things you did while on a trip, physical objects purchased while away can hold their own special memories.

Souvenir collecting is a tradition that dates back thousands of years. Often when families would travel they would bring back with them a piece of something they had encountered as they ventured into a new land.

The souvenir is coveted, not for its monetary value, but because it is a proof. It is a proof that someone has visited another land and brought back a piece of history, or an artifact or object native to that land to show for it.

Why it is important to allow children to purchase their own souvenirs

Souvenir collecting, if done right, can be a very positive experience for your children and teens. A souvenir does not have to be expensive to be coveted by your family. In fact, a lot of the souvenirs you can get are free! Your children and teens will love showing off a souvenir they acquired on your travels, because it is unique and is a great conversation starter. It is also something you can use in conjunction with photographs and brochures to remind your teens and children of places you've visited and to inspire meaningful thought and conversation with them.

Sometimes the act of purchasing a souvenir can be part of the memory in itself. It may be that a child has a chance to hone their negotiating skills, and this foreign practice may provide for a fun memory and a sense of accomplishment when they get to bring home their reward. Even if they don't get to try a hand at haggling, particularly quaint and memorable shops, or fun, bustling marketplaces can provide shopping opportunities that are out of the ordinary and meaningful for children.

Allowing children to browse souvenir shops for gifts can also be rewarding. It may be to get something to bring home to a family member, friend, or teacher. Whether it is your child's chance to bring a bit of vacation to someone they care about (and share about your trip with others) or an opportunity to relive a bit of your shared adventure at an upcoming holiday, this sort of thoughtful shopping and giving can help a child cement special memories, and share their fun with people they care about.

What kinds of souvenirs are appropriate?

The answer to this question depends on where you're visiting, your budget, the cultural importance of the item as it relates to your family's trip, and your child's age.

Younger children often enjoy collecting things such as rocks, because it is a rock they've never seen before and they know they cannot obtain back home. Older children may want to visit souvenir shops, but you should encourage them to stay within their budget and buy something that has personal meaning to them; something that will remind them of the trip they have taken with their parents and siblings.

Stamps, old coins, and hand-crafted artwork and sculptures from natives are often offered at reasonable prices and can make a great decoration for your teen to bring home and hang in a frame on their wall if it's a picture, or place atop a dresser or bookcase. Some children like to collect the same type of souvenir from each location. In our family, our kids collect shot glass, postcards, magnets, and snow globes - depending on which child you ask.

This idea of setting and working within a budget will provide an additional opportunity for education while traveling. whether your children use money they have earned or been given, or you provide a small amount for each child at the start of the trip - allowing them to make their own choices will teach them about the value of money, and keep them thinking about what part of the trip means the most to them.

Encourage your children to obtain souvenirs, so that they can bring back a little piece of their journey back home, which will invoke memories that will last for a lifetime.

Other ideas for keepsakes

You may also want to encourage your children to save some of the things you collect along the way, even if they may not hold any physical value. Ticket stubs, brochures, information from museums, even a napkin from a hotel or restaurant you enjoyed might be nice things for a family scrapbook. You might also consider putting together a shadow box, or a board of your vacation memories from each trip, or your collected travels, to display in your home.

Anything of meaning to you can be a keepsake and treasured possession when it reminds you of important time shared together.

Besides creating and collecting reminders for yourselves, one of the main reasons to involve children in both the taking of photographs and the collecting of souvenirs, is to encourage them to think critically about a trip.

When you have children insisting that you take one more picture, or saying that they really want something from that shop because they want to remember the city, you know you are on the right page. These keepsakes will provide a window into what matters most to your children, and allow them to treasure the time away just as you will.

While taking photos and buying souvenirs shouldn't be a main focus of your trip, it would be a shame to overlook them. Allow yourselves to dedicate most of your time to making memories, with a nod to keeping them close as well.

Other Types of Vacations

We have spent a great deal of this book focusing on "big trips." The sort of all-out, boundary pushing vacations that up the ante for your family by taking you farther and pushing you a little harder.

We have also chosen to focus mainly on the more standard model of planning a trip together, as a family.

Before we close, we would like to touch on a few other types of vacations as food for thought. Again, in keeping with our desire to promote great travel as a way of life and an ongoing pursuit, we would like you to consider different ways to travel, and vacations of different scope and size with equal measure. There is something to be gained from each experience, and some of these ideas may help you arrive at new, better ideas about how to spend family time.

Day Trips

As you continue to look at your family's travel pursuits in the bigger picture, you should never rule out day trips. While talking about grand and exciting vacations, it can be easy to become narrow minded and focus all of your time and energy on these. With most people only able to take these sorts of "big trips" on a more limited basis, if you are really going to grow your travel world, you should start thinking smaller in order to think bigger.

Day trips keep the excitement and fun of seeing new places alive. They allow children to exercise their creative and critical thought on a more regular basis, and to kindle the flames of curiosity. They allow you to further develop and cement bonds formed on your bigger trips by continuing to explore together, even if it is on a smaller scale.

In Part I we covered the idea of exploring locations both ordinary and extraordinary with equal zeal. Chances are that when you are talking about day trips, you are talking about packing up the car and driving somewhere. Depending on where you live, there might also be trains that serve as options, but the scale and scope of these experience will be much smaller.

The trick is to try to approach each day trip with the same careful thought and consideration with which you approach your "big vacations."

Don't simply think of a day trip as a chance to drive to one place and see one thing for as long as it lasts, then drive home. Take it as an opportunity to plan a mini vacation (even if it is only one day). This may or may not mean planning multiple stops (depending on your family, your schedule, and the location in question) but should involve doing some research beforehand.

See what the available options are. If you plan on visiting a museum, a state park, or other location of interest - see what is there for your family to learn about and enjoy. Have a plan of attack regarding a few key points of interest, and visit armed with a little information about what things mean, and about how long you want to spend there.

If you do construct a day with multiple stops, act as if it is a day on a longer trip. Think about the logistics of getting from place to place, and ordering stops so that they both make sense logistically, and help you form a cohesive experience that mixes a bit of fun and activity with some meaningful experiences.

By practicing this way of day tripping with care and thought, you will benefit in two ways. The first benefit is that your day trips themselves will be better, more fun, and more meaningful. Just as on your larger vacations, they will help your family enjoy the many benefits of traveling together. You will learn, grow, and feel closer to one another as you experience new things - even if they are just down the road.

The other benefit will be a sort of "practice" for planning your bigger trips. As you get used to the idea of researching a destination, and planning your activities before you arrive, you will begin to internalize concepts that will aid you in making the most of that dream destination when you get there. The idea of creating itineraries and trying to maximize the benefits of each stop will start to become real for you.

Also, don't think that a day trip doesn't mean there aren't opportunities to try and save. Check deal and coupon websites for "local deals" and see if you can't secure a better price or an applicable discount for your admission. The more aspects of family travel you practice on a regular basis, the more experience you will be able to call on for each future trip - whether it be a day or two weeks.

There are a number of reasons that all the itineraries on RealFamilyTrips.com constitute a single day. We often group a few together in a "Spotlight" article to show how you could easily build a bigger trip out of several individual days, but they are all intended to stand alone. One of the reasons for this is customization. By creating individual days, even the family spending a week somewhere can pick and choose from many options to enjoy days that work for them. The other reason is to encourage this vision that "vacation" doesn't have to only apply when you get to go away for several days or more at a time.

Enjoying an amazing day together somewhere can be just as rewarding as a longer trip. When taken as a chance to grow, each time your family leaves the house and embarks on an adventure, you are setting yourselves up for an opportunity to create a memory and to grow in each other's company.

"Planned Surprise" Trips

A concept that can apply to both day trips and bigger vacations is that of the "planned surprise" getaway. This is a different way to think about booking and planning that may just make things simpler for you, or offer a welcome change of pace once you have a wealth of travel experience and need to shake things up.

Planning a vacation can sometimes cause stress. One cause of this stress is the realization that between the schedules of work and school (possibly further complicated by different schools and multiple jobs) there are a finite number of days that "work," and making the most of them leaves little room for error. Add to this the financial burden, the varying tastes of multiple family members, and the limitations associated with children's ages, and you have something that at first might look a bit more like a puzzle than a relaxing time away.

With the difficult realization that there are only so many years left before the children "leave the nest" and shared time becomes less common, planning "perfection" in family vacations can be even more challenging. If any of this sounds familiar to you, don't worry - there is a creative solution.

The perfect family vacation combines careful planning and spontaneity in a healthy balance.

Part of what makes vacation planning stressful is the notion that the majority of planning tends to become muddled when everyone inserts their opinions. If you do decide to share the planning process, it is hampered by squeezing in time around work schedules and kids' activities, leaving a small amount of time to sit down and hash out the details. If everyone is involved in the equation, differing opinions can create a set of disparate ideas that make pulling the trigger on anything more difficult. If a child is set on not enjoying a vacation before even boarding the plane, it will taint the entire experience.

Consider the idea of designating one family member as the trip planner for a certain vacation, based on a budget you agree on, and letting them plan the trip from top to bottom. For everyone else in the family, all they will be told is when the trip is planned for. Let the details be a surprise. The very nature of the surprise vacation can get you over a lot of humps. Someone who may not love the idea of a city walking tour may try to talk you out of it if given months to overanalyze. When everything feels spontaneous, everyone in the family (especially children) is that much more likely to remain open to ideas and just "go with the flow."

The idea of keeping the trip a surprise for most of the family enables the planner to have free reign and keep the process as simple as possible. It allows everyone being surprised to add an extra element of excitement to their vacation experience. The time you hopped on a plane without knowing where you were going is sure to be a memory that will last a lifetime, and bring you all closer together as you explore and experience off-the-cuff vacationing together.

Consider the idea of planning a "surprise" trip for your family and see how it feels. By relieving the pressure to craft a "perfect trip" and adding the fun of going along for an incredible ride, you might just find the perfectly imperfect way to appease everyone in your busy family with a trip that they'll cherish forever.

Closing Thoughts and Additional Information

Our Goals and Hope for You

Throughout this book, our goal has been to share our experiences in order to save you some of the hassle of things that took us years to learn. We have also hoped to demystify some of the more confusing and misunderstood aspects of travel, in order to demonstrate that a great vacation is within the reach of any family.

Finally, we hope we have been able to inspire you. Whether it be with real stories from great trips, outstanding destinations you may not have considered, or thoughts about planning or booking that made you say "oh yeah!"

As we continue our own travels, we continue to tour and to grow, as well as to help others to enjoy the same wonder and amazement that we find in these experiences.

The joy really is in exploring, in growing, and in enjoying our time together. As amazing as any one vacation may be, it is the lives that we share together and with each other that matter most.

We ask you now to think about your own goals. Having experienced all that we have offered throughout this book, you surely have a lot to think about. We hope that it will lead you to planning a great vacation, a great series of vacations, each of which we hope will open new doors and provide incredible new opportunities for your family.

As important as the destinations, the logistics, the booking and planning information may be - we also ask you to walk away from this book first and foremost with thoughts about your own family.

As you look to plan that first vacation in your lifetime of new travel experiences - think of those people and what you want to share with them.

Are you itching for adventure, and can't wait to climb that mountain, or soak in that hot spring? Are you excited to wander the streets of an exotic, faraway city, or to eat something you have never heard of before? Are you looking to just feel closer to your children by tucking them into a new bed framed by a stunning view that you could never have imagined?

Think about the experiences that you want to share as well as the emotions. Think about how you can nurture your children's unique gifts. Think about how you can share the things that are important to you with them. Think about ways that you can provide the very best for your family - not of material things, but of love, growth, and opportunity.

Before you jump into booking that first flight and taking that first trip, sit down and create a list for yourself of the things you would like to see happen for your family. It could be qualities you want to instill, experiences you want to share, or feelings you want to enjoy together with your children.

Armed with these important goals, you have a chance to always keep a watchful eye on your family's growth. Travel will have its share of logistics, and you will see a good number of places, but you must always keep an eye on the biggest picture of all: your family members themselves.

We hope you have learned something from this book, and that we have been able to provide useful advice and lots of inspiration. We hope that our ideas and suggestions about great travel can carry you to new heights and exciting opportunities.

We wish you the very best on your journey.

-The Team at RealFamilyTrips.com

Other Books by Us

If you have enjoyed this book, we hope that you will take a look at some of the others we have written. With this being a distillation of our travel values, experience, and expert opinions - we also have even more practical advice to share. As you look to start planning your own amazing adventures, we hope that you will consider our series of guidebooks for destinations we love. They come with the same kind of careful thought, attention to detail, and real family experience that we share throughout this volume.

Our Current Guidebooks:

- "Israel for Families: An Adventure in 12 Days"
- "New York City for Families: 5 Boroughs in 7 Days"
- Coming soon, more titles for more great locations…

Where to Find and How to Buy:

- Both books are available in print through Amazon.com ($14 for Israel, $16 for NYC).
- Both books are available on Amazon.com for Kindle eBook readers and apps ($5 for Israel, $6 for NYC).
- Both books are available on Smashwords. They offer a variety of eBook formats that work on Nook, Apple iBooks, Kobo, and virtually any other reader ($5 for Israel, $6 for NYC).

Two Different Guidebooks, Same Great Features:

- **A pre-planned, out-of-the box vacation.** "Israel For Families" features 12 days, spanning the entire country, while "New York City For Families" features 7 days, that span all 5 boroughs. We take out all the guesswork with days that encompass a variety of activities, spanning the same benefits discussed in this book. Our days are designed to work for most any family, and keep in mind what it means to travel with kids in tow. Each day provides a detailed list of stops, contact information and background on each destination, and a comprehensive list of logistics, including how to get there and what to bring.

- The books feature **detailed background information on the destination**, each area and neighborhood visited, and each stop made. Learn not only what to see, but why. Help lend context to your vacation with notes about historical significance, cultural exposure, and a variety of other ways to look at the locations you visit and activities you enjoy. We feature a combination of "the usual suspects" as far as famous attractions, coupled with off the beaten path adventures, and tie them all together with background information that helps lend them significance.

- The books include a **robust selection of alternate activities for each location**, organized for easy reference. Something on our trip doesn't catch your fancy? Already been there? Our alternate activities and resources, located in the back of the book, allow you to swap out one idea for another and create a customized trip for you and your family. Alternately, our alternate activities can serve as a handy "a la carte" menu for day trips.

- Both books also include an **innovative selection of original stories** help make the guide (and the trip itself) more engaging for children. The stories are historical fiction, appropriate for ages 4-17 for Israel, 6-17 for NYC), and take place at locations actually visited on the trip. Allow your children to learn about the stops you will make, gain context and grow excited by learning about what they will see on their own level.

- The expert guide contains **useful travel tips designed with families in mind.** Other guides may have ideas on what to see; we go much further. Learn what days to take public transit, and what days it makes more sense to go by cab. We recommend the best times to stop for a snack, which tickets you need to buy in advance - and much, much more. Prepared by real families, for real families, our information takes into account how you travel and what is important when traveling with the kids.

Our comprehensive guides are designed to be the only resource your family needs to take a fantastic vacation. If it isn't in the book itself, we point you to where to find it - from great vendors to discount tickets.

Everyone wants to take an amazing family vacation, and we hope the book you are holding now has inspired you to take one. If you still feel that the time spent planning on is beyond your reach, consider our guidebooks as another option. We did the work for you, by presenting a great vacation that will teach you a lot and allow you quality time to bond and grow closer to one another. Just read, book, and go!

The Team at RealFamilyTrips.com

Who Helped Put This Book Together

Our team works tirelessly to bring you the best in travel information and writing, from one real family to countless others. Get to know the group at RealFamilyTrips.com and what makes us different from other family travel resources.

Noah Greenblatt

Noah is almost 17 years old and just started his junior year in high school. He takes his studies seriously, and loves science. His hobbies include skiing, basketball, baseball, and of course, travel. Noah enjoys hanging out with friends and family. Noah loves time spent vacationing with family and all it has taught him.

Julia Greenblatt

Julia is also almost 17 years old and started her junior year in high school. She enjoys playing soccer and drawing. In her free time, she volunteers for The Friendship Circle, something she loves to do. Julia's favorite subject is history, and she loves learning about different cultures and civilizations. Julia enjoys the opportunities traveling with family affords her to learn firsthand about the world around her.

Anna Greenblatt

Anna is also an almost 17 year old junior in high school (see a pattern?). She enjoys playing soccer, drawing, reading, and hanging out with her family and friends. Anna is very enthusiastic about helping to make the world a better place through her involvement in charity work, and the chance to see the world through travel helps motivate this passion for service.

Sophia Greenblatt

Sophia just began 7th grade. She loves ice skating and soccer. Sophia's favorite subject is English. Sophia is excited to share about vacationing with her family and looks forward to time spent with her parents and siblings when they go away together.

Avery Greenblatt

Avery is 9 years old. He just started 4th Grade. His favorite hobbies are playing basketball and football. He also loves learning math in school. He enjoys the time that he spends with his family. He is excited to have joined the team at Real-FamilyTrips.com and hopes to have a great impact on the site and its goals.

Vera Greenblatt

Vera is a four year old girl (going on 16!) who loves to have fun. She enjoys doing ballet and playing with her siblings. When Vera grows up she wants to be just like her mom! She is the newest member of RealFamilyTrips.com and we look forward to seeing what she can do!

Naomi Greenblatt

Dr. Naomi Greenblatt is an NYU educated psychiatrist who maintains a private practice in reproductive psychiatry. Dr. Greenblatt is a diplomate of the American Board of Psychiatry. She is a frequent lecturer and has been featured on the radio as well as in numerous publications. She is proud to be a co-founder of RealFamilyTrips.com and hopes to help other families achieve the sort of meaningful growth through travel that she has enjoyed with her family.

Jason Greenblatt

Jason Greenblatt Esq is a well-known real estate attorney. In addition to his successful career in law, he is an accomplished public speaker and adjunct professor who teaches real estate related courses. As a co-founder of RealFamilyTrips.com, Jason recognizes travel as an important part of his treasured family time, as well as a powerful tool for growth and education.

Ryan Kagy

Ryan is the Head Writer at RealFamilyTrips.com. Born to a family that valued and celebrated travel, he has known and enjoyed the benefits of a good trip from a young age. He is proud to lead content generation for RealFamilyTrips.com, this volume, and InspireConversation.com. He would like to thank Laura and his parents for their continued love, inspiration, and support in his life.

The "Fine Print"

This book is provided without any guarantees or warranties of any kind, express or implied. Your use of the book, and the services and vendors mentioned, is at your sole risk. Real Family Trips, Inspire Conversation LLC and each of their members, shareholders, partners, owners and affiliates (all of the foregoing, collectively, the "Publisher and Related Parties") will not be held responsible for any damages of any type due to your use of the book or services and vendors mentioned.

Although Real Family Trips has made every effort to ensure that the information in this book was correct at press time, the author and publisher do not assume and hereby disclaim any liability to anyone for any loss, damage, or disruption caused by errors or omissions, whether such errors or omissions result from negligence, accident, or any other cause.

All information provided in this book is intended for informational and entertainment purposes only. The views expressed are personal opinions only. Neither Real Family Trips nor its parent company Inspire Conversation LLC is responsible for any legal, medical, financial, or other hardships caused by acting on the information provided in this book. Unless otherwise noted, all material in the book is the legal property of Real Family Trips and/or Inspire Conversation LLC and may not be reprinted or republished without the express written consent of Real Family Trips and/or Inspire Conversation LLC. When applicable, every attempt has been made to correctly credit the legal owners of photos and other various media. Please contact us if you feel that you have not been credited properly.

Your use of the book constitutes your agreement and acknowledgment that you hold the Publisher and Related Parties harmless and understand that the Publisher and Related Parties are not liable in any way for any claims, causes of action, liability, damage, or other actions or obligations that may arise from your use of the book or any products, vendors or services contained therein.

Image Credits

We thank all those who contributed photos and images to help bring this book to life.

Cover - Summer Landscape with Train, Ship, Airplane and Bus - jazzia © 123RF.com; thank you to Derek Aubie for cover formatting and image preparation.

Dedication

Mixed Ethnic Children, popocorn © 123RF.com

Part I

Family Vector, Kirsty Pargeter © 123RF.com

Part II

Illustration of Airplane Flight Paths Over Earth, dmstudio © 123RF.com

Part III

Vector Set of Icons, Alexandr Rozhkov © 123RF.com

Part IV

Black Outline Vector Computer, Thanarat Boonmee © 123RF.com

Part V

Black and White Icon of Luggage, print2d © 123RF.com

www.ingramcontent.com/pod-product-compliance
Lightning Source LLC
Chambersburg PA
CBHW071147300426
44113CB00009B/1114